P9-DIA-291

Careers in Business

Careers in Business

Editor
Michael Shally-Jensen, Ph.D.

SALEM PRESS
A Division of EBSCO Information Services, Inc.
Ipswich, Massachusetts

GREY HOUSE PUBLISHING

Library of Congress Cataloging-in-Publication Data

Careers in business / editor, Michael Shally-Jensen, Ph.D. -- [First edition].

   pages : illustrations, charts ; cm. -- (Careers in--)

Edition statement supplied by publisher.
Includes bibliographical references and index.
ISBN: 978-1-61925-537-1

   1. Business--Vocational guidance--United States. I. Shally-Jensen, Michael.

HF5382.5.U5 C37 2015
650/.023/73

First Printing

CONTENTS

Publisher's Note vii

Editor's Introduction ix

Accountant   1

Accounts Payable Specialist 17

Administrative Assistant 29

Advertising & Marketing Manager 41

Auditor 56

Bookkeeper 70

Budget Analyst 82

Buyer 93

Cost Estimator 106

Credit & Loan Officer 119

Credit Manager 131

Customer Service Representative 143

Executive Secretary 155

Financial Manager 168

Human Resources Manager 183

Management Consultant 200

Market Researcher 214

Network & Computer Systems Administrator 228

Operations Director 245

Payroll Administrator 260

Purchasing Agent 273

Receptionist and Office Assistant 285

Retail Store Sales Manager 297

Services Sales Representative 311

Technical Sales Representative 325

Appendix A: Holland Code. 338

Appendix B: Bibliography 342

Index 343

PUBLISHER'S NOTE

Careers in Business contains twenty-five alphabetically arranged chapters describing general fields of interest in business and business administration. Merging scholarship with occupational development, this single comprehensive guidebook provides business and business administration students with the necessary insight into potential careers, and provides instruction on what job seekers can expect in terms of training, advancement, earnings, job prospects, working conditions, relevant associations, and more. *Careers in Business* is specifically designed for a high school and undergraduate audience and is edited to align with secondary or high school curriculum standards.

Scope of Coverage

Understanding the wide net of jobs in business and business administration is important for anyone preparing for a career within them. *Careers in Business* comprises twenty-five lengthy chapters on a broad range of occupations including traditional jobs such as Accountant, Receptionist, and Payroll Administrator, as well as more recently established positions including Market Researcher, Network Administrator, and Financial Manager. This excellent reference also presents possible business career paths and occupations within high-growth and emerging fields.

Careers in Business is enhanced with numerous charts and tables, including projections from the US Bureau of Labor Statistics, and median annual salaries or wages for those occupations profiled. Each chapter also notes those skills that can be applied across broad occupation categories. Interesting enhancements, like **Fun Facts**, **Famous Firsts**, and dozens of photos, add depth to the discussion. A highlight of each chapter is **Conversation With** – a two-page interview with a professional working in a related job. The respondents share their personal career paths, detail potential for career advancement, offer advice for students, and include a "try this" for those interested in embarking on a career in their profession.

Essay Length and Format

Each chapter ranges in length from 3,500 to 4,500 words and begins with a Snapshot of the occupation that includes career clusters, interests, earnings and employment outlook. This is followed by these major categories:

- **Overview** includes detailed discussions on: Sphere of Work; Work Environment; Occupation Interest; A Day in the Life. Also included here is a Profile that outlines working conditions, educational needs, and physical abilities. You will also find the occupation's Holland Interest Score, which matches up character and personality traits with specific jobs.

- **Occupational Specialties** lists specific jobs that are related in some way, like Electronic Commerce Specialist and Online Merchant, and Cost Estimator and Production Coordinator. Duties and Responsibilities are also included.

- **Work Environment** details the physical, human, and technological environment of the occupation profiled.

- **Education, Training, and Advancement** outlines how to prepare for this field while in high school, and what college courses to take, including licenses and certifications needed. A section is devoted to the Adult Job Seeker, and there is a list of skills and abilities needed to succeed in the job profiled.

- **Earnings and Advancements** offers specific salary ranges, and includes a chart of metropolitan areas that have the highest concentration of the profession.

- **Employment and Outlook** discusses employment trends, and projects growth to 2020. This section also lists related occupations.

- **Selected Schools** list those prominent learning institutions that offer specific courses in the profiles occupations.

- **More Information** includes associations that the reader can contact for more information.

Special Features

Several features continue to distinguish this reference series from other career-oriented reference works. The back matter includes:
- Appendix A: Guide to Holland Code. This discusses John Holland's theory that people and work environments can be classified into six different groups: Realistic; Investigative; Artistic; Social; Enterprising; and Conventional. See if the job you want is right for you!
- Appendix B: General Bibliography. This is a collection of suggested readings, organized into major categories.
- Subject Index: Includes people, concepts, technologies, terms, principles, and all specific occupations discussed in the occupational profile chapters.

Acknowledgments

Special mention is made of editor Michael Shally-Jensen, who played a principal role in shaping this work with current, comprehensive, and valuable material. Thanks are due to Allison Blake, who took the lead in developing "Conversations With," with help from Vanessa Parks, and the professionals who communicated their work experience through interviews. Their frank and honest responses provide immeasurable value to *Careers in Business*. The contributions of all are gratefully acknowledged.

EDITOR'S INTRODUCTION

An Occupational Overview

Business careers entail the planning, organizing, and execution of business operations. It encompasses many occupations, from professional managers of all kinds to administrative support personnel. Some of the principal career areas are finance, sales, marketing, operations, and human resources. Many organizations, including those specializing in particular industries, sub-industries, or areas of expertise, have departments or staff units that come under the heading of business or business administration.

Business Careers

Because of its broad usefulness in so many areas of economic activity, from private industry to government service, the general business administration field has long been one of the top choices for career seekers. In a spring 2013 report in the *Occupational Outlook Quarterly*, published by the U.S. Bureau of Labor Statistics (BLS), the authors use employment data to highlight occupations that have considerable flexibility in terms of their utility in different industries. Business administration jobs, that is, are present in a wide variety of settings, and because of that they often provide workers job mobility and career flexibility.

"Workers in some occupations spend most of their careers in just one industry. Teachers, for example, often work only in schools," write the authors of the BLS report. "But in other occupations such as network and computer systems administrators, workers have technical skills that are sought after in more than 200 industries."

The occupations with significant career mobility, as identified by BLS, fall into four main groups: 1) business and financial operations; 2) management; 3) computer systems; and 4) office and administrative support. Occupational employment may be concentrated in a few industries or dispersed among many, but workers in almost every one of these occupations have at least some ability to change jobs or industries. Many types of employers require workers with knowledge of business and financial operations, management practices, computers and networks, and office and administrative support activities. The more widely an occupation has jobs in a variety of industries, the more versatile or mobile it usually is.

Business and Financial Operations

The success of almost any business depends on its finances and operational efficiency. For this reason, many industries need workers in occupations related to business and financial operations. These occupations usually pay well, but most require at least a bachelor's degree at the entry level.

Management

Management includes leadership positions such as general manager and operations director; sales and administrative managers; marketing and human resources managers; and many others. Here too compensation can be good, even exceptional, and many of the highest positions require at least some post-secondary education.

Computer Systems

Computer systems occupations include everything from software developers to network and system administrators to web developers and information security analysts. These positions often pay well, with most having a median wage more than double the median for all occupations.

Office and Administrative Support

Finally, office and administrative support includes jobs such as administrative assistant and customer service representative, among many others. Many of these have high employment rates and are versatile.

Looking more closely, here are some of the specific professions within these four groups that the authors of the BLS report point to as among the most versatile:

- Accountants and auditors, who analyze and prepare financial records for organizations, were employed in 280 industries in 2013, according to the BLS. The bulk of the jobs were in business services firms specializing in accounting, tax preparation, and payroll. But many accountants and auditors also worked in government, health care, and the retail industry.
- Financial managers, who oversee an organization's or a department's financial operations, worked in over 260 industries. Most of the jobs were in banks and credit unions, but also in other financial services industries and general business operations.
- General and operations managers, who have a broad range of duties related to running a business, worked in the highest number of distinct industries: 290. A small percentage of these jobs were at the top level, that of overseeing a large enterprise; but many were also at the level of managing smaller operations such as a store or an equipment contractor.
- Management consultants, who study business operations and suggest improvements, worked in 200 industries in 2013. Most of these were in business and technical consulting services firms, but many also were in government, education, and information technology.
- Human resources specialists, who recruit employees and oversee employee benefits, worked in about 260 industries. A significant number of these jobs were in employment services firms, but most of them were in the health care, retail, and transportation industries.

- Computer network and systems administrators worked in up to 180 industries – even more if one counts specialists who handle such tasks along with other computer-related work for small- and medium-sized organizations. A sizeable percentage of these jobs were in computer services firms, but the bulk of them were in banking and insurance, health care, and government.
- Sales representatives and managers have always had flexibility in their profession. These workers facilitate the movement of products and services from one business to another business or to the consumer. A wide variety of industries, 250 in all, made direct use of fulltime sales reps and sales managers in 2013. Manufacturers, insurance companies, the food industry, and many others were among the top employers of these professionals.
- Finally, office and administrative support occupations include office assistants, customer service representatives, secretaries, accounts payable staff, data entry personnel, and payroll associates, among others. Many of these have high employment rates and substantial versatility in terms of the types of organizations making use of them. Between 270 and 290 industries counted these occupations as necessary components in their field of operations.

Which industry one chooses to work in will, of course, determine the working conditions that go with the job, including work schedules, wages, benefits, and advancement opportunities. Industry matters, but perhaps less so in the case of business administration occupations than other occupations. There is more flexibility to move between jobs and industries with a business administration background. And, the more options one has when considering one's career, the better the chances are of landing the ideal job.

Business Administration Education

The individual's career options in business administration will also depend on his or her education level and other qualifications. For example: Do you have prior work experience in the field? Do you have a proven record of performance? Are you a capable leader? What special skills do you have? Do you have any certifications? All of these things help determine whether a person is qualified for a specific position.

Equally important is educational background. Some business administration jobs require an advanced degree, such as the master's of business administration (MBA). Others require no postgraduate degree at all, or a two-year associate's degree rather than a four-year bachelor's degree. There are many different options regarding training in business administration. The option that you choose should depend on what you want to achieve in a business administration career. Some people take a part-time, entry-level position while beginning to work toward completion of degree requirements. Others go straight to college after high school, working intermittently and doing internships along the way, only begin their fulltime career after graduating. There is also on-the-job training, seminars, and certificate programs to consider in advancing in one's career. In addition, online training is popular in the business administration field. Whatever one chooses, a career in business administration can be an exciting and rewarding experience.

Sources

Bureau of Labor Statistics. "Business and Financial Occupations," *Occupational Outlook Handbook*.
    Washington, DC: BLS, 2014. Available at: http://www.bls.gov/ooh/business-and-financial/home.htm

Torpey, Elka, and Audrey Watson. "Careers with Options: Occupations with Jobs in Many Industries,"
    Occupational Outlook Quarterly (Bureau of Labor Statistics), spring 2013; pp. 15-24.

U.S. News & World Report. "Best Business Jobs 2014." Available at: http://money.usnews.com/careers/best-
    jobs/rankings/best-business-jobs?page=2

—M. Shally-Jensen, Ph.D.

ACCOUNTANT

Snapshot

Career Cluster: Banking & Finance; Business Administration; Government & Public Administration

Interests: Keeping records, working with numbers, offering guidance, analyzing data

Earnings (Yearly Average): $65,080

Employment & Outlook: Average Growth Expected

OVERVIEW

Sphere of Work

Accountants are responsible for the financial record keeping, financial efficiency, and fiduciary reporting of individuals, corporations, non-profit organizations, and government entities. Accountants offer diverse financial services, including financial document preparation and review, payroll, budget analysis, investment guidance, auditing, bankruptcy filing, and tax preparation. The main fields of accounting include internal accounting, public accounting, managerial accounting, and government accounting. Certified public accountants (CPAs) are the most common accounting position. CPAs may be independent

contractors or employed by public accounting firms providing financial services to businesses and individuals.

Work Environment

An accountant's work environment is generally office-based. Depending on the employer and particular job description, an accountant may telecommute from a home office, visit client offices as a contractor, or work on a full-time basis in an employer's office. Accountants may work as a full-time member of a team responsible for targeted financial responsibilities or may be hired as a project contractor. An accountant's work environment is dependent on technology (computers and accounting software programs), as well as having access to the most recent government regulations.

Profile

Working Conditions: Work Indoors
Physical Strength: Light Work
Education Needs: Bachelor's Degree
Licensure/Certification: Required
Physical Abilities Not Required: No Heavy Labor
Opportunities For Experience: Internship, Military Service, Part-Time Work
Holland Interest Score*: CRS

* See Appendix A

Occupation Interest

Individuals attracted to the accounting profession tend to be well-organized and detail-oriented people who find satisfaction in manipulating numbers and tracking financial trends. Accountants may also have an interest and affinity for technology and regulatory issues. For instance, those who excel in accounting tend to be adept at educating themselves about and responding to technological and regulatory change. Analytical people choosing to pursue the occupation of accountant may find satisfaction in implementing and auditing financial record keeping, as well as staying up to date on accounting best practices, ethical issues, and legal matters in accounting.

A Day in the Life—Duties and Responsibilities

TTypical daily work tasks of a general accountant will include activities such as tax preparation, payroll, bookkeeping, and auditing. Organizations may also require accountants to select, implement, and troubleshoot accounting software systems, as well as stay up to date with regulatory and ethical issues and news in accounting by reading accounting industry journals and participating in industry associations. An accountant's daily occupational duties and responsibilities may also include meeting with clients, colleagues, supervisors, and employees as needed.

Clients, on a daily basis, may require accountants to provide financial counseling, tax preparation, payroll management, purchase order tracking, auditing, bankruptcy help, and contract preparation. Colleagues, on a daily basis, may require accountants to participate in discussions of work teams, workflows, dynamics, and best practices. Supervisors, on a daily basis, may require accountants to present their work and account for their work hours, take on extra work as needed, and strategize about organizational operations and best practices.

The duties of those accountants who have or supervise employees in their organizations will include managerial roles and responsibilities. Employees, on a daily basis, may need their supervising accountants to provide a review of the employee's financial document preparation or specific training related to accounting practices or technology. It is not unusual for accountants to advise or provide analysis to senior management on the financial implications of corporate performance, growth or acquisitions. Periodically, supervising accountants will also need to perform employee performance reviews.

External accountants who work for organizations with remote or multiple locations often travel to those locations to perform in-house auditing and bookkeeping work. Busy accountants will need to accommodate educational training, certification renewal, extended work travel, and commuting into their daily work schedules.

Duties and Responsibilities

- Designing or modifying accounting systems and procedures
- Maintaining accounts or records
- Auditing contracts, purchase orders and vouchers and preparing related reports
- Preparing periodic financial statements and other management reports
- Directing and coordinating activities of workers engaged in keeping accounts and records

OCCUPATION SPECIALTIES

Public Accountants

Public Accountants prepare federal, state and local tax returns of individuals, businesses or other organizations.

Budget Analysts

Budget Analysts apply principles of accounting to analyze past and present financial operations in order to prepare a budget.

Management Accountants

Management Accountants plan, set up and direct the operation of an accounting system to determine the cost of producing or selling an item or service.

Property Accountants

Property Accountants identify and keep records of company owned or leased equipment, buildings and other property.

Systems Accountants

Systems Accountants devise and install customized accounting systems and related procedures in establishments that do not use a standardized system.

Internal Auditors

Internal Auditors examine and analyze the accounting records of a business and prepare reports concerning its financial status and operating procedures.

WORK ENVIRONMENT

Physical Environment

Accountants generally work in office environments. The work of an accountant largely requires sitting at a desk and using computers for long periods of time each day. Accountants often meet with their immediate staff, and may be required to meet with corporate officers and outside auditing firms. Access to meeting spaces is often necessary.

Relevant Skills and Abilities

Analytical Skills
- Analyzing data

Communication Skills
- Speaking effectively
- Writing concisely

Interpersonal/Social Skills
- Being able to work independently
- Working as a member of a team

Organization & Management Skills
- Paying attention to and handling details

Research & Planning Skills
- Laying out a plan
- Organizing information

Technical Skills
- Working with data or numbers
- Working with machines, tools or other objects

Human Environment

An accountant's human environment may be social or isolated depending on the assignment and organization. Accountants, depending on their work assignments and organization, may interact with clients, employees, supervisors, or colleagues.

Technological Environment

An accountant's technological environment will generally include computers, financial software packages for bookkeeping and auditing, telecommunication tools, and reference materials outlining legal and regulatory matters.

EDUCATION, TRAINING, AND ADVANCEMENT

High School/Secondary

High school students interested in someday pursuing a career in accounting should prepare themselves by building good study habits and exercising personal discipline. For those who feel at ease with numbers and mathematical functions, it is helpful to maximize the school's offering of mathematical and business courses, as well participate in any extracurricular activities relative to business and mathematics. Students should consider applying for internships or even volunteer work with local accountants or financial organizations to learn what it is accountants do on a daily basis.

Suggested High School Subjects
- Accounting
- Algebra
- Business
- Business & Computer Technology
- Business Data Processing
- Business Law
- College Preparatory
- Computer Science
- Economics
- English
- Mathematics
- Social Studies

Famous First

The first Certified Public Accountant (CPA) was Frank Broaker of New York City, who was certified on December 1, 1896. Several other candidates were certified on the same day, but Broaker's name appeared first in the alphabetical list. Later, he was criticized for publishing a crib sheet to aid other aspiring CPAs in their effort to pass the state exam.

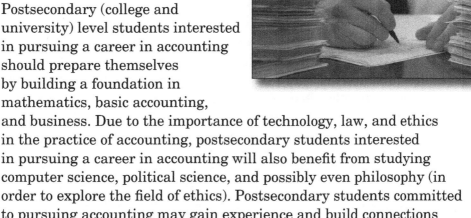

Postsecondary

Postsecondary (college and university) level students interested in pursuing a career in accounting should prepare themselves by building a foundation in mathematics, basic accounting, and business. Due to the importance of technology, law, and ethics in the practice of accounting, postsecondary students interested in pursuing a career in accounting will also benefit from studying computer science, political science, and possibly even philosophy (in order to explore the field of ethics). Postsecondary students committed to pursuing accounting may gain experience and build connections through accounting internships and entry-level employment with accounting businesses and firms. It's important to note that a college degree is a condition of CPA licensure in most states.

Related College Majors
- Accounting
- Business Administration
- Financial Management

Adult Job Seekers

Adults seeking accounting jobs have generally earned a bachelor's degree and, in some cases, an MBA. Adult job seekers will benefit from joining professional accounting associations as a means of professional networking. Professional accounting associations generally maintain job lists advertising open accounting positions. Adult job seekers who wish to join the accounting profession, but who lack a college degree, may gain access to the field by seeking out entry-level bookkeeping and clerk positions. Supervisors and mentors can help junior accountants to plan their career and educational choices.

Professional Certification and Licensure

Professional recognition through certification and licensure is extremely valuable in the job market. Most states require CPA candidates to complete 150 semester hours of college coursework - an additional 30 hours beyond the usual 4-year bachelor's degree. Prospective accounting majors should research the requirements of any states in which they hope to become licensed.

To become a CPA, it is also necessary to take a four-part two-day examination that is the same for all states. Candidates are not required to pass all four parts at once, but most states require they pass all four parts within 18 months of passing the first part. Most states also require applicants for a CPA certificate to have some public accounting experience. Accountants may join professional associations, although membership is not required.

Additional Requirements

Individuals dedicated to training and advancing in the accounting field generally work to develop their analytical, mathematical, and business abilities. Written and verbal communication skills are also important for accountants, as is proficiency with accounting software. High levels of integrity and ethics are required of accountants, as accountants often work with confidential documents. Membership in professional accounting societies is encouraged among junior and senior accountants as a means of building status within a professional community and networking.

Fun Fact

Roll over, Rock & Roll Hall of Fame. Ohio houses another hall of fame: The Accounting Hall of Fame, established at Ohio State University in 1950. As of 2014, 92 accountants had been elected to it.
Source: http://fisher.osu.edu/departments/accounting-and-mis/the-accounting-hall-of-fame/

EARNINGS AND ADVANCEMENT

Earnings depend upon the accountant's experience, level of education and certification as a public accountant. While larger firms usually pay higher starting salaries than small or medium-sized firms, the small and medium-sized firms usually offer the well-qualified employee an opportunity for more rapid advancement. Generally, certified public accountants (CPAs) and those with graduate degrees earn a higher beginning salary.

According to a salary survey conducted by the National Association of Colleges and Employers, graduates with a Bachelor's degree in accounting received average annual starting salaries of $53,536 in 2012; graduates with a Master's degree in accounting earned $54,403 annually.

Median annual earnings of accountants were $65,080 in 2013. The lowest ten percent earned less than $41,000, and the highest ten percent earned more than $113,000.

Accountants may receive paid vacations, holidays, and sick days; life and health insurance; and retirement benefits. These are usually paid by the employer.

Metropolitan Areas with the Highest
Employment Level in this Occupation

Metropolitan area	Employment[1]	Employment per thousand jobs	Hourly mean wage
New York-White Plains-Wayne, NY-NJ	71,070	13.56	$44.94
Los Angeles-Long Beach-Glendale, CA	43,490	10.94	$37.55
Washington-Arlington-Alexandria, DC-VA-MD-WV	35,350	14.93	$40.82
Chicago-Joliet-Naperville, IL	31,340	8.47	$35.80
Houston-Sugar Land-Baytown, TX	29,650	10.75	$38.74
Atlanta-Sandy Springs-Marietta, GA	28,460	12.33	$36.56
Dallas-Plano-Irving, TX	25,300	11.77	$37.07
Boston-Cambridge-Quincy, MA	24,150	13.81	$38.28
Philadelphia, PA	22,040	11.98	$37.58
Denver-Aurora-Broomfield, CO	21,360	16.68	$35.95

[1] Does not include self-employed. Source: Bureau of Labor Statistics

EMPLOYMENT AND OUTLOOK

Accountants and auditors held about 1.3 million jobs in 2012. Employment is expected to grow about as fast as the average for all occupations through the year 2022, which means employment is projected to increase 10 percent to 15 percent. Stricter financial laws and regulations, recent financial crises, and increased scrutiny of company finances will drive job growth. In addition, the need to replace accountants and auditors who retire or transfer to other occupations will produce thousands of additional job openings annually, reflecting the large size of this occupation. The changing role of accountants and auditors will also spur job growth. In response to market demand, accountants and auditors will offer more financial management and consulting services. By focusing on analyzing operations, rather than simply providing financial data, accountants will help to boost demand for their services.

Opportunities are expected to be favorable for college graduates seeking accounting and auditing jobs who have worked part-time in a business or accounting firm while in school. In fact, experience has become so important that some employers in business and industry seek persons with one or two years experience for beginning positions.

Employment Trend, Projected 2010–22

Accountants and Auditors: 13%

Business and Financial Occupations: 13%

Total, All Occupations: 11%

Note: "All Occupations" includes all occupations in the U.S. Economy. Source: U.S. Bureau of Labor Statistics, Employment Projections Program

Related Occupations

- Auditor
- Bookkeeper & Accounting Clerk
- Budget Analyst
- Credit Manager
- Energy Auditor
- Financial Analyst
- Financial Manager
- Personal Financial Advisor
- Public Administrator

Related Military Occupations

- Finance & Accounting Manager

Conversation With . . .
LYNN AMORE

Accountant
The Hanover Insurance Group
Accounting professional, 10 years

1. What was your individual career path in terms of education, entry-level job, or other significant opportunity?

When I got out of high school, I worked for Digital Equipment Corporation as a secretary. I took a lot of night classes. Then I got married and had a child. In 1996, I was laid off, so I went back to school full-time to finally get my degree. I was always good with numbers and got my degree in business administration. During that time, I took an internship at Hanover Insurance with no pay, but I got three credits. I was 36 years old! When my internship ended, they asked me to work through the summer as a temp. It was accounting work, reconciliations and so forth. At the end of the summer, they offered me a 30-hour permanent position as a reconciliation specialist, which is making sure that money that comes in the door is applied to a policy. I did that for a few years. During that time, I got a Series 6 license, which allows you to sell mutual funds and variable annuities. I always took advantage of the classes offered by Hanover. It's important to always keep improving. In my late 40s, I interviewed for a job that I didn't get. That motivated me to get my INS Certificate in General Insurance. You have to pass exams to get it. That made me more marketable, because I was 50 years old and I knew I was going to be up against younger people, competing for the same jobs. After that, I applied for an accountant's position that I wanted, and I got it.

2. What are the most important skills and/or qualities for someone in your profession?

It seems obvious, but you really need to understand basic accounting rules. You definitely need to know the Microsoft Office products: Excel, Access, Microsoft Word. You have to be a team player and be open to other people's ideas and new ideas. You must be organized and be thorough. You have to always double-check work. You have to deal with deadlines. In accounting, the end of the month can be a very busy time.

3. What do you wish you had known going into this profession?

I wish I had known how to deal with different personalities and how to not take things personally. My first boss was a very critical person and I took it very personally. You have to know how to stand up for yourself.

4. Are there many job opportunities in your profession? In what specific areas?

There are a lot of opportunities. Most businesses or organizations really want you to be a Certified Public Accountant (CPA). If you are a CPA or have your master's degree, or both, you're really golden. There are opportunities in finance, management, products.

5. How do you see your profession changing in the next five years? What role will technology play in those changes, and what skills will be required?

You have to be proficient with Microsoft Access and Microsoft Excel and know the products inside and out, how to work with pivot tables that slice data and work with macros. You have to stay on top of the software because it's always changing. It's awesome. You have to like that stuff. One thing that they tell you at Hanover is you're in charge of your own career. We have to write development goals and progress reports. You can just sit back and do your job and do it every day, or you can learn and be ready as the profession changes. Always take advantage of training opportunities. You'll be lucky if you can work for a company that offers a lot of training.

6. What do you enjoy most about your job? What do you enjoy least about your job?

It's close to home! But, seriously, I like working with the spreadsheets. I like getting creative with the databases and figuring out process improvements. I find that fun. And I like the people I work with. That said, though, what I like least is working alongside one of my coworkers who just talks so much about herself. She's a narcissist.

7. Can you suggest a valuable "try this" for students considering a career in your profession?

Try to get an internship. That's such a great way to just sort of try it. But, short of that, create a spreadsheet or put a budget together. Create tabs and link all the data together. Kids—actually, everyone—should always do a budget.

SELECTED SCHOOLS

Many large universities, especially those with business schools, offer programs in accounting. The student can also gain initial training through enrollment at a liberal arts college or community college. Below are listed some of the more prominent institutions in this field.

Brigham Young University
Marriott School of Management
Campus Drive
Provo, UT 84602
801.422.4121
marriottschool.byu.edu

Indiana University—Bloomington
Kelley School of Business
1309 E. 10th Street
Bloomington, IN 47405
812.855.8100
kelley.iu.edu

New York University
Stern School of Business
665 Broadway, 11th Floor
New York, NY 10012
212.998.4500
www.stern.nyu.edu

Ohio State University
Fisher College of Business
120 Schoenbaum Hall
210 W. Woodruff Avenue
Columbus, OH 43210
614.292.2715
fisher.osu.edu

University of Illinois—Urbana-Champaign
College of Business
1515 East Gregory Drive
Champaign, IL 61820
217.333.2740
business.illinois.edu

University of Michigan—Ann Arbor
Ross School of Business
701 Tappan Avenue
Ann Arbor, MI 48109
734.763.5796
michiganross.umich.edu

University of Notre Dame
Mendoza College of Business
Notre Dame, IN 46566
574.631.7505
business.nd.edu

University of Pennsylvania
The Wharton School
1 College Hall
Philadelphia, PA 19104
215.898.6376
www.whatron.upenn.edu

University of Southern California
Marshall School of Business
3670 Trousdale Parkway
Los Angeles, CA 90089
213.740.8674
www.marshall.usc.edu

University of Texas—Austin
McCombs School of Business
1 University Station, B6000
Austin, TX 78712
512.471.5921
www.mccombs.utexas.edu

MORE INFORMATION

Accreditation Council for Accountancy and Taxation
1010 North Fairfax Street
Alexandria, VA 22314-1574
888.289.7763
www.acatcredentials.org

American Accounting Association
5717 Bessie Drive
Sarasota, FL 34233-2399
941.921.7747
info@aaahq.org
aaahq.org/index.cfm

American Institute of Certified Public Accountants
1211 Avenue of the Americas
New York, NY 10036
212.596.6200
www.aicpa.org

The American Institute of CPA Student Scholarships
www.aicpa.org/BecomeACPA/
Scholarships/Pages/default.aspx

Institute of Internal Auditors
247 Maitland Avenue
Altamonte Springs, FL 32701
407.937.1100
www.theiia.org

Institute of Management Accountants
10 Paragon Drive
Montvale, NJ 07645-1718
800.638.4427
www.imanet.org

National Association of State Boards of Accountancy
150 4th Avenue North, Suite 700
Nashville, TN 37219
615.880.4200
www.nasba.org

Simone Isadora Flynn/Editor

Accounts Payable Specialist

Snapshot

Career Cluster: Business Administration

Interests: Accounting, business administration, mathematics, solving problems, customer service

Earnings (Yearly Average): $33,820

Employment & Outlook: Average Growth Expected

OVERVIEW

Sphere of Work

Accounts payable specialists, also known as billing clerks, oversee all stages of the billing process. Tasks completed by accounts payable specialists may include reviewing financial records and data such as charge slips or purchase orders, calculating charges and fees for goods, preparing and sending invoices, assisting customers with billing inquiries, and resolving billing disputes. Accounts payable specialists often work in billing and payroll departments.

Work Environment

Accounts payable specialists work in offices in businesses, hospitals, insurance companies, educational institutions, among other organizations. Depending on employer and particular job description, an accounts payable specialist may work on a full-time or part-time basis in an employer's office. Accounts payable specialists typically work standard forty-hour weeks, but overtime may be necessary during periods of increased business and billing.

Profile

Working Conditions: Work Indoors
Physical Strength: Light Work
Education Needs: On-The-Job Training, High School Diploma
Licensure/Certification: Usually Not Required
Physical Abilities Not Required: No Heavy Labor
Opportunities For Experience: Internship, Part-Time Work
Holland Interest Score*: CRS, CSE

* See Appendix A

Occupation Interest

Individuals attracted to the billing clerk profession tend to be organized and detail-oriented people who find satisfaction in tracking financial information. Those who excel as accounts payable specialists demonstrate good judgment, financial and mathematical abilities, focus, responsibility, and effective time management. Prospective accounts payable specialists must be honest and trustworthy as they handle sensitive financial information. Accounts payable specialists should also be problem solvers attuned to the concerns of the client as well as their employer. .

A Day in the Life—Duties and Responsibilities

Although the exact daily occupational duties and responsibilities of accounts payable specialists vary by job specification and work environment, all accounts payable specialists submit bills to customers, maintain fiscal records, and resolve any problems that arise. They are also responsible for complying with regulatory requirements for financial institutions.

After goods are delivered or services are rendered, accounts payable specialists calculate the charges and fees owed to the company or organization, making adjustments for discounts or credits and shipping costs. They may enter billing and insurance codes into specialized billing software programs if needed. Accounts payable specialists also review and verify the accuracy of financial records and data such as charge slips, purchase orders, and hospital records. They then prepare invoices or statements that detail the charges incurred, type shipping labels on a computer or typewriter, and send the bills and invoices to clients. Accounts payable specialists assist customers with billing inquiries as necessary. They must keep meticulous documentation and provide financial records to accountants who handle tax preparation, payroll, and auditing for their employer.

The billing clerk's level of work experience also influences the type of duties he or she receives. Entry-level accounts payable specialists must accept supervision and instruction from a billing manager or office manager. Experienced accounts payable specialists may be assigned more complex tasks or train new billing clerk hires in office procedures and processes. They may themselves become billing machine operators or billing managers. Some accounts payable specialists select, implement, and troubleshoot the accounting software systems they use for billing. They may also participate in discussions of work teams, workflows, dynamics, and best practices.

Duties and Responsibilities

- Computing amounts due from purchase orders and sales receipts
- Figuring discounts
- Completing invoices or billing forms
- Maintaining billing files
- Creating shipping labels and credit memoranda
- Handling customer's inquiries about their account

WORK ENVIRONMENT

Physical Environment

Accounts payable specialists generally work in bright, pleasant office environments in businesses, hospitals, and insurance companies. Their work requires sitting at a desk and using computers and telephones for long periods each day.

Relevant Skills and Abilities

Communication Skills
- Communicating effectively

Interpersonal Skills
- Working both independently and as part of a team

Organization & Management Skills
- Following instructions
- Organizing information or materials
- Paying attention to and handling details
- Performing routine work

Technical Skills
- Working with data or numbers
- Working with machines, tools or other objects

Plant Environment

Accounts payable specialists working in plant or manufacturing environments supervise the ordering, billing, and bookkeeping of the organizations. While an accounts payable specialist's office in a plant environment is most often kept separate from production lines, he or she may experience physical risks resulting from production fumes, noise, or plant accidents.

Human Environment

An accounts payable specialist's human environment may be social or isolated, depending on assignment and organization. Accounts payable specialists may interact with clients, employees, supervisors, or colleagues. Strong interpersonal and communication skills are useful in this occupation as accounts payable specialists may encounter uncooperative or unresponsive clients.

Technological Environment

To complete their work, accounts payable specialists use Internet communication tools, telephones, electronic databases, accounting and basic office software programs, bookkeeping and billing machines, calculators, fax machines, photocopying machines, scanners, and postal machines. For specialized billing services, clerks may also need to access electronic patient or client records and have familiarity with coding software.

EDUCATION, TRAINING, AND ADVANCEMENT

High School/Secondary

High school students interested in pursuing a career as an accounts payable specialist should prepare themselves by building good study habits as well as by developing an ease with numbers and mathematical functions. High school-level study of English, typing, computer science, business, bookkeeping, and mathematics will provide a strong foundation for future work as an accounts payable specialist. Emphasis on the life sciences is helpful for those who intend to work in medical facilities. As work experience is more important than educational attainment in this occupation, high school students interested in this career path will benefit from seeking internships or part-time work with local businesses or financial organizations.

Suggested High School Subjects
- Accounting
- Applied Communication
- Bookkeeping
- Business
- Business & Computer Technology
- Business Data Processing
- Business English
- Business Math
- Keyboarding

Famous First

The first successful adding machine was invented by William Seward Burroughs of St. Louis, Missouri, in 1886 and patented in 1888. Burroughs' company later developed electronic billing machines and mainframe computers, and eventually merged with Sperry Corporation to form Unisys. Burroughs' grandson is the Beat writer William S. Burroughs, who wrote *The Adding Machine.*

Postsecondary

Postsecondary education is not required for work as an accounts payable specialist; however, students interested in becoming accounts payable specialists should consider pursuing vocational training of an associate's degree in bookkeeping, accounting, secretarial science, or general business. Coursework in mathematics and business also prove useful in their future work. Accounts payable specialists who complete a formal postsecondary program may have greater opportunities for employment or advancement in the field. Job placement is available through some programs. Internships or part-time employment with local businesses or financial organizations may provide relevant work experience and potential advantage in future job searches..

Related College Majors
• Accounting Technician Training

Adult Job Seekers

A high school diploma or vocational training and basic computer skills are the minimum requirements for accounts payable specialists. Some billing clerk jobs require extensive experience, on-the-job training, and an associate's degree. Adult job seekers should educate themselves about the educational and professional certification requirements of the organizations where they seek employment. Adults seeking employment as accounts payable specialists may benefit from joining professional accounting or financial associations to help with networking and job searching. Professional financial associations, such as the American Medical Billing Association (AMBA), generally offer networking opportunities and maintain lists of available jobs. Members of the Office and Professional Employees International Union and similar unions may receive benefits and job protection.

Professional Certification and Licensure

Certification and licensure is not required for general accounts payable specialists but may be required as a condition of employment for specialized billing clerks such as medical billing clerks. Many community colleges offer the one-year Medical Billing Assistant Certificate of Proficiency, which involves completing an educational program and passing a competency examination.

Additional Requirements

Individuals who find satisfaction, success, and job security as accounts payable specialists are knowledgeable about the profession's requirements, responsibilities, and opportunities. Membership in professional financial associations is encouraged among all accounts payable specialists as a means of building professional community and networking. Association members must comply with the standards of ethics and conduct established by their professional organization.

Fun Fact

Disorganization is costly: an estimated $89,840,657,069 is spent looking for misplaced items in the office among full-time office professionals. An estimated 38 working hours – nearly a full work week – per person per year are lost as a result of looking for misplaced items, and 46% of office workers have lost one of the following items in the past year—a file folder, mobile phone, calculator, flash or memory drive, a briefcase, suitcase, or luggage, lap top computer, or a PDA.

Source: Completely Organized, Inc., http://www.completelyorganized.com/facts-about-being-organized/.

EARNINGS AND ADVANCEMENT

Earnings depend on the type and size of business, geographic area and the employee's skills. Accounts payable specialists had median annual earnings of $33,820 in 2013. The lowest ten percent earned less than $24,000, and the highest ten percent earned more than $47,000. Accounts payable specialists may receive paid vacations, holidays, and sick days; life and health insurance; and retirement benefits. These are usually paid by the employer.

Metropolitan Areas with the Highest Employment Level in this Occupation

Metropolitan area	Employment[1]	Employment per thousand jobs	Hourly mean wage
New York-White Plains-Wayne, NY-NJ	19,450	3.71	$19.52
Los Angeles-Long Beach-Glendale, CA	17,330	4.36	$17.54
Houston-Sugar Land-Baytown, TX	11,200	4.06	$17.90
Philadelphia, PA	11,000	5.98	$17.33
Chicago-Joliet-Naperville, IL	10,990	2.97	$17.45
Dallas-Plano-Irving, TX	9,420	4.38	$17.47
Atlanta-Sandy Springs-Marietta, GA	8,060	3.49	$16.52
Phoenix-Mesa-Glendale, AZ	7,890	4.43	$16.92
Santa Ana-Anaheim-Irvine, CA	6,360	4.38	$18.89
Minneapolis-St. Paul-Bloomington, MN-WI	6,350	3.55	$18.38

[1] Does not include self-employed. Source: Bureau of Labor Statistics

EMPLOYMENT AND OUTLOOK

Accounts payable specialists held about 600,000 jobs in 2012. One third of the jobs were in health services. Wholesale trade and retail trade industries also employed a large number of accounts payable specialists. Employment is expected to grow about as fast as the average for all occupations through the year 2022, which means employment is projected to increase 9 percent to 14 percent.

Automated and electronic billing processes are greatly simplifying billing and allowing companies to send out bills faster without hiring additional workers. However, due to the increasing number of billing transactions in the growing health care industry, which employs many accounts payable specialists due to the complicated nature of medical billing, demand for jobs is expected to be high. Job openings will also occur as workers transfer to other occupations or leave the labor force.

Employment Trend, Projected 2010–22

Accounts Payable Specialists: 11%

Total, All Occupations: 11%

Office and Administrative Support Occupations: 7%

Note: "All Occupations" includes all occupations in the U.S. Economy. Source: U.S. Bureau of Labor Statistics, Employment Projections Program

Related Occupations

- Bank Teller
- Bookkeeper & Accounting Clerk
- Cashier
- General Office Clerk
- Office Machine Operator
- Payroll Clerk
- Shipping & Receiving Clerk
- Statistical Assistant

Conversation With . . .
MICHELLE GORDON

Accounts Payable & Accounting Manager
A.F. Amorello & Sons Construction
Worcester, MA
Accounting professional, 20 years

1. What was your individual career path in terms of education/training, entry-level job, or other significant opportunity?

When I graduated from high school, I didn't know what I wanted to do with my fu-ture. I had worked part-time jobs in retail and customer service and knew that wasn't the path I wanted to take. When I started college, I took classes ranging from criminal justice to business and explored my options. I obtained a work-study job in a variety of departments and positions, including financial aid, administrative assistant, receptionist and accounts payable. I realized that I liked working in an office environment, so I changed my major to Organization Management and received my Bachelor's degree. I was later hired by the college as an Accounts Payable Clerk. I held this position for a few years before moving onto another company. Since that time I've held a number of different positions, such as Accounts Payable Clerk, Purchasing Agent, Purchasing Manager and Accounting Manager.

2. What are the most important skills and/or qualities for someone in your profession?

I believe the most important skills are the ability to multitask and great organizational skills.

3. What do you wish you had known going into this profession?

I'm not really sure how to answer this. I will say that your ability to do your job effectively is heavily reliant on everybody else doing theirs, and vice versa. It's good to have clear policies and procedures in place, as well as good communication with your peers. I've also found that when you're in an office position, you may be required to do a lot of miscellaneous tasks that don't necessarily fall under Accounts Payable functions: insurance claims, subcontractor agreements and insurance, office supplies, fleet (vehicle) management, or cash receipts. That's when organization skills and multitasking come into play.

4. Are there many job opportunities in your profession? In what specific areas?

There are a lot of opportunities in Accounts Payable. You have the ability to obtain employment in almost any industry; every company needs some sort of accounting work. As long as you are computer literate, able to work with or learn different software packages, and willing to learn the different facets of the industry where you are looking to obtain employment, you will have a lot of versatility.

5. How do you see your profession changing in the next five years? What role will technology play in those changes, and what skills will be required?

I think technology will play a big part in how this profession changes in the next five years. The accounting part will be similar, but the programs you utilize will affect how you do your job. For instance, companies now receive payments, pay invoices, and make deposits electronically. More companies are leaning towards being paperless as they utilize scanning software or electronic signatures. You don't need to be sitting at your desk to do your job. We use smart phones, tablets and whatever new technology becomes available.

6. What do you enjoy most about your job? What do you enjoy least about your job?

What I enjoy most is the work. I was never one to work in retail or out in front with customers. I was always better suited to working behind the scenes. I know what is expected of me and when it's expected. I work toward my deadlines and am able to handle whatever comes up in between.

In the past, I worked for a company that had cash flow problems and as a result I had to field phone calls from vendors looking for money. The company was a start-up and their customers weren't paying their invoices, so the adverse affect was that the company couldn't pay its invoices. Making phone calls to customers about payment status and talking to vendors on the other side looking for money is a tough position to be in professionally

7. Can you suggest a valuable "try this" for students considering a career in your profession?

See if you can become an intern or get a work-study job at school. You could shadow someone you know who works in an accounting department, and take a few business and accounting classes. The time will not be wasted because even if you decide to work in a different field, or maybe run your own business someday, understanding the behind-the-scenes picture will help you succeed.

SELECTED SCHOOLS

Many technical and community colleges offer programs in business administration and accounting. Interested students are advised to consult with their school guidance counselor or to research area postsecondary schools and training programs.

MORE INFORMATION

Accounts Payable Network
Institute of Finance and
Management
PO Box 781
Williamsport, PA 17703
207.842.5557
www.theaccountspayablenetwork.
com

**American Medical Billing
Association**
2465 East Main Street
Davis, OK 73030
580.369.2700
www.ambanet.net/AMBA.htm

**Office & Professional Employees
International Union**
265 W. 14th Street, 20th Floor
New York, NY 10011
800.346.7348
www.opeiu.org

Simone Isadora Flynn/Editor

Administrative Assistant

Snapshot

Career Cluster: Business Administration
Interests: Office management; managing people, projects, and schedules; information management technology; communication; meeting/event planning
Earnings (Yearly Average): $32,840
Employment & Outlook: Average Growth Expected

OVERVIEW

Sphere of Work

An administrative assistant is an office professional who performs various clerical tasks to assist the executives, presidents, or owners of a corporate business or government agency with the smooth operation of the office. An administrative assistant is responsible for managing and completing a wide range of short- and long-term duties and projects, and frequently takes on executive responsibilities in the absence, or under the direction, of the executive.

Work Environment

An administrative assistant generally works from an indoor office and takes all directions from his or her employer. An assistant usually works in a space that is near, or in some cases connected to, the workspace of the executive to whom he or she reports. Administrative assistants interact with other office personnel, other executives or company vice presidents, and external vendors. They must often assume office management responsibilities, frequently delegating tasks and projects to secretaries, interns, and other subordinates. They usually work a standard forty-hour week but may be expected to work longer hours, depending on the nature of the business.

Profile

Working Conditions: Work Indoors
Physical Strength: Light Work
Education Needs: High School Diploma or GED, Technical/Community College
Licensure/Certification: Recommended
Physical Abilities Not Required: No Heavy Labor
Opportunities For Experience: Apprenticeship, Military Service, Part-Time Work
Holland Interest Score*: ESC

* See Appendix A

Occupation Interest

Those interested in pursuing a career as an administrative assistant must be highly detail-oriented with the desire to complete any task, big or small, quickly and efficiently. An administrative assistant must have a passion for working with and managing people and must maintain a positive attitude. Because employers expect extremely efficient results from their office personnel, an administrative assistant should possess the desire to please and sometimes to exceed what would normally be expected of an office worker.

A Day in the Life—Duties and Responsibilities

An administrative assistant's typical workday consists of performing standard, high-level clerical tasks as needed, as well as completing additional errands and assignments as directed by the employer. Administrative assistants provide information management support to top company executives. These tasks may include organizing conference calls, arranging itineraries and travel plans, reviewing correspondence, and preparing the office for large meetings. They may also supervise other employees and provide training and orientation to new office personnel. Throughout the day, they manage all communications for their employers, including scheduling appointments, maintaining paper and electronic files, overseeing large projects, conducting research, and handling messages and mail services.

In addition to regular administrative tasks, administrative assistants often perform duties outside of the administrative sphere, such as running personal errands, meeting with external vendors, and conducting an employer's business in his or her absence. Some administrative assistants, like those who operate within a specialized field, may be required to learn and understand technical terminology and procedures used in that field.

Administrative assistants are sometimes expected to be on call for last minute or emergency projects outlined by their employers.

Duties and Responsibilities

- Coordinating office services
- Overseeing record-keeping and scheduling of executives
- Reviewing budgets, personnel performance, and work schedules
- Acting as a liaison between executives and other staff personnel

WORK ENVIRONMENT

Physical Environment

Administrative assistants usually work in clean, comfortable, and well-maintained offices located in close proximity to that of their employer. Some administrative assistants have their own offices where they work alone, and some work in large, open spaces with many other office employees. Most administrative assistants work in corporate business offices, hospitals, schools, government agencies, law firms, or nonprofit organizations. A virtual administrative assistant works remotely, from a home or private office.

Relevant Skills and Abilities

Communication Skills
- Speaking effectively
- Writing concisely

Interpersonal/Social Skills
- Cooperating with others
- Motivating others
- Providing support to others
- Working as a member of a team

Organization & Management Skills
- Following instructions
- Managing people/groups
- Managing time
- Organizing information or materials

Research & Planning Skills
- Solving problems

Human Environment

Administrative assistants interact with numerous people on a daily basis and must maintain a pleasant attitude. They may greet guests or customers, direct and supervise office employees and vendors, and interact with high-level executives.

Technological Environment

An administrative assistant commonly uses a computer equipped with standard office software, e-mail, and Internet applications, as well as any custom software the company may use. Administrative assistants also use transcription and dictation software, copy and fax machines, scanners, telephone systems, and audio recorders.

EDUCATION, TRAINING, AND ADVANCEMENT

High School/Secondary

High school students interested in becoming administrative assistants should focus on subjects like business, communications, computers, technology, economics, and English. High school graduates who have some basic knowledge of office management can apply to become administrative assistants. Students can also take independent classes to learn the fundamentals of office management. They can also participate in a job shadowing project or mentorship program.

Suggested High School Subjects
- Business
- Business & Computer Technology

- Business Data Processing
- Business Law
- College Preparatory
- Composition
- English
- Mathematics

Famous First

The first business high school was the Washington Business High School in Washington, DC, which opened in 1890. The school's first principal, Allan Davis, held a law degree. The school functioned for some thirty years before it was finally closed.

College/Postsecondary

Interested postsecondary students should complete a vocational education program that offers training in office skills or a one- or two-year program in office administration at a community college or vocational school. Administrative assistants in a specialized field, like law or medicine, must complete specialized training programs designed to familiarize new employees with the culture and language of the specialty.

A postsecondary degree is not formally required for administrative assistant positions; however, it has become increasingly helpful to have a college degree, as employers are looking for polished, knowledgeable individuals who are able to interact intelligently and effectively with top executives.

Postsecondary students are also encouraged to seek internships or part-time volunteer positions in local corporate offices to gain real-world experience and to further their knowledge of the trade.

Related College Majors

- Administrative Assistant/Secretarial Science
- Business Administration & Management
- Executive Assistant/Secretary Training
- General Office/Clerical & Typing Services
- Office Supervision & Management

Adult Job Seekers

People applying for administrative assistant jobs through a temporary placement agency often receive training in computer and office skills through the agency. Other job seekers apply directly with a business or company, and some are hired after completing an internship or volunteer assignment. Most businesses offer administrative on-the-job training in new technologies and software. Continuing education classes also give administrative assistants the tools they need to stay abreast of changes in the industry.

Professional Certification and Licensure

Though administrative assistants are not required to receive formal certification or licensure, certification has become increasingly beneficial. An administrative assistant can become a Certified Administrative Professional (CAP) by meeting specific requirements and successfully completing an examination. Professional administrative organizations like the International Association of Administrative Professionals and the International Virtual Assistants Association offer testing and certification in office administration and management. Administrative assistants working in a specialized field like law or medicine may need to pass specific courses and tests in order to receive certification. Consult credible professional associations within the field and follow professional debate as to the relevancy and value of any certification program.

Additional Requirements

A successful administrative assistant must pay impeccable attention to detail. Executives expect their administrative assistants to complete all daily tasks pleasantly, accurately, and in a timely fashion. Employers want to hire administrative assistants they can implicitly trust to assist them, so loyalty, good judgment, a friendly attitude, and the ability to multitask are extremely valuable traits in the office environment.

Fun Fact

In 1942, the National Secretaries Association was formed "to elevate the standards of the secretarial profession." The group defined a secretary as "an executive assistant who possesses a mastery of office skills, who demonstrates the ability to assume responsibility without direct supervision, who exercises initiative and judgment, and who makes decisions within the scope of assigned authority."

Source: http://library.temple.edu/scrc/national-secretaries

EARNINGS AND ADVANCEMENT

Swift advancement is possible for able and hard-working individuals. Though entry level positions in business are paid an hourly rate, administrative assistants are almost always salaried positions. Earnings depend on the size of the organization and the level of responsibility and experience.

Median annual earnings of administrative assistants were $32,840 in 2013. The lowest ten percent earned less than $21,000, and the highest ten percent earned more than $49,000.

Salaries in different parts of the country vary. Earnings are generally lowest in southern cities and highest in northern and western cities. In addition, salaries vary by industry; salaries tend to be highest in transportation, legal services, and public utilities, and lowest in retail trade, finance, insurance and real estate. Certification in this field is usually rewarded with a higher salary.

Administrative assistants may receive paid vacations, holidays, and sick days; life and health insurance; and retirement benefits. These are usually paid by the employer.

Metropolitan Areas with the Highest Employment Level in This Occupation

Metropolitan area	Employment[1]	Employment per thousand jobs	Hourly mean wage
New York-White Plains-Wayne, NY-NJ	107,230	20.46	$19.00
Los Angeles-Long Beach-Glendale, CA	60,250	15.16	$18.27
Chicago-Joliet-Naperville, IL	45,600	12.32	$16.95
Houston-Sugar Land-Baytown, TX	42,140	15.28	$16.39
Washington-Arlington-Alexandria, DC-VA-MD-WV	34,730	14.67	$20.61
Philadelphia, PA	34,180	18.58	$17.47
Atlanta-Sandy Springs-Marietta, GA	32,320	14.00	$16.85
Denver-Aurora-Broomfield, CO	31,500	24.59	$17.96
Nassau-Suffolk, NY	31,150	25.21	$18.18
Dallas-Plano-Irving, TX	31,030	14.44	$16.42

[1] Does not include self-employed. Source: Bureau of Labor Statistics.

EMPLOYMENT AND OUTLOOK

Administrative assistants and secretaries held about 2.3 million jobs in 2012. Employment of administrative assistants is expected to grow about as fast as the average for all occupations through the year 2022, which means employment is projected to increase 10 percent to 15 percent. There will always be a need for individuals that can effectively carry out the wishes and plans of executives. Conscientious and hard working people will find no shortage of opportunities in this occupation.

Employment Trend, Projected 2012–22

Administrative Assistants and Secretaries: 12%

Total, All Occupations: 11%

Office and Administrative Support Occupations: 7%

Note: "All Occupations" includes all occupations in the U.S. Economy. Source: U.S. Bureau of Labor Statistics, Employment Projections Program.

Related Occupations

- Administrative Support Supervisor
- Customer Service Representative
- Executive Secretary
- General Office Clerk
- Legal Secretary
- Medical Assistant
- Secretary

Related Military Occupations

- Administrative Support Specialist
- Finance & Accounting Specialist
- Legal Specialist & Court Reporter
- Management Analyst
- Personnel Specialist
- Postal Specialist
- Religious Program Specialist

Conversation With . . .
RILEY CLARK

Executive Assistant
Anne Arundel Community College, Arnold, MD
Administrative Assistant, 7 years

1. What was your individual career path in terms of education/training, entry-level job, or other significant opportunity?

I received my bachelor's degree in Communication from Boston University, and worked part-time throughout college as an administrative assistant at a law firm. When I graduated, I spent some time traveling, but returned to a less than ideal job market. I found an entry-level position at a not-for-profit, and worked very hard to steadily increase my responsibilities. Through connections I made in that role, I was informed of an open position at a local university. Currently, I am Executive Assistant to the Vice President for Learning at a community college. Some of my previous titles have included Program Assistant, Program Coordinator, and Assistant to the Dean.

2. What are the most important skills and/or qualities for someone in your profession?

For administrative support positions, the most important skills to hone are problem solving and the ability to adapt to changing environments. With those two skills, you can handle any task asked of you.

3. What do you wish you had known going into this profession?

I think people in my profession develop intimate relationships with the people they support. Some people are just not compatible in a work environment, so I wish I had known how to interview a potential supervisor while being interviewed for a position.

4. Are there many job opportunities in your profession? In what specific areas?

I believe there are entry-level opportunities for administrative support staff, but the higher ranking administrative support positions are much less common, in my experience.

5. **How do you see your profession changing in the next five years, what role will technology play in those changes, and what skills will be required?**

    I think the key role for people in administrative support and related positions will be to act as a liaison between the emerging advancements in technology and the people we are assisting. I can generate reports much faster using my computer skills than someone from the generation above me, and the generation below will be even faster. To prepare for that, I take classes in commonly used software to make sure I can provide the best support to my manager.

6. **What do you like most about your job? What do you like least about your job?**

    What I enjoy most about my job is the diverse range of operations I'm asked to conduct on a daily basis. My least favorite aspect of this profession is a general misunderstanding of the breadth and scale of the operations that administrative support staff conduct.

7. **Can you suggest a valuable "try this" for students considering a career in your profession?**

    Evaluate your personal relationships—friendships, family, romantic relationships. If you find that you do more for the people in your life than you receive from them, you might be very satisfied in an administrative support role. If taking care of others makes you happy, you should definitely explore the possibility of an administrative support position.

SELECTED SCHOOLS

Many technical and community colleges offer programs in business administration and/or secretarial science. Interested students are advised to consult with their school guidance counselor or to research area postsecondary schools and training programs.

MORE INFORMATION

American Society of Administrative Professionals
121 Free Street
Portland, ME 04101
888.960.2727
www.asaporg.com

Association of Executive and Administrative Professionals
900 S. Washington Street, Suite G-13
Falls Church, VA 22046
703.237.8616
www.theaeap.com

International Association of Administrative Professionals
P.O. Box 20404
Kansas City, MO 64195-0404
816.891.6600
www.iaap-hq.org

International Virtual Assistants Association
375 N. Stephanie Street, Suite 1411
Henderson, NV 89014
877.440.2750
www.ivaa.org

Office and Professional Employees International Union
80 8th Avenue, Suite 610
New York, NY 10011
800.346.7348
www.opeiu.org

Briana Nadeau/Editor

Advertising and Marketing Manager

Snapshot

Career Cluster: Business Administration; Media & Communications; Sales & Marketing

Interests: Animals and Animal Maintenance and Training

Earnings (Yearly Average): $123,220

Employment & Outlook: Average Growth Expected

OVERVIEW

Sphere of Work

Advertising and marketing managers work as staff members in corporate marketing and advertising departments. They can also work in specialized ad agencies or marketing firms. Their work falls within the communication, information, and business sectors. They serve as one of the main links or points of contact between the marketplace and the company or agency for which they work. Advertising and marketing managers coordinate print, television, radio, and digital media advertising campaigns and projects; in some cases, they may also be responsible for sales and developing new business opportunities.

While advertising and marketing managers contribute to campaign development, they are not technically part of an agency's creative (or design) team. Their primary role is to ensure that campaigns are priced, administered, and executed smoothly and efficiently, and with the company's (or client's) interests in mind. They ensure that campaign milestones are met and elements of the campaign are delivered on time and within budget. Aside from working closely with the director of advertising and marketing, they coordinate the work activities of personnel such as copywriters, graphic designers, production assistants, public relations personnel, and market researchers. They may interact with sales representatives and have additional project management responsibilities, as well. Advertising and marketing managers are generally supervised by a departmental director or client services supervisor.

Work Environment

Advertising and marketing managers work in an office environment within small to large companies or agencies. Air and car travel may be occasionally required to attend trade conferences or meet with clients. Evening and weekend work is also often required. Advertising and marketing managers frequently work under pressure and adhere to strict budgets and tight deadlines.

Profile

Working Conditions: Work Indoors
Physical Strength: Light Work
Education Needs: Bachelor's Degree
Licensure/Certification: Usually Not Required
Physical Abilities Not Required: No Heavy Labor
Opportunities For Experience: Internship, Apprenticeship, Volunteer Work
Holland Interest Score*: AES

* See Appendix A

Occupation Interest

Graduates and professionals with a strong interest in advertising and marketing, mass media and communications, and project management are often attracted to the advertising industry. In particular, the role suits people who have an interest in coordinating multiple activities in a fast-paced environment and who are comfortable working closely with others.

Aside from excellent collaborative, communication, and organizational skills, advertising and marketing managers must also possess strong research and analytical skills and solid business acumen. They may be expected to formulate and execute budgets, monitor expenses, and assist with financial reporting. In some instances, they will be expected to make sales calls or develop and present new business proposals.

Successful advertising and marketing managers must be able to speak and write fluently, work with a diverse range of people, adapt to new industries, clients, products and services, and deliver consistent results under pressure. The role also requires considerable tact and diplomacy.

A Day in the Life—Duties and Responsibilities

TThe typical work day of an advertising and marketing manager includes frequent meetings with staff, supervisors, department heads, and, in the case of independent agencies, clients. The campaign deliverables, which advertising and marketing managers coordinate, are usually subject to tight timeframes and strict deadlines. Therefore, on a daily basis, the role demands excellent organizational and time management skills. Advertising and marketing managers must be adept at multi-tasking, adapting to change, and problem solving.

Advertising and marketing managers generally gain a high level of exposure to different customer types, industries, products, and services (although some may specialize in specific industries). The role demands high business (and possibly sales) acumen and the ability to analyze new information quickly and effectively. An advertising and marketing manager is expected to thoroughly research and understand the industry in which their company operates, as well as their competitors and any competing products and marketing campaigns. This includes developing a deep understanding of the company's (or client's) customer base, methods and processes, challenges and opportunities, and target markets.

Advertising and marketing managers are expected to have competent computing skills to help them prepare campaign-related and organizational materials, such as financial and marketing reports, budget proposals, "pitches" (presentations) to acquire new business, and other work-related documents. They may also be expected to develop and manage spreadsheets and databases for project management and accounting purposes.

Duties and Responsibilities

- **Preparing advertising and marketing campaigns, schedules, and budgets**
- **Consulting with people in sales, market research, and creative departments**
- **Overseeing staff in layout, copy, and production**

OCCUPATION SPECIALTIES

Advertising Managers

Advertising managers seek to generate interest in a product or service by means of ads placed in various media. They work with sales staff and others to create ideas for an advertising campaign. Some advertising managers specialize in a particular field or type of advertising. For example, media directors determine the way in which an advertising campaign reaches customers; they can use any or all of various media, including radio, television, newspapers, magazines, the Internet, and outdoor signs. Advertising managers known as account executives manage clients' accounts, but they do not necessarily develop or supervise the creation or presentation of the advertising. That is the work of the creative services department.

Marketing Managers

Marketing managers gather and use data to estimate the demand for products and services that an organization and its competitors offer. They identify potential markets, develop pricing strategies to help maximize profits, and ensure that customers are satisfied (by using surveys, etc.). They work with sales, advertising, and product development staffs to identify and target customers and keep the firm's products or services competitive in the marketplace. In smaller firms individuals may function as both marketing and advertising managers as well as promotions managers.

Promotions Managers

Promotions managers oversee programs that combine advertising with purchasing incentives to increase sales. Often, the programs use direct mail, inserts in newspapers, Internet advertisements, in-store displays, product endorsements, or special events to target customers. Purchasing incentives may include discounts, samples, gifts, rebates, coupons, sweepstakes, and contests.

WORK ENVIRONMENT

Relevant Skills and Abilities

Analytical Skills
- Critical thinking and reasoning
- Information processing

Communication Skills
- Listening to others
- Persuading others
- Speaking and writing effectively

Interpersonal/Social Skills
- Being able to work both independently and on a team
- Cooperating with others
- Having good judgment
- Motivating others

Organization & Management Skills
- Making sound decisions
- Managing time and money
- Meeting goals and deadlines
- Paying attention to and handling details
- Solving problems
- Supervising others as necessary

Other Skills
- Appreciating both the business and the creative sides

Physical Environment

Office settings predominate. Advertising and marketing managers work for small to large advertising and marketing departments or agencies, usually in urban or semi-urban locations. Some travel may be required.

Job security is sometimes tenuous in the advertising industry. Economic or sector downturns, changes to a firm's customer base, or reduced customer spending can lead to layoffs. This tends to create an atmosphere of intense competition.

Human Environment

Advertising and marketing manager roles demand strong collaborative and team skills. Advertising and marketing managers interact with sales, advertising, business, and creative specialists, such as brand and product managers, marketing managers, brand strategists, public relations executives, graphic designers, art directors, multimedia technicians, copywriters, production assistants, and editors. They are likely to work with multiple departmental or client contacts, as well as outside service providers or freelancers. They usually report to an agency/department director or owner, or to an area supervisor.

Technological Environment

Advertising and marketing managers use standard business technologies, including computer systems and networks, telecommunications tools, Internet and social media tools, presentation tools and software, and financial and database software. In smaller firms, where greater overlap between marketing and design functions often exists, managers sometimes need to be familiar with graphic design software and basic production technologies (such as desktop publishing)

EDUCATION, TRAINING, AND ADVANCEMENT

High School/Secondary

High school students can best prepare for a career as an advertising and marketing manager by taking courses in business, math (with an accounting focus), computer literacy, and communications (for example, journalism or business communications). Courses such as social studies, history, and economics will also prepare the student for synthesizing research into written materials. The creative aspects of the advertising industry may be explored through art and graphic design. However, it is important to note that advertising and marketing managers work in an administrative, rather than a creative, capacity. In addition, psychology and cultural studies may provide an understanding of group and individual responses to advertising and other forms of communication.

Students should also become involved in extracurricular school activities and projects that develop business and communication skills to gain hands-on experience prior to graduation. Additionally, serving as a club secretary, treasurer, or other office holder will help to develop organizational skills. Participation in student newsletters and similar publications will help to build an understanding of print and multimedia communications.

Suggested High School Subjects

- Business Data Processing
- Business Math
- Communications
- Composition
- Computer Science
- Economics
- English
- Graphic Arts
- Journalism
- Psychology
- Statistics

Famous First

The first use of coupons in a promotional campaign was in 1865, when soap maker B. T. Babbitt of New York City began selling soap bars in wrappers. He printed the word "coupon" on the wrapper and gave away a lithographic print for every 10 coupons returned. The strategy was so successful that Babbitt had to create a "premium department" to manage this and other such giveaways.

College/Postsecondary

At the college level, students interested in becoming an advertising and marketing manager should work toward earning an undergraduate degree in communications, advertising, marketing, or business administration. Alternatively, they should build a strong liberal arts background. Owing to strong competition among professional business candidates, a master's degree is sometimes expected, although practical experience is often more highly regarded than formal qualifications.

A large number of colleges and universities offer advertising, marketing, communications, and business degree programs. Some programs offer internships or work experience with advertising departments or agencies. These experiences may lead to entry-level opportunities. Aspiring advertising and marketing managers can also gain entry into the advertising industry via other roles, such as market research, administration, or sales.

Related College Majors
- Advertising
- Business Administration
- Communications
- Journalism
- Management/Management Science
- Marketing & Merchandising
- Psychology
- Public Relations
- Statistics

Adult Job Seekers

Adults seeking a career transition into or return to an advertising and marketing manager role will need to highlight qualifications, skills, and experience in areas such as business administration, advertising, and marketing. Necessary skills for a successful transition include account coordination, client liaison, and project management.

Marketing and advertising experience with a non-agency corporation is often highly regarded because agency firms value employees who understand the client side of the relationship.

Networking is critical—candidates should not rely solely on online job searches and advertised positions to explore work opportunities. As with recent college graduates, adult job seekers may wish to consider entry to the advertising industry via an alternative route, such as market research, administration, or sales.

Professional Certification and Licensure

There are no formal professional certifications or licensing requirements for advertising and marketing managers.

Additional Requirements

The most important attributes for advertising and marketing managers are a passion for advertising and marketing communications, coupled with excellent business, organizational, and people skills. Advertising and marketing managers must be skilled and diplomatic coordinators, negotiators, and problem solvers. They should be willing to persist under often heavy workloads and with demanding stakeholders..

Fun Fact

Marketers are using Facebook and Twitter more and more to take advantage of the fact that one of every seven minutes users surf the web is spent on Facebook, and 340 million Tweets were posted each day in 2012.

Source: http://www.i7marketing.com/internetmarketing/10-interesting-social-media-facts/

EARNINGS AND ADVANCEMENT

Earning potential increases as advancement occurs. Advancement may be quick in corporate ranks, partly because turnover can be high as a result of account success or failure. Many firms provide their employees with continuing education opportunities, either in-house or at local colleges and universities, and encourage employee participation in seminars and conferences.

According to a salary survey by the National Association of Colleges and Employers, graduates with a bachelor's degree in advertising had starting salaries of $47,343 in 2012. Advertising and marketing managers had median annual earnings of $123,220 in 2013. The lowest ten percent earned less than $65,000, and the highest ten percent earned more than $200,000. Performance incentives and bonuses are granted according to the employee's record of performance.

Advertising and marketing managers may receive paid vacations, holidays, and sick days; life and health insurance; and retirement benefits. These are usually paid by the employer. Top executives in the field may receive additional benefits (such as stock options).

Metropolitan Areas with the Highest Employment Level in This Occupation

Metropolitan area	Employment[1]	Employment per thousand jobs	Hourly mean wage
New York-White Plains-Wayne, NY-NJ	11,630	2.22	$85.29
Los Angeles-Long Beach-Glendale, CA	7,360	1.85	$65.55
Chicago-Joliet-Naperville, IL	7,100	1.92	$55.55
Minneapolis-St. Paul-Bloomington, MN-WI	6,460	3.61	$61.66
Boston-Cambridge-Quincy, MA	5,780	3.31	$67.72
San Jose-Sunnyvale-Santa Clara, CA	5,320	5.72	$88.36
San Francisco-San Mateo-Redwood City, CA	4,700	4.50	$83.57
Washington-Arlington-Alexandria, DC-VA-MD-WV	4,330	1.83	$73.15
Atlanta-Sandy Springs-Marietta, GA	4,300	1.86	$64.06
Santa Ana-Anaheim-Irvine, CA	3,570	2.46	$70.23

[1] Does not include self-employed. Source: Bureau of Labor Statistics.

EMPLOYMENT AND OUTLOOK

There were approximately 215,000 advertising and marketing managers employed nationally in 2012. Positions exist not only in advertising agencies, but also with public relations firms, printing and publishing firms, computer services firms, and many others. There is also a strong demand for advertising and marketing managers in the non-profit sector, including colleges/universities and philanthropic organizations. Employment is expected to grow about as fast as the average for all occupations through the year 2022, which means employment is projected to increase 10 percent to 15 percent. Increasingly intense domestic and global competition in products and services offered to consumers should require greater need for this occupation as companies want to maintain and expand their share of the market.

Many of the high-level jobs are very competitive. College graduates with extensive experience, a high level of creativity, and strong communication skills should have the best job opportunities.

Employment Trend, Projected 2012–22

Marketing Managers: 13%

Advertising, Promotions, and Marketing Managers: 12%

Total, All Occupations: 11%

Advertising and Promotions Managers: 7%

Note: "All Occupations" includes all occupations in the U.S. Economy. Source: U.S. Bureau of Labor Statistics, Employment Projections Program.

Related Occupations
- Advertising Director
- Advertising Sales Agent
- Copywriter
- Electronic Commerce Specialist
- Market Research Analyst
- Public Relations Specialist
- Sales Manager

Conversation With . . .
EVELYN KERRIGAN

Marketing Manager
East Coast 3rd-Party Freight and Logistics
Management Company
Marketing/sales profession, 25 years

1. What was your individual career path in terms of education/training, entry-level job, or other significant opportunity?

In college I studied anthropology and English. I also took some art and design courses as electives. The English and writing became important components of my career in marketing, as did the art and design aspects of my education. I was in sales positions for many years that required writing, and even marketing department administration at one point. Those led to my first marketing position, which fell into my lap. The employer knew I had writing and sales experience, and I realized that everything I had been doing was geared to that job.

2. What are the most important skills and/or qualities for someone in your profession?

Diversifying your abilities and being flexible are the most valuable attributes you offer a company. Small- to mid-sized companies view marketing as a bleed to the bottom line versus sales, which is a revenue stream. Companies want to optimize their marketing budget by finding someone who can be the whole marketing package. That means someone who possesses the ability to write press releases, do graphics for ads, punch up social media stats with engaging copy, run e-marketing campaigns using the latest CRM (customer relationship management) platform, while organizing the trade show schedule. You have to have a well-rounded mix of tools.

Companies with a larger budget may look for more specialized marketing positions, but you limit yourself by over-specializing. Companies can always outsource functions such as creating ads, which is less expensive than hiring a graphic designer. You must be flexible because you have to be able to change direction at a moment's notice. You also have to be a good listener with a solid grasp of what your company's goals and visions are from a brand and marketing perspective.

The ability to either prepare or propose a budget and maintain that budget is usually another important part of the position.

Finally, I think marketing requires a person who is very personable. You're dealing with a lot of people in a lot of different areas.

3. What do you wish you had known going into this profession?

How intense it can be. This industry is not for slackers. You have to be on your toes and the expectations are high. You have to produce results. You have to be an ideas person as well as someone who can execute those ideas. And most of all, you have to be able to negotiate with those with whom you work, such as sales and upper management, who aren't always going to agree with your ideas and plans.

4. Are there many job opportunities in your profession? In what specific areas?

Yes. There are opportunities in just about all industries, but there is also a ton of competition. It seems like there are more marketing majors out there than anything else. You'll find most jobs in the B2B and B2C markets. The turnover is pretty high. Honestly, there is a three to five year burnout factor for most marketers before they are looking for the next challenge.

5. How do you see your profession changing in the next five years, what role will technology play in those changes, and what skills will be required?

Marketing automation is huge now and will become more and more advanced. This includes all online systems that engage the person reading whatever you are sending out, such as an email.

You also have to understand how sales integrate with marketing via the company's CRM platform.

Inbound marketing (driving engagement through content such as white papers, blogs or social media) is also becoming more the norm, rather than outbound marketing, this is another term for traditional marketing, such as print ads, mailers, or TV and radio spots. It is a pull mentality rather than a push.

6. What do you like most about your job? What do you like least about your job?

The creativity and the challenge of a successful campaign are what make the job rewarding. Being constantly creative and "on" is a challenge. Having to come up with the next awesome ad or campaign can be a lot of pressure. Some days it just isn't there.

7. Can you suggest a valuable "try this" for students considering a career in your profession?

Find a local company that's just starting out. Offer to do a trial marketing campaign for them, gratis. You don't even have to spend any money to do this. Just give them a well-documented, thought-out plan. It can be a social media campaign, for example. Then be prepared to show the results with real metrics. It could be a fun project, and who knows, it might just land you a job!

SELECTED SCHOOLS

Many colleges and universities, especially those with business schools, offer programs in marketing and advertising. The student can also gain initial training at a technical or community college. Below are listed some of the more prominent institutions in this field.

Indiana University—Bloomington
Kelley School of Business
1309 E. 10th Street
Bloomington, IN 47405
812.855.8100
kelley.iu.edu

New York University
Stern School of Business
665 Broadway, 11th Floor
New York, NY 10012
212.998.4500
www.stern.nyu.edu

University of California—Berkeley
Haas School of Business
S450 Student Services Building #1900
Berkeley, CA 94720
510.642.1421
haas.berkeley.edu

University of Michigan—Ann Arbor
Ross School of Business
701 Tappan Avenue
Ann Arbor, MI 48109
734.763.5796
michiganross.umich.edu

University of North Carolina—Chapel Hill
Kenan-Flagler Business School
Campus Box 3490, McColl Building
Chapel Hill, NC 27599
919.962.3235
www.kenan-flagler.unc.edu

University of Pennsylvania
The Wharton School
1 College Hall
Philadelphia, PA 19104
215.898.6376
www.whatron.upenn.edu

University of Southern California
Marshall School of Business
3670 Trousdale Parkway
Los Angeles, CA 90089
213.740.8674
www.marshall.usc.edu

University of Texas—Austin
McCombs School of Business
1 University Station, B6000
Austin, TX 78712
512.471.5921
www.mccombs.utexas.edu

University of Virginia
McIntire School of Commerce
125 Ruppel Drive
PO Box 400173
Charlottseville, VA 22903
434.924.3176
www.commerce.virginia.edu

**University of Wisconsin—
Madison**
Wisconsin School of Business
Grainger Hall
975 University Avenue
Madison, WI 53706
608.262.1550
bus.wisc.edu

MORE INFORMATION

**Advertising Research
Foundation**
432 Park Avenue South, 6th Floor
New York, NY 10016-8013
212.751.5656
thearf.org

Advertising Women of New York
25 West 45th Street, Suite 403
New York, NY 10036
212.221.7969
www.awny.org

American Advertising Federation
1101 Vermont Avenue, NW
Suite 500
Washington, DC 20005-6306
800.999.2231
www.aaf.org

**American Association of
Advertising Agencies**
405 Lexington Avenue, 18th Floor
New York, NY 10174-1801
212.682.2500
www.aaaa.org

American Marketing Association
311 S. Wacker Drive
Suite 5800
Chicago, IL 60606
312.542.9000
www.marketingpower.com

**Association of National
Advertisers**
708 Third Avenue, 33rd Floor
New York, NY 10017-4270
212.697.5950
www.ana.net

Kylie Grimshaw Hughes/Editor

Auditor

Snapshot

Career Cluster: Banking & Finance; Business Administration; Government & Public Administration

Interests: Analyzing data, accounting, finances, record-keeping, detail work

Earnings (Yearly Average): $65,080

Employment & Outlook: Average Growth Expected

OVERVIEW

Sphere of Work

Auditors use their training in accounting to review the accuracy of an organization's financial records. Auditors work for and verify the financial records of the public sector (including government agencies and departments) and the private sector (including large corporations, small businesses, and non-profit organizations). There are two main areas of auditing internal auditing and external auditing. Internal auditors review their organization's internal financial controls and record keeping for evidence of waste or fraud. External auditors are hired, often as a condition of regulatory and stakeholder compliance,

from an outside organization to review and verify the accuracy of an organization's financial controls and record keeping. .

Work Environment

An auditor's work environment is generally desk-based. Depending on the employer and particular job description, an auditor may telecommute from a home office, visit client offices as a contractor, or work on a full-time basis in an employer's office. Auditors may work as a full-time member of a work team responsible for ongoing financial document review and documentation or may be hired as a contractor. An auditor's work environment is dependent on technology, including computers and financial software programs, as well as having access to the most recent government regulations.

Profile

Working Conditions: Work Indoors
Physical Strength: Light Work
Education Needs: Bachelor's Degree
Licensure/Certification: Required
Physical Abilities Not Required: No Heavy Labor
Opportunities For Experience: Internship
Holland Interest Score*: RCS

* See Appendix A

Occupation Interest

Individuals interested in the auditing profession tend to be well-organized and detail-oriented people who find satisfaction in reviewing and analyzing systems, processes, and large amounts of data. Auditors may also have an interest and affinity for technology and regulatory issues. For instance, those who excel in auditing tend to be adept at educating themselves about and responding to frequent technological and regulatory changes. Analytical people choosing to pursue the occupation of auditor may find satisfaction in staying up-to-date on auditing best practices.

A Day in the Life—Duties and Responsibilities

An auditor's daily occupational duties and responsibilities include reviewing, verifying, and certifying the accuracy and authenticity of financial records. Specific duties, schedules, and assignments vary between internal and external auditors. Further specialization can occur, as some choose to pursue interests in information technology (IT) auditing, environmental auditing, financial auditing, and compliance auditing.

Internal auditors will review their organization's financial records on an ongoing basis, looking for regulatory compliance or indications of employee mismanagement, waste, or fraud. Internal auditors review all financial records including ordering, payroll, inventory, expenses, work orders, equipment purchasing, profit/loss statements, and taxes. Internal auditors are also increasingly responsible for reviewing and overseeing financial software, as organizations move to automate financial transactions. Internal auditors report findings to management and often participate in developing the organization's financial policies and best practices.

External auditors, usually employed by public accounting firms, will be hired on a contract basis quarterly or annually to review the financial documents of businesses or government departments. Stakeholder and state and federal laws generally require businesses to seek an external independent audit of all financial records on a regular basis. External auditors most often report their findings to regulatory agencies such as the Securities and Exchange Commission (SEC) and the Internal Revenue Service (IRS).

Duties and Responsibilities

- Auditing contracts, purchase orders and vouchers and preparing related reports
- Directing and coordinating activities of workers engaged in keeping accounts and records
- Writing opinions on financial statements
- Giving advice on profit planning, budgeting, and cost control

OCCUPATION SPECIALTIES

Internal Auditors

Internal Auditors examine and evaluate financial and information systems, management procedures, and internal controls. They check records to assure accuracy and to protect against fraud and waste.

County/City Auditors

County/City Auditors direct activities of personnel engaged in recording deeds and similar legal instruments, keep records of county or municipal accounts, compile and transmit fiscal records, prepare financial statements, and audit books of city or county offices.

Tax Auditors

Tax Auditors audit financial records to determine tax liability. They review information gathered from the taxpayer, such as material assets, income, surpluses, liabilities and expenditures to verify net worth or reported financial status.

WORK ENVIRONMENT

Immediate Physical Environment

Auditors generally work in office environments. The work of an auditor requires sitting at a desk and using computers for long periods of time each day. Auditors hired to perform external audits may be required to travel to client offices to review financial records and attend meetings.

Human Environment

An auditor's human environment may be social or isolated depending on the assignment and the organization. These factors will influence interaction with clients, employees, supervisors, or colleagues. It must be noted that auditors—who are by their job definition responsible for finding problems, waste, and fraud—may be perceived in an adversarial or hostile way by some organizational employees.

Relevant Skills and Abilities

Interpersonal/Social Skills

- Being able to work independently
- Being honest
- Being patient
- Cooperating with others
- Working as a member of a team

Organization & Management Skills

- Paying attention to and handling details

Research & Planning Skills

- Analyzing information
- Solving problems

Technical Skills

- Performing scientific, mathematical and technical work
- Using technology to process information
- Working with machines, tools or other objects

Technological Environment

An auditor's technological environment will generally include computers, financial and auditing software, and telecommunication tools.

EDUCATION, TRAINING, AND ADVANCEMENT

High School/Secondary

High school students interested in pursuing an auditing career should prepare themselves by building good organizational skills and developing strong study habits. They should also develop strong mathematical skills. Students should consider applying for internships, part-time work if available, or even volunteer work with local financial organizations in order to learn what it is that auditors do on a daily basis.

Suggested High School Subjects
- Accounting
- Algebra
- Applied Communication
- Bookkeeping
- Business
- Business Law
- Calculus
- Computer Science
- English
- Geometry
- Mathematics
- Statistics
- Trigonometry

Famous First

The first auditing firms to become prominent nationally were Deloitte & Touche, Coopers & Lybrand, Arthur Young (Ernst & Young), and Arthur Anderson, founded in 1896, 1898, 1906, and 1913, respectively. They were long known as the "Big Four." Today, we still have the "Big Four" consisting of Deloitte & Touche, Pricewaterhouse Coopers, Ernst & Young (now called EY), and KPMG.

Postsecondary

Postsecondary students interested in pursuing an auditing career should prepare themselves by building a foundation in mathematics, accounting, and business courses. Due to the importance of technology, law, and ethics in the practice of auditing, postsecondary students interested in pursuing a career in auditing will also benefit from studying both computer and political science. Postsecondary students committed to pursuing auditing will gain experience and build connections through auditing internships and part-time employment with financial businesses, such as accounting and auditing firms.

Related College Majors
- Accounting
- Business Administration & Management, General
- Economics, General
- Mathematics

Adult Job Seekers

Adults seeking auditing jobs have generally earned a bachelor's degree in accounting, business administration, or another closely related profession. Those individuals who intend to work toward managerial or supervisor roles in the auditing world may choose to earn a master's of business administration (MBA) or law degree. Adult job seekers will benefit from joining professional auditing associations as a means of professional networking. Professional auditing associations generally offer job-finding workshops and maintain job lists advertising open auditing positions. Adult job seekers who wish to join the auditing profession, but who lack a college degree, may be able to gain access to the field by seeking entry-level bookkeeping and clerk positions. Supervisors and mentors can help junior auditors plan their career and educational choices.

Professional Certification and Licensure

Auditors are required to have the same professional certification and licensure required of accountants. The most common professional license for auditors and accountants is the CPA certification issued by state boards of accountancy. Only licensed CPAs are legally allowed to submit financial reports to the SEC. CPA licensure is based on three elements: education, examination, and experience. CPAs are required to have at least 150 semester hours of college coursework, pass the CPA exam, and fulfill state experience requirements. The American Institute of Certified Public Accountants administers the universal CPA examination accepted by all states. The CPA examination includes four discrete parts that must be passed within an eighteen-month period. The CPA examination is computerized and offered multiple times a year at state testing centers.

In addition to the CPA certification, professional auditors may choose to pursue auditing-specific designations such as the Certified Internal Auditor license and the Certified Information Systems Auditor license. These two licenses, achieved through passing examinations, are the industry standard for demonstrating professional auditing competencies. As in any venture, a candidate should consult credible professional associations within their prospective field and follow professional debate as to the relevancy and value of any certification program.

Additional Requirements

Individuals who find satisfaction, success, and job security in the auditing profession will be knowledgeable about the profession's requirements, responsibilities, and opportunities.

Individuals dedicated to training and advancing in the auditing field generally work to develop their analytical, mathematical, and business abilities. Written and verbal communication skills are also important for auditors, as is proficiency with auditing software. High levels of integrity and ethics are required of auditors, as they often work with private and confidential documents. Additionally, external auditors often do their work within a corporation's offices—sometimes outside of the normal workday. Discretion and trust are essential to an effective working relationship between the outside auditor and his or her client.

Membership in professional auditing associations is encouraged among both junior and senior auditors as a means of building status within a professional community and networking.

Fun Fact

Before he was a disciple, Matthew was a tax collector for the Romans. Today, St. Matthew is the Roman Catholic patron saint of a multitude of financial professionals: accountants, tax collectors, bookkeepers, stock brokers and bankers.

Source: http://catholicherald.com/stories/A-Patron-Saint-for-Bankers-and-Accountants,1953.

EARNINGS AND ADVANCEMENT

According to a salary survey conducted by the National Association of Colleges and Employers, graduates with a bachelor's degree in accounting received annual starting salary offers averaging $53,536 in 2012; master's degree candidates in accounting were offered $53,785 in 2012.

Median annual earnings of auditors were $65,080 in 2013. The lowest ten percent earned less than $41,000, and the highest ten percent earned more than $113,000.

Auditors may receive paid vacations, holidays, and sick days; life and health insurance; and retirement benefits. These are usually paid by the employer.

Metropolitan Areas with the Highest Employment Level in This Occupation

Metropolitan area	Employment[1]	Employment per thousand jobs	Hourly mean wage
New York-White Plains-Wayne, NY-NJ	71,070	13.56	$44.94
Los Angeles-Long Beach-Glendale, CA	43,490	10.94	$37.55
Washington-Arlington-Alexandria, DC-VA-MD-WV	35,350	14.93	$40.82
Chicago-Joliet-Naperville, IL	31,340	8.47	$35.80
Houston-Sugar Land-Baytown, TX	29,650	10.75	$38.74
Atlanta-Sandy Springs-Marietta, GA	28,460	12.33	$36.56
Dallas-Plano-Irving, TX	25,300	11.77	$37.07
Boston-Cambridge-Quincy, MA	24,150	13.81	$38.28
Philadelphia, PA	22,040	11.98	$37.58
Denver-Aurora-Broomfield, CO	21,360	16.68	$35.95

[1] Does not include self-employed. Source: Bureau of Labor Statistics

EMPLOYMENT AND OUTLOOK

Auditors and accountants held about 1.3 million jobs nationally in 2012. Employment is expected to grow about as fast as the average for all occupations through the year 2022, which means employment is projected to increase 10 percent to 15 percent. An increase in the number of businesses, changing financial laws and regulations, and increased scrutiny of company finances will drive job growth. In addition, the need to replace auditors and accountants who retire or transfer to other occupations will produce thousands of additional job openings annually, reflecting the large size of this occupation. The changing role of auditors and accountants will also spur job growth. In response to market demand, auditors and accountants will offer more financial management and consulting services. By focusing on analyzing operations, rather than simply providing financial data, auditors and accountants will help to boost demand for their services.

Opportunities are expected to be favorable for college graduates seeking auditing and accounting jobs who have worked part-time in a business or accounting firm while in school. In fact, experience has become so important that some employers in business and industry seek persons with one or two years experience for beginning positions. A master's degree or computer experience also offer more advantages for employment.

Employment Trend, Projected 2012–22

Auditors and Accountants: 13%

Business and Financial Occupations: 13%

Total, All Occupations: 11%

Note: "All Occupations" includes all occupations in the U.S. Economy. Source: U.S. Bureau of Labor Statistics, Employment Projections Program.

Related Occupations

- Accountant
- Actuary
- Budget Analyst
- Credit Manager
- Energy Auditor
- Financial Analyst
- Financial Manager
- Insurance Underwriter
- Personal Financial Advisor
- Public Administrator

Conversation With . . .
LARRY HARRINGTON

Internal Auditor, Vice President
Raytheon Company, Waltham, MA
Auditor, 25 years

1. What was your individual career path in terms of education/training, entry-level job, or other significant opportunity?

I graduated from Bentley University in Waltham, Massachusetts, with a degree in accounting. I worked for a number of years before attending and graduating from the Advanced Management Program at Harvard Business School. My advice for people starting out in their careers is to gain valuable work experience for a few years before seeking an advanced degree; this will leverage your business experience with real-time learning. I strongly suggest a program with an international focus.

I started my career in public accounting before moving into the corporate world, as an internal auditor. The skills I gained as an internal auditor enabled me to be viewed as an agent of change. Companies could trust me to lead new functions even if I didn't have core skills in that discipline because of my leadership, creativity and ability to work with others who did have those core skills. Eventually, I held vice president roles in finance, human resources and operations before moving into my current role as the chief audit executive at Raytheon Company, creating positive change with a sense of urgency.

2. What are the most important skills and/or qualities for someone in your profession?

The most important skills and qualities for an internal auditor can, appropriately, be encapsulated with the acronym CHANGE:

Communicating with persuasion; both verbal and written.

Helping others succeed through critical thinking and change management skills.

Accounting, IT and other business skills help you to accomplish positive change.

Networking and building relationships within your business, industry, and
    profession; most jobs come through networking.

Growing: invest in your own learning as employers seldom invest enough in you.

Enquiring mindset. Auditors are people who wonder about how businesses work.

3. What do you wish you had known going into this profession?

The importance of leadership (even without the title), the power of networking, and the necessity to continually self-invest in my knowledge and skill, rather than relying solely on a company to provide training. I also would have sought an international assignment.

4. Are there many job opportunities in your profession? In what specific areas?

Internal audit is a growth profession. All public companies have a requirement for internal auditors. There are also private companies that have an internal audit function to ensure they can get an internal objective view on their processes and any risks to the company. There are lots of early career positions as well as management positions.

5. How do you see your profession changing in the next five years, what role will technology play in those changes, and what skills will be required?

The profession is forever morphing as businesses morph due to global competition, big data, and technology. Many internal audit groups are working to analyze data in real-time, using continuous monitoring so that we can spot problems sooner and fix them quicker.

6. What do you like most about your job? What do you like least about your job?

The most enjoyable part is the development and coaching of people. I enjoy sharing my knowledge and mentoring people to create a career path and a plan to achieve that success. I learn from the people working for me as they help me continually learn and change, even at this point in my career.

The least enjoyable part is people thinking that internal audit is here to make them look bad. We have to work hard to change our professional image, so that people know our role is to help them succeed by helping them improve processes, reduce costs, meet their business objectives, and help them avoid surprises.

7. Can you suggest a valuable "try this" for students considering a career in your profession?

When you are out in your day-to-day life think critically about the processes you see, think about ways that you could improve those processes. An example may be the flow at a restaurant or the timing of the stoplights in a high traffic area. These are simple examples of logistical issues that may benefit from process improvement.

SELECTED SCHOOLS

Many colleges and universities, especially those with business schools, offer programs in accounting. The student can also gain initial training at a technical or community college. For some of the more prominent institutions in this field, see the list of selected schools in the "Accountant" chapter.

MORE INFORMATION

Accreditation Council for Accountancy and Taxation
1010 North Fairfax Street
Alexandria, VA 22314-1574
888.289.7763
www.acatcredentials.org

American Institute of Certified Public Accountants
1211 Avenue of the Americas
New York, NY 10036
888.777.7077
www.aicpa.org

Information Systems Audit and Control Association
3701 Algonquin Road, Suite 1010
Rolling Meadows, IL 60008
847.253.1545
www.isaca.org

Institute of Internal Auditors
247 Maitland Avenue
Altamonte Springs, FL 32701-4201
407.937.1100
www.theiia.org

Institute of Management Accountants
10 Paragon Drive
Montvale, NJ 07645-1718
800.638.4427
www.imanet.org

National Association of State Auditors, Comptrollers and Treasurers
449 Lewis Hargett Circle, Suite 290
Lexington, KY 40503
859.276.1147
www.nasact.org

Simone Isadora Flynn/Editor

Bookkeeper

Snapshot

Career Cluster: Banking & Finance; Business Administration
Interests: Accounting, finance, business management, mathematics, analyzing information
Earnings (Yearly Average): $35,730
Employment & Outlook: Average Growth Expected

OVERVIEW

Sphere of Work

Bookkeepers are responsible for administering the financial records of a business. This may include the business's payroll, invoices, expenses, receipts, and other accounting matters. While bookkeepers fulfill an accounting function, they are generally not qualified accountants. A certified accountant must possess graduate qualifications and professional certification, whereas bookkeeping requires no formal qualifications.

Generally speaking, bookkeepers work for smaller businesses and handle all accounting functions, whereas workers known as accounting clerks or accounting assistants usually work for larger companies performing particular tasks as members of an accounting team. A bookkeeper may work alone, in which case they usually interact with external financial service providers such as an auditor and tax accountant.

Bookkeeping is a general business administration function, but many bookkeepers and accounting assistants will develop specialized industry experience as a result of the employers they work for.

Work Environment

Bookkeepers can expect to work in office settings. Depending on the size and nature of the organization they serve, they may manage financial record keeping alone or as part of an accounting team. Internally, they will interact with other administrators, business support staff, and management. Externally, they may interact with customers, suppliers, vendors, wholesalers, contractors, and other service providers.

Bookkeepers engaged in full-time work for an employer usually work a standard forty-hour week, although they may be required to work longer hours during a company's busy periods or to meet financial reporting deadlines. Self-employed bookkeepers may serve a number of small- to medium-sized firms, each on a part-time basis. They may work from home or on-site.

Profile

Working Conditions: Work Indoors
Physical Strength: Light Work
Education Needs: High School Diploma, Technical/Community College
Licensure/Certification: Usually Not Required
Physical Abilities Not Required: No Heavy Labor
Opportunities For Experience: Internship, Military Service
Holland Interest Score*: CRE, CSE

* See Appendix A

Occupation Interest

Bookkeeping attracts people who have an interest in accounting, numbers, and business transactions. This work may also attract candidates who would like to gain entry-level experience in accounting and financial administration before committing to studies in accounting, finance, or economics.

The often meticulous and repetitive nature of bookkeeping

demands sustained attention to detail. Bookkeepers may spend long periods of time sitting at a desk or workstation crunching numbers and doing data entry. Therefore, attention to accuracy and the ability to meet deadlines are important.

These roles also offer potential opportunities to learn a variety of allied skills and specialist business functions, such as purchasing, quoting, budgeting, and payroll.

A Day in the Life—Duties and Responsibilities

Accounting clerks are usually members of an accounting team. As such, they may spend periods of their day working alone and with others. Bookkeepers may work as part of a team or independently. Much of the day will be spent at a desk doing financial data entry into specialized accounting and bookkeeping systems.

Bookkeepers and accounting assistants may also assist with payroll processing, invoicing and receipting, accounts payable and receivable administration, reconciling bank statements, writing checks, making bank deposits, doing petty cash reimbursements, completing forms, and preparing financial reports such as profit and loss statements or balance sheets. They may also assist in processes such as budgeting and purchasing.

They may be expected to attend meetings and to contribute to projects, groups, and committees. General administrative tasks are likely to include opening and sending mail and generating correspondence, memos, and other written communications.

Duties and Responsibilities

- Calculating employees' wages and preparing payroll checks
- Recording data from sales slips, statements, check stubs and inventory records in general ledgers, journals or on data processing sheets or computers
- Preparing financial reports
- Balancing books

WORK ENVIRONMENT

Immediate Physical Environment

Office settings predominate. Bookkeepers and accounting assistants are found in nearly every type of industry and business. Self-employed bookkeepers may work from home.

Relevant Skills and Abilities

Communication Skills
- Expressing thoughts and ideas
- Writing concisely

Interpersonal/Social Skills
- Cooperating with others
- Having good judgment
- Working as a member of a team

Organization & Management Skills
- Following instructions
- Organizing information or materials
- Paying attention to and handling details
- Performing routine work

Research & Planning Skills
- Using logical reasoning

Technical Skills
- Performing scientific, mathematical and technical work
- Working with data or numbers
- Working with machines, tools or other objects

Human Environment

Bookkeepers must be able to sustain relatively detailed and repetitive work for long periods of time. They must also be able to work collaboratively with colleagues, supervisors, managers, members of other departments, and external stakeholders such as customers and vendors.

Technological Environment

Bookkeepers are expected to use specialized accounting software and systems, as well as general office computing programs. Daily operations will also demand the use of standard office technologies, including telephone, e-mail, photocopiers, and the Internet.

EDUCATION, TRAINING, AND ADVANCEMENT

High School/Secondary

High school students can best prepare for a career in bookkeeping by taking courses in business mathematics and administration, accounting, bookkeeping, communications, and business law. Foreign languages are also increasingly valued as businesses find themselves operating in global and cross-cultural contexts.

Becoming involved in extracurricular school activities that develop business competencies will also provide students with an opportunity to develop relevant skills and learn from others prior to graduation. This could include, for example, participating in business incubation projects.

Suggested High School Subjects
- Accounting
- Applied Communication
- Bookkeeping
- Business
- Business & Computer Technology
- Business Data Processing
- Business English
- Business Law
- Business Math
- Keyboarding

Famous First

The first account ledgers were clay tablets written in cuneiform script (perhaps the oldest form of written language) dating from 10,000 years ago or earlier in parts of the Middle East. Daily transactions were collected in a basket and the contents summarized in a larger, multi-columned tablet that showed the totals.

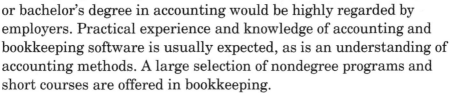

Postsecondary

There are no formal educational qualifications required for bookkeeping, although an associate or bachelor's degree in accounting would be highly regarded by employers. Practical experience and knowledge of accounting and bookkeeping software is usually expected, as is an understanding of accounting methods. A large selection of nondegree programs and short courses are offered in bookkeeping.

Opportunities for career advancement will depend largely on the size and type of organization in which the candidate works and their breadth of experience. Bookkeepers and accounting assistants who wish to become accountants or financial controllers will need to complete a bachelor's degree in accounting, finance, or economics, as well as postgraduate professional certification.

Related College Majors
- Accounting Technician Training
- Bookkeeping

Adult Job Seekers

AAdults seeking a career transition into or return to bookkeeping are advised to refresh their skills and update their resume. A number of agencies and institutions provide self-guided continuing education and professional development modules. Candidates may make themselves more attractive to employers by gaining specialist knowledge in certain fields, such as payroll, taxation preparation, wholesale accounting, credit applications and collections, financial statement analysis, double-entry bookkeeping, and fraud prevention. Experience in relevant specialty areas or industries should be highlighted in the candidate's resume and application letter.

Networking, job searching, and interviewing are critical. Aspiring bookkeepers may be well-counseled also to consider allied roles, such as payroll specialist and purchasing clerk.

Professional Certification and Licensure

There are no formal professional certifications or licensing requirements for bookkeeping. Certification with and/or membership in national or state-based professional associations is optional.

Additional Requirements

Bookkeeping balances the demands of data entry and transactional work with potentially more complex and strategic accounting activities. These are roles, therefore, in which there are often opportunities to learn a variety of allied skills and business functions.

EARNINGS AND ADVANCEMENT

Earnings depend on the type, size, and geographic location of the employer as well as the employee's ability and length of experience. Median annual earnings of bookkeepers and accounting clerks were $35,730 in 2013. The lowest ten percent earned less than $23,000, and the highest ten percent earned more than $55,000.

Bookkeepers and accounting assistants may receive paid vacations, holidays, and sick days; life and health insurance; and retirement benefits. These benefits are usually paid by the employer

Metropolitan Areas with the Highest Employment Level in This Occupation

Metropolitan area	Employment[1]	Employment per thousand jobs	Hourly mean wage
New York-White Plains-Wayne, NY-NJ	63,210	12.06	$20.95
Los Angeles-Long Beach-Glendale, CA	48,720	12.26	$19.63
Chicago-Joliet-Naperville, IL	34,270	9.26	$19.31
Houston-Sugar Land-Baytown, TX	30,010	10.88	$18.62
Dallas-Plano-Irving, TX	26,380	12.27	$18.75
Atlanta-Sandy Springs-Marietta, GA	25,810	11.18	$18.07
Philadelphia, PA	22,380	12.16	$19.61
Washington-Arlington-Alexandria, DC-VA-MD-WV	22,010	9.30	$21.52
Minneapolis-St. Paul-Bloomington, MN-WI	21,650	12.08	$19.10
Boston-Cambridge-Quincy, MA	20,880	11.94	$21.66

[1] Does not include self-employed. Source: Bureau of Labor Statistics

EMPLOYMENT AND OUTLOOK

AThere were about 1.8 million bookkeepers and accounting assistants employed nationally in 2012. Employment is expected to grow about as fast as the average for all occupations through the year 2022, which means employment is projected to increase 10 percent to 15 percent. These workers will be needed as there is more attention being paid to the level of accuracy, accountability and transparency that public companies must use when reporting financial information, including the use of International Federal Reporting Standards. Still, most job openings will stem from replacement needs, due to workers who transfer to other occupations or leave the labor force.

Employment Trend, Projected 2012–22

Bookkeepers and Accounting Assistants: 11%

Total, All Occupations: 11%

Office and Administrative Support Occupations: 7%

Note: "All Occupations" includes all occupations in the U.S. Economy. Source: U.S. Bureau of Labor Statistics, Employment Projections Program.

Related Occupations
- Accountant
- Bank Teller
- Billing Clerk
- Cashier
- General Office Clerk
- Medical Records Administrator
- Office Machine Operator
- Payroll Clerk
- Statistical Assistant

Related Military Occupations
- Finance & Accounting Specialist

Conversation With . . .
KAREN MILLER

Bookkeeper/Accountant/Office Manager
New Orleans, LA
5 1/2 years

1. What was your individual career path in terms of education/training, entry-level job, or other significant opportunity?

I received a Bachelor's Degree in Business Administration from the University of New Orleans and went straight into a large corporation. I started as an executive assistant and I thought once I got my foot in the door I could work my way up, which I did. I spent the 10 years in human resources as a benefits clerk and then as a compensation analyst. However, I learned over the years that I really wanted to work for a small business because I felt a corporation has so much bureaucracy and I'd lost the personal touch. When I was in HR, I had to do exit interviews whenever there were layoffs and it was just a very cold process. So I joined my family's business in payphones, back before cellphones prospered. I became operations manager and ran every aspect of the business until we sold the business after the proliferation of cellphones. During this time, I found that I really enjoyed accounting, specifically working with numbers and analyzing profits. By this time I was in my 50's and wanted to "slow" down, so I started working part-time as a bookkeeper/accountant. That's what I am currently doing.

2. What are the most important skills and/or qualities for someone in your profession?

The most important skills for a bookkeeper/accountant are definitely organization and attention to detail.

3. What do you wish you had known going into this profession?

I always assumed the position of bookkeeper/accountant was a boring job, but I've learned that I like the process. I like entering numbers, having clean numbers, and having them balance. If I'd know that earlier, I would have gotten into it much sooner, and possibly gone for CPA accreditation.

4. **Are there many job opportunities in your profession? In what specific areas?**

There are plenty of job opportunities in this profession. A working mother could do something as basic as part-time bookkeeping, or someone could establish a career in accounting and go as high as CFO of a major corporation. The options are very diverse in this field.

5. **How do you see your profession changing in the next five years, what role will technology play in those changes, and what skills will be required?**

I think this profession will stay in great demand for two reasons: 1) Technology helps streamline the job greatly, but a human brain will always need to analyze the data. 2) Technology enables this job to be done remotely - such as at home - or on a part-time basis, which is a wonderful alternative for many employees.

6. **What do you like most about your job? What do you like least about your job?**

I enjoy organizing things, and when I analyze reports and make recommendations, and when they result in favorable numbers, it is a source of pride in the job! There's nothing really that I enjoy the least. I don't mind being at a desk for hours, but I'm sure lots of people would not like that aspect of the job.

7. **Can you suggest a valuable "try this" for students considering a career in your profession?**

When I was in college, I got a part-time job at the university in their financial services department, and that is when I became exposed to the "numbers" world. Even though my degree is not in accounting, my bachelor's degree program in business administration required that I take three different accounting courses. The rest I learned from on-the-job exposure. A real "try this" would be to use the Quickbooks accounting program in your own life for your personal finances, and get a real feel for income/expense analysis. This profession has greatly helped me plan my personal finance spending and retirement planning.

SELECTED SCHOOLS

Many technical and community colleges offer programs in business administration and accounting. Interested students are advised to consult with their school guidance counselor or to research area postsecondary schools and training programs. For those interested in pursuing a bachelor's degree, see the list of schools in the "Accountant" chapter in the present volume.

MORE INFORMATION

American Accounting Association
5717 Bessie Drive
Sarasota, FL 34233-2399
941.921.7747
aaahq.org/index.cfm

American Institute of Professional Bookkeepers
6001 Montrose Road, Suite 500
Rockville, MD 20852
800.622.0121
www.aipb.org

National Association of Certified Public Bookkeepers
140 N. Union Street, Suite 240
Farmington, UT 84025
866.444.9989
www.nacpb.org

Kylie Grimshaw Hughes/Editor

Budget Analyst

Snapshot

Career Cluster: Banking & Finance; Business Administration; Government & Public Administration

Interests: Economics, accounting, strategic planning, finance

Earnings (Yearly Average): $70,110

Employment & Outlook: Slightly Slower Than Average Growth Expected

OVERVIEW

Sphere of Work

A budget analyst is a professional who helps in the development and implementation of a business or government budget. Budget analysts review revenues and expenses, study the cost-effectiveness of an organization's activities, research alternative courses of action, and make recommendations for a balanced annual budget. Budget analysts play an important role in an organization's financial planning for the fiscal year. For government agencies and non-profit organizations, a budget analyst can help the group efficiently and effectively distribute funds for programs and departments. For businesses, a budget analyst can help maximize profits and reduce expenditures.

Work Environment

The work of a budget analyst is performed primarily in an office setting. In a government agency, the analyst may work as part of a team, each member of which focuses on selected budget areas. A budget analyst frequently meets with his or her superiors, department heads, managers, and other members of the organization with insight on how the organization's money is being spent. Budget analysts normally work a regular forty-hour workweek, although during periods in which the budget is being finalized, their hours may be extended temporarily. At these peak times, the work environment may be somewhat stressful when budget deadlines loom.

Profile

Working Conditions: Work Indoors
Physical Strength: Light Work
Education Needs: Bachelor's Degree, Master's Degree
Licensure/Certification: Recommended
Physical Abilities Not Required: No Heavy Labor
Opportunities For Experience: Military Service, Part-Time Work
Holland Interest Score*: CER

* See Appendix A

Occupation Interest

Budget analysts use their extensive research and analysis experience to help an organization map out its future, finding and making recommendations concerning the best financial course of action for the short- and long-term. Budget analysts are able to perceive and grasp the complete and often complex inner workings of a government agency, non-profit organization, or business in such a way that few other employees can..

A Day in the Life—Duties and Responsibilities

A budget analyst is responsible for monitoring the past, present, and short- and long-term fiscal health of an organization or government agency. He or she will research the organization's past financial activities and health, reviewing financial reports and other related documents from previous years. Additionally, the budget analyst analyzes monthly budgets for each department (or applicable business activity) to ensure that the current year's budget requirements are being followed and that no extraordinary costs or revenue drops are occurring. The budget analyst researches current trends in the marketplace, the economy, and between vendors to see if there are any trends that may positively or negatively impact the organization for which he or she works. This research includes reviewing documents and meeting with key officials and personnel for more information.

Using this past and present information, the budget analyst will put together the framework for the organization's annual spending plan for the coming fiscal year. This budget will feature revenues and profits generated from each activity in the previous year, the costs involved for those activities, the amounts the business will invest in employee pay and benefits, and any other information of importance to the organization's financial health. In addition to the annual budget, these analysts may be called upon to create smaller budgets for individual activities and projects and/or short-term programs. In each of these activities, the analyst will be focused on ensuring that investments are cost-effective—in other words, that the program will generate as much revenue as possible while costs and expenses are held to a minimum.

The budget analyst may also be called upon by executives, legislators, and other officials to present their findings and opinions about how best to proceed with financial plans. This component of a budget analyst's job may include testifying at legislative and agency hearings, speaking at board of directors meetings, or meeting directly with executives and high-level officials

Duties and Responsibilities

- Providing technical advice and assistance in preparing annual budgets
- Reviewing financial requests by departments within the organization
- Examining past budgets in relation to the current budget
- Reporting on budgetary discrepancies
- Conducting in-house seminars on new budgetary guidelines

WORK ENVIRONMENT

Physical Environment

Budget analysts generally work in office environments, either in their own individual offices or sharing open office space with other personnel. These settings will be busy, especially during periods closest to budget deadlines. Many meetings between these analysts and key personnel will take place in conference rooms and similar settings within the main office.

Relevant Skills and Abilities

Analytical Skills
- Analyzing data

Communication Skills
- Speaking effectively
- Writing concisely

Interpersonal/Social Skills
- Being able to work independently

Organization & Management Skills
- Paying attention to and handling details
- Performing routine work

Research & Planning Skills
- Using logical reasoning

Technical Skills
- Using technology to process information
- Working with data or numbers
- Working with machines, tools or other objects

Human Environment

Although budget analysts often work independently on their individual areas of focus, they typically work in a team dynamic, particularly when putting together large government or corporate budgets. They frequently interact with one another as well as with superiors and department heads during the course of developing an annual or quarterly budget.

Technological Environment

Budget analysts typically need to have knowledge of computers and be proficient in the use of business and accounting software. Such software includes spreadsheet and database programs and word processing systems.

EDUCATION, TRAINING, AND ADVANCEMENT

High School/Secondary

High school students interested in becoming budget analysts should take courses in business and accounting, mathematics, and computer science. They may also benefit from developing better writing and communications skills.

Suggested High School Subjects
- Accounting
- Business
- Business Data Processing
- Business Law
- Business Math
- Computer Science
- English

Famous First

The first Bureau of the Budget within the federal government was started by President Warren G. Harding in 1921. Originally part of the US Treasury, the bureau helped to plan the federal budget and monitor government accounts in relation to it. Later, the bureau was moved to the Executive Office of the President and, in 1970, renamed the Office of Management and Budget (OMB).

College/Postsecondary

Budget analysts generally choose to complete bachelor's degrees in business, finance, accounting, and management. Because this field is highly competitive, individuals who obtain a master's degree tend to have an edge over other candidates.

Related College Majors
- Accounting
- Business
- Business Administration & Management, General
- Finance, General

Adult Job Seekers

Individuals with an interest in becoming budget analysts will often find positions posted on government jobs websites. They may also consult with state and municipal government websites. Trade associations such as the National Association of State Budget Officers and the American Association for Budget and Program Analysis can also offer opportunities for candidates..

Professional Certification and Licensure

Federal, state, and local government budget analysts are sometimes asked to obtain training and certification through Advancing Government Accountability's Certified Government Financial Manager program. Advancing Government Accountability's program requires that the candidate have two years of financial management experience, a bachelor's degree, and twenty-four credit hours in financial management.

Additional Requirements

Government budget analysts are often called upon to testify on their research findings at legislative and agency hearings. They must therefore have the ability not only to understand the often complex nature of budgets, but be able to effectively communicate with those individuals who are not as well-versed on the subject. Additionally, budget analysts are expected to be critical thinkers; they should be able to carefully analyze a budget area for strengths and weaknesses, explore alternatives, and offer new ideas and approaches to budgets.

EARNINGS AND ADVANCEMENT

Earnings of both private and public sector budget analysts vary considerably based on education, experience and the organization for which they work. Beginning budget analysts work under close supervision, but rapid advancement is possible for those with exceptionally good analytical ability and work ethic. As budget analysts rise in position, their jobs become increasingly supervisory.

Median annual earnings of budget analysts were $70,110 in 2013. The lowest ten percent earned less than $46,000, and the highest ten percent earned more than $104,000.

Budget analysts may receive paid vacations, holidays, and sick days; life and health insurance; and retirement benefits. These are usually paid by the employer.

Metropolitan Areas with the Highest Employment Level in This Occupation

Metropolitan area	Employment[1]	Employment per thousand jobs	Hourly mean wage
Washington-Arlington-Alexandria, DC-VA-MD-WV	4,700	1.98	$42.72
Los Angeles-Long Beach-Glendale, CA	2,710	0.68	$39.05
New York-White Plains-Wayne, NY-NJ	1,670	0.32	$37.58
Atlanta-Sandy Springs-Marietta, GA	1,310	0.57	$34.17
Boston-Cambridge-Quincy, MA	1,300	0.75	$37.31
Baltimore-Towson, MD	1,200	0.94	$36.25
Chicago-Joliet-Naperville, IL	1,030	0.28	$36.89
St. Louis, MO-IL	1,010	0.78	$36.17
Dallas-Plano-Irving, TX	970	0.45	$34.83
Philadelphia, PA	920	0.50	$35.52

[1] Does not include self-employed. Source: Bureau of Labor Statistics

EMPLOYMENT AND OUTLOOK

Nationally, there were 62,000 budget analysts employed in 2012. Employment is expected to grow slightly slower than the average for all occupations through the year 2022, which means employment is projected to increase 3 percent to 9 percent. Though computers can perform most of the work of analyzing and projecting budgets, job growth for budget analysts will occur due to the increased demand for financial analysis in the public and private sectors. Because of the growing complexity and specialization in the business world, more attention is being given to financial planning and control.

Employment Trend, Projected 2012–22

Business and Financial Operations Occupations: 13%

Total, All Occupations: 11%

Budget Analysts: 6%

Note: "All Occupations" includes all occupations in the U.S. Economy. Source: U.S. Bureau of Labor Statistics, Employment Projections Program.

Related Occupations

- Accountant
- Actuary
- Auditor
- Cost Estimator
- Energy Auditor
- Financial Analyst
- Personal Financial Advisor

Related Military Occupations

- Finance & Accounting Manager
- Management Analyst

Conversation With . . .
CLAIRE LODGE

Finance Consultant and Former Budget Analyst, 6 years
Arlington, VA
Financial profession, 7 years

1. What was your individual career path in terms of education/training, entry-level job, or other significant opportunity?

I thought I wanted to do International Development/Development Economics. In fact, I have a B.A. in International Studies from American University and an M.S. in Development Economics from the University of Manchester in England. After graduation, however, I fell into budgeting. I had a job interview and the day-to-day tasks seemed analytical - which I liked from my economics background - but with a lot of people interaction. It seemed like a good fit for me.

To be a budget analyst, a specific degree is not needed. I'm good at math, but I think it's more important to be a logical thinker. The main thing, at least at the government agency where I worked, is writing ability and analytical skills. So, even though I went in without a budget-related educational background, I was hired and excelled.

We developed the budget by working within the department, then the Office of Management and Budget that is basically the White House budget wing, and, finally, with Congress.

2. What are the most important skills and/or qualities for someone in your profession?

Writing is really important. You have to be able to effectively write responses to inquiries from government departments and Congress and to write the agency's budget for Congress. But the other aspect of writing, which I think is sometimes taken for granted, is email writing. Tone is important. Sometimes you are giving bad news. So, even if it's only a four sentence email, you have to be willing to reread it three times to make sure nothing can be misconstrued.

Analytical skills are critical. In the federal budgeting world, there is a mantra: Come to me with solutions, not problems. My boss actually wanted three solutions. You can't come up with solutions if you don't know how to analyze the problem.

You need to be organized. If you can't multi-task and keep track of your assignments, you will not excel in this career. Oftentimes, I was working on three different assignments and something time-pressing would come up. I had to know what I could afford to put to the back burner, what couldn't be left behind, and then communicate that to my bosses.

3. What do you wish you had known going into this profession?

I asked a lot of questions in my job interviews so I knew what to expect, at least as much as one can. The interviewee should ask questions to see if the job is a good fit.

4. Are there many job opportunities in your profession? In what specific areas?

Yes. The federal government needs budget analysts, as do state and local governments.

5. How do you see your profession changing in the next five years, what role will technology play in those changes, and what skills will be required?

I think that there will always be budget analysts in the public sector. Technology has made their jobs easier. I have no idea how budget analysts were able to do what they do before computers, and really before Excel.

6. What do you like most about your job? What do you like least about your job?

Being a budget analyst is not a routine job. I might do something different every day. Also, there may be crunch times, especially in public sector budgeting where you can plan on working later than normal at times like the end of a fiscal year. The lack of daily routine was a negative only because I couldn't make plans for the same time every day.

7. Can you suggest a valuable "try this" for students considering a career in your profession?

A lot of budget analysts learn on the job. The closest "try this" would be budgeting in your own life, but that leaves out some of the big parts of the federal budgeting process such as questions from Congress, submitting your budget for approval, and working with different entities.

SELECTED SCHOOLS

Many colleges and universities, especially those with business schools, offer programs in accounting and business finance. The student can also gain initial training at a technical or community college. For some of the more prominent institutions in this field, see the lists of selected schools in the "Accountant" and "Financial Manager" chapters.

MORE INFORMATION

More Information
American Association for Budget and Program Analysis
P.O. Box 1157
Falls Church, VA 22041
703-941-4300
www.aabpa.org

Association of Government Accountants
2208 Mount Vernon Avenue
Alexandria, VA 22301
703.684.6931
www.agacgfm.org

Government Finance Officers Association
203 N. LaSalle Street, Suite 2700
Chicago, IL 60601-1210
312.977.9700
www.gfoa.org

National Association of State Budget Officers
444 N. Capitol Street NW, Suite 642
Washington, DC 20001
202.624.5382
www.nasbo.org

Michael AuerbachEditor

Buyer

Snapshot

Career Cluster: Business Administration; Sales & Marketing
Interests: Purchasing, sales negotiations, retail management, advertising, marketing
Earnings (Yearly Average): $52,370
Employment & Outlook: Slower Than Average Growth Expected

OVERVIEW

Sphere of Work

Buyers, also called wholesale and retail buyers, select merchandise to be sold either to purchasers of wholesale items, such as large retailers, or to the public. In other words, they buy products or finished goods for resale. They negotiate the purchase of goods directly from manufacturers or purchase items from wholesalers for retail purposes. Buyers arrange for transportation and delivery of goods, and they make branding and purchasing decisions for clients based on customer feedback and industry trends.

Work Environment

Buyers generally split their time between office or store environments—where they meet with management, manage online transactions, and attend meetings—and trade shows, conferences, markets, and manufacturing centers. Hours are often irregular and may include weekends and evenings. .

Profile

Working Conditions: Work Indoors
Physical Strength: Light Work
Education Needs:
  Technical/Community College,
  Bachelor's Degree
Licensure/Certification:
  Recommended
Physical Abilities Not Required: No
  Heavy Labor
Opportunities For Experience:
  Internship, Part Time Work
Holland Interest Score*: ESA

* See Appendix A

Occupation Interest

Individuals drawn to the profession enjoy working in fast-paced, competitive environments. They must be able to interact with many different types of people, and they are often required to negotiate sales in high-pressure situations. They should also enjoy identifying and following trends. Buyers must keep track of prices, sales records, and quality standards, and they often employ spreadsheet and retail-management software to do so. Buyers are often expected to train and mentor entry-level staff and should be comfortable supervising others.

A Day in the Life—Duties and Responsibilities

The daily duties of a buyer vary according to the commodity or merchandise that he or she purchases. Buyers may visit factories and manufacturing facilities directly, review available products, and perform quality tests or review testing data. They then negotiate the price of merchandise and arrange the transportation of goods. Some buyers, particularly for retail establishments, conduct business at trade shows and markets or in one-on-one meetings with wholesalers. Buyers work closely with vendors and manufacturers to develop and purchase desirable products. They analyze market and industry data to anticipate customer needs and buying patterns, and they determine the quantity of goods needed. They are also sometimes required to work with point-of-sale and retail-management software, set prices and discount levels for goods, and provide inventory information.

Buyers work with manufacturers and vendors to develop quality standards and inspect and return merchandise if it fails to meet them. They introduce new merchandise to other sales staff and train them to sell it. Buyers also monitor competitors' activities by following advertising and sales information and keep abreast of industry and economic trends. Retail buyers may work for multiple independent businesses and meet with owners and managers to ascertain their needs. They may help marketing staff determine which products should be featured in advertisements and when. Seasonal fluctuations and sales can influence the pace of this work.

Duties and Responsibilities

- Supplying wholesale and retail businesses with products for resale
- Consulting with a store or merchandise manager on a budget and items to be purchased
- Analyzing sales records to determine what products are currently in demand
- Selecting and ordering manufactured products and finished goods
- Inspecting, grading or appraising merchandise
- Visiting manufacturers' showrooms
- Assisting in establishing markup rates and prices of new merchandise
- Determining necessary markdowns to sell slow-moving merchandise
- Traveling throughout various market areas in the United States or foreign countries to examine and select merchandise

OCCUPATION SPECIALTIES

Wholesale and Retail Buyers

Wholesale and Retail Buyers purchase finished goods, such as clothing or electronics, for resale. Those who work for large organizations usually specialize in one or two lines of merchandise (for example, men's clothing or women's shoes or children's toys) and are often known as merchandise managers. Those who work for small stores or suppliers may be responsible for purchasing all merchandise lines sold by the business.

Purchasing Agents

Purchasing Agents obtain goods and services for the operation of an organization, including raw materials, equipment, tools, parts, and supplies. In other words, they handle not finished goods for resale but rather the materials and operational supplies that go into the making of finished goods.

Procurement and Contract Managers

Procurement Managers are usually engineers who develop specifications and performance tests in order to get parts and equipment for high-tech applications, such as in the aeronautical and aerospace industry. Contract Managers usually work in manufacturing firms or government agencies and specialize in negotiating and supervising contracts for supplies and services.

WORK ENVIRONMENT

Physical Environment

Buyers work in a variety of environments, depending on the merchandise or commodities they purchase. Most travel frequently and often work from off-site locations and hotels. They spend time inspecting goods in factories or attending large conferences and trade shows, where they may negotiate purchases with many vendors simultaneously.

Relevant Skills and Abilities

Communication Skills
- Persuading others
- Speaking effectively
- Writing concisely

Interpersonal/Social Skills
- Cooperating with others
- Working as a member of a team

Organization & Management Skills
- Coordinating tasks
- Making decisions
- Managing people/groups
- Managing time
- Meeting goals and deadlines
- Performing duties that may change frequently

Research & Planning Skills
- Using logical reasoning

Work Environment Skills
- Traveling

Human Environment

As interacting with others is a crucial part of their job, buyers must have excellent interpersonal skills. They must be energetic and persuasive negotiators to ensure the best pricing and quality for their clients. Buyers must have strong critical-thinking skills and be able to develop close professional relationships with vendors and clients alike. They often work on sales teams and collaborate with other staff within their organizations as well as with off-site colleagues.

Technological Environment

Buyers must be comfortable with point-of-sale, inventory, and spreadsheet software. They travel frequently and often work remotely, so they must be able to manage the technology that makes this possible. Buyers often use planning and management programs as well as presentation and word processing software.

EDUCATION, TRAINING, AND ADVANCEMENT

High School/Secondary

Students interested in the position of buyer should work to develop strong speaking and writing skills. They should take courses in business management, if available, and in English and math. Entry-level retail experience is also helpful.

Suggested High School Subjects
- Applied Communication
- Arts
- Bookkeeping
- Business
- Business Data Processing
- Business Law
- Clothing & Textiles
- College Preparatory
- Economics
- English
- Mathematics
- Merchandising
- Psychology
- Speech

Famous First

The first law requiring professional buyers not to mark up items for resale excessively was California's Fair Trade Act, authorized in 1931. The law was designed to "protect trade-mark owners, distributors and the public against injurious and uneconomic practices in the distribution of articles of standard quality under a distinguished trade-mark, brand or name."

College/Postsecondary

Buyers are typically required to have completed some postsecondary study, though requirements vary from employer to employer. Large firms often require at least a two-year degree and two to five years of work experience. Some firms require a bachelor's degree in a business-related field. Manufacturing buyers may need degrees in engineering or applied sciences to understand the needs of their clients fully. Sales and marketing degrees are available from both two- and four-year programs, and internships in this field are virtually mandatory. Most companies have comprehensive training programs for new employees and require a significant training and trial period.

Related College Majors

- Business Administration
- Marketing Management & Research
- Purchasing, Procurement & Contracts Management
- Retail & Wholesale Operations

Adult Job Seekers

AAdults interested in the wholesale or retail buying field should investigate internship opportunities, which may be available for adult job seekers as well as college students and young professionals. In addition, they may benefit from gaining retail sales experience, which can be readily obtained and allows workers to explore the field. The most important characteristics of a successful buyer are negotiating ability, high energy, and a willingness to work hard. Internal training programs ensure that candidates from various backgrounds are given an equal start.

Professional Certification and Licensure

Certification and licensure are generally not required but may be preferred by some employers. The Institute for Supply Management offers various certifications to buyers, including the Accredited Purchasing Practitioner (APP) and Certified Purchasing Manager (CPM) certifications. The American Purchasing Society grants Certified Purchasing Professional (CPP) and Certified Professional Purchasing Manager (CPPM) designations. Governmental supply purchasers are awarded other designations through written and oral examinations. Professional development is very important in the field, and buyers participate regularly in training sessions and seminars offered by industry trade associations.

Additional Requirements

Buyers work in a fast-paced, competitive field that is stimulating for high-energy individuals who enjoy negotiating and travel. Buyers must demonstrate leadership and ethical behavior, since they often train and supervise assistants and trainees and also represent the company in meetings with outside vendors and suppliers.

Fun Fact

According to the website statisticbrain.com, Americans spend $121 on clothing every month on average. Of that amount, $59 is spent on women's clothing; $35 is spent on men's clothing; $21 on shoes; and $5 on children's clothing.

EARNINGS AND ADVANCEMENT

Earnings depend on the size and geographic location and the experience of the employee. Median annual earnings of buyers were $52,370 in 2013. The lowest ten percent earned less than $30,000, and the highest ten percent earned more than $93,000.

Buyers may receive paid vacations, holidays, and sick days; life and health insurance; and retirement benefits. These are usually paid by the employer. Buyers may also receive employee discounts on merchandise.

Metropolitan Areas with the Highest Employment Level in This Occupation

Metropolitan area	Employment[1]	Employment per thousand jobs	Hourly mean wage
New York-White Plains-Wayne, NY-NJ	5,560	1.06	$34.27
Los Angeles-Long Beach-Glendale, CA	5,520	1.39	$26.90
Chicago-Joliet-Naperville, IL	4,280	1.16	$25.75
Seattle-Bellevue-Everett, WA	2,960	2.04	$29.04
Houston-Sugar Land-Baytown, TX	2,620	0.95	$29.64
Dallas-Plano-Irving, TX	2,300	1.07	$33.17
Fayetteville-Springdale-Rogers, AR-MO	2,070	9.97	$31.94
Boston-Cambridge-Quincy, MA	1,790	1.02	$32.13
Atlanta-Sandy Springs-Marietta, GA	1,760	0.76	$34.83
Philadelphia, PA	1,690	0.92	$30.09

[1] Does not include self-employed. Source: Bureau of Labor Statistics

EMPLOYMENT AND OUTLOOK

There were approximately 125,000 buyers employed nationally in 2012. Employment of buyers is expected to grow slower than the average for all occupations through the year 2022, which means employment is projected to increase 1 percent to 7 percent. Most job opportunities will result from the need to replace workers who leave the work force or transfer to other occupations.

Employment Trend, Projected 2012–22

Total, All Occupations: 11%

Buyers and Purchasing Agents: 4%

Note: "All Occupations" includes all occupations in the U.S. Economy. Source: U.S. Bureau of Labor Statistics, Employment Projections Program.

Related Occupations
- Online Merchant
- Purchasing Agent
- Retail Salesperson
- Retail Store Sales Manager
- Wholesale Sales Representative

Conversation With . . .
KRISTEN LONGHENRY

Associate Buyer
Bed Bath & Beyond
Buyer, 5 years

1. What was your individual career path in terms of education/training, entry-level job, or other significant opportunity?

I always loved shopping. I was very fortunate to go to a high school that had fashion classes. I was always sewing my own clothes; I made my prom dress. Between my junior and senior years, I attended a program at the Fashion Institute of Technology (FIT) for high school students. That was a great program. I majored in fashion merchandising and marketing at Mount Ida College near Boston. I studied abroad in London, and that gave me exposure to international markets. When I graduated, I managed a Hollister store for a year. I moved to New York City and took a paid internship with a small company as a merchandise coordinator. Then I took an entry-level job as an assistant buyer for a year and half with Ross Stores, which is an off-price chain. From there, I moved into Bed Bath & Beyond as an assistant buyer. I'm in the bath area; I buy shower heads, shower hooks, shower curtains and shower accessories.

2. What are the most important skills and/or qualities for someone in your profession?

Critical thinking is very important. Every day I'm dealing with a puzzle. I have 1,000 stores I am buying for. Also, you need to know Excel. I live in Excel all day. You have to have strong negotiating skills—and with that comes confidence. You have to have the ability to push back. Finally, you have to have business acumen. Math is very important in this business. I'm no math genius by any stretch, but I do know how to arrive at the answer. I need my calculator, but I know how to get the answer.

3. What do you wish you had known going into this profession?

I wish that I had know more about working in a large company versus a small company. If you're working in a small company, you can get things done so much faster. In a large company, there are processes you have to follow, a chain of command, and it's much more political. Also, in a small company, you can get promoted much faster.

4. Are there many job opportunities in your profession? In what specific areas?

There are plenty of jobs. There's home, there's footwear, there's media, there's accessories, there's grocery stores. At a company like Bed Bath or Macy's, there are buyers and merchandising. The people in merchandising work with the design team and the buyers buy from the collection they come up with. But the buyers can drive merchandising to tell designers what to produce. There's also planning. They're the numbers people. Every single company has a planner to match their buyer. They deal with things like how much inventory you can buy.

5. How do you see your profession changing in the next five years, what role will technology play in those changes, and what skills will be required?

Omni-channel Retail—merging a customer's experiences online and in the store—is huge. It's important to stay on top of technology. We are in a completely different place than we were two years ago and we will be somewhere completely different in another two years. Foot traffic is down and e-commerce is up.

We're all trying to figure out how to deal with "showrooming" (when consumers examine goods in a store, but purchase online at a better price). Inventory is an expense

6. What do you like most about your job? What do you like least about your job?

To be honest, what I enjoy most is that I get to shop all day. What I like least is the analysis. Yes, I'm shopping, but there's a lot of analysis behind what I chose, so sometimes that can take the fun out of. Sometimes trying to get approval to carry a new product can be like hitting your head against the wall.

7. Can you suggest a valuable "try this" for students considering a career in your profession?

Definitely work in retail. I even recommend taking a year after college and being a store manager. It just teaches you what a store is, how it runs. Yes, I can purchase an item to be placed in a store, but someone has to unpack that item, someone has to put a price tag on it, someone has to put it on the shelf, and so on. At the time I didn't realize it, but in hindsight, working at Hollister was one of the most valuable experiences I had. Additionally, study abroad. Companies are becoming increasingly global. If they're not now, they're going to be. It helps if you understand what retail is in another country.

SELECTED SCHOOLS

Many colleges and universities, especially those with business schools, offer programs in marketing and merchandising, the foundation of the buyer's profession. The student can also gain initial training at a technical or community college. For some of the more prominent institutions to this field, see lists of selected schools in the "Advertising and Marketing Manager" and "Operations Manager" chapters.

MORE INFORMATION

American Purchasing Society
North Island Center, Suite 203
8 East Galena Boulevard
Aurora, IL 60506
630.859.0250
www.american-purchasing.com

APICS
8430 West Bryn Mawr Avenue
Suite 1000
Chicago, IL 60631
800.444.2742
www.apics.org

Institute for Supply Management Information Center
P.O. Box 22160
Tempe, AZ 85285-2160
800.888.6276
www.ism.ws

NGIP—The Institute for Public Procurement
151 Spring Street
Herndon, VA 20170-5223
800.367.6447
www.nigp.org

National Retail Federation
325 7th Street NW, Suite 1100
Washington, DC 20004
800.673.4692
www.nrf.com

Bethany Groff/Editor

Cost Estimator

Snapshot

Career Cluster: Architecture & Construction; Business Administration; Manufacturing

Interests: Mathematics, engineering, accounting, solving problems, working with a team

Earnings (Yearly Average): $59,460

Employment & Outlook: Faster Than Average Growth Expected

OVERVIEW

Sphere of Work

Cost estimators forecast the budgets of projects in a variety of industries. They usually work in the construction industry, where they estimate the costs and duration of projects, but they can also work in the manufacturing industry. The forecasts developed by cost estimators are used by others in the industry to make bids on construction or manufacturing contracts. They are essential to their respective industries, as they help determine the profitability of construction or manufacturing projects and products.

Work Environment

Cost estimators spend a majority of their time in offices. However, visiting construction sites and manufacturing plants is usually necessary for them to forecast costs accurately. Cost estimators must be aware of the various hazards present at these sites. They work closely with business owners, contractors, and project managers to help ensure an accurate cost is forecasted.

Profile

Working Conditions: Work both Indoors and Outdoors
Physical Strength: Light Work
Education Needs: Bachelor's Degree
Licensure/Certification: Recommended
Physical Abilities Not Required: No Heavy Labor
Opportunities For Experience: Internship
Holland Interest Score*: ESR

* See Appendix A

Occupation Interest

The cost-estimator profession involves a great deal of working with numbers, so the job tends to attract individuals who enjoy mathematics, engineering, and accounting. Anyone with a strong background in these fields can find success as a cost estimator, but the field does welcome people from a broad range of backgrounds. Cost estimators are detail-oriented problem solvers who enjoy working as part of a team in both an office and a construction or manufacturing environment. Many companies require a cost estimator to be certified, so individuals should be willing to further their training in order to excel.

A Day in the Life—Duties and Responsibilities

Cost estimating for construction and manufacturing involves collecting information and analyzing data on a large variety of factors. These factors vary for each project, but they typically include labor, materials, location, length of the project, and any specialized hardware and software that may be needed. Multiple cost estimators may work together on very large projects, with each providing estimates for a specific area of work.

A cost estimator establishes a budget through a variety of methods. For construction projects, cost estimation begins by reviewing the relevant drawings and specifications submitted for the project. Once these are analyzed and the construction company decides to make a bid, the cost estimator typically visits the location of the future construction project. At the site, he or she collects all relevant information, including the required utilities, material, insurance, labor, taxes or fees, and projected duration of the project, and estimates all of the costs needed for the contractor to complete the project. Included in these estimates are incidentals such as inclement weather and wasted material.

After a cost estimator surveys all of these aspects, he or she puts together a cost summary for the whole project. This summary is presented to everyone involved in the project, including business owners, engineers, and subcontractors. During the project's development and duration, an estimator tracks and manages the costs and may also be expected to negotiate costs, moderate any extra costs that arise, or suggest cost-saving measures.

Cost estimators in manufacturing perform similar tasks as those in construction. They forecast all costs associated with the development and production of products.

Duties and Responsibilities

- Compiling lists of the type of materials, tools, fixtures, equipment, and personnel required for a job
- Figuring the duration of a job and the costs associated with it
- Presenting a detailed cost estimate
- Consulting with personnel or other departments relating to cost problems

OCCUPATION SPECIALTIES

Construction Estimators

Construction Estimators estimate the cost of construction work. They may, for example, estimate the total cost of building a bridge or commercial shopping center. They may identify direct costs, such as the cost of raw materials and the cost of labor, and set a timeline for how long the project will take.

Manufacturing Cost Estimators

Manufacturing Cost Estimators calculate the costs of developing, producing, or redesigning a company's goods or services. For example, a cost estimator working for a home appliance manufacturer may determine whether a new type of dishwasher will be profitable to manufacture.

Software Development and Services Cost Estimators

Some cost estimators work in software development. Many high-technology products require a considerable amount of computer programming, and calculating the costs of software development requires great expertise. Similarly, firms involved in services, such as design services, may employ cost estimators to develop quotes on services offered to clients.

WORK ENVIRONMENT

Physical Environment

The majority of cost estimation is done in an office environment. Related research is typically performed on-site at construction work sites and manufacturing plants. These environments can pose a variety of hazards, so proper safety precautions must be taken. To evaluate these sites, travel may be required.

Relevant Skills and Abilities

Analytical Skills
- Analyzing data

Communication Skills
- Speaking effectively
- Writing concisely

Organization & Management Skills
- Paying attention to and handling details

Research & Planning Skills
- Analyzing information
- Developing evaluation strategies
- Using logical reasoning

Technical Skills
- Applying the technology to a task
- Performing technical work
- Working with machines, tools or other objects

Human Environment

To forecast a project's budget accurately, cost estimators work closely with others in their industry, including business owners, accountants, contractors, subcontractors, manufacturers, architects or designers, and supervisors. They may be required to negotiate costs.

Technological Environment

Cost estimators rely heavily on computers and scanners for their profession. Software for accounting, statistics, mathematics, modeling, and project management is frequently used. Cost estimators also use blueprints and schematics to help estimate cost precisely.

EDUCATION, TRAINING, AND ADVANCEMENT

High School/Secondary

Education requirements for a cost estimator vary by industry, but employers commonly require an individual to have at least completed high school or an equivalent degree program. High school students considering a profession as a cost estimator will benefit from courses in mathematics, computer science, and statistics, as well as any course that involves finance or economics. Those interested in cost estimating should strongly consider pursuing a postsecondary degree in a relevant subject area..

Suggested High School Subjects
- Blueprint Reading
- Building Trades & Carpentry
- College Preparatory
- English

Famous First

The first successful cost estimating software developed for Microsoft Windows was the Success Estimating and Cost Management System, created in 1991 by U.S. Cost, an architectural and engineering firm based in Atlanta. Other versions were released in subsequent years, and in 2002 the program was renamed SuccessEstimator. It remains in use today by a wide variety of commercial firms and government agencies.

College/Postsecondary

Employers in the construction and manufacturing industry usually require a cost estimator to have a bachelor's degree in a relevant field. Exceptions are sometimes made for individuals who have years of experience in the construction industry and obtain a relevant associate's degree. Relevant fields include civil and industrial engineering, finance, business management, operations research, and mathematics. These course programs are offered in a range of institutions, including colleges and universities. Technical and trade schools offer construction-related programs that can teach and train an individual in construction fields related to cost estimating.

Many schools that offer civil and industrial engineering degrees include cost estimating as part of the program, as do schools that offer master's degrees in construction science or construction management.

Related College Majors
- Business Administration & Management
- Construction/Building Technology
- Purchasing, Procurement & Contracts Management

Adult Job Seekers

Those interested in becoming a cost estimator should consider finding an internship, co-op, or entry-level position in construction or manufacturing to gain hands-on experience and on-the-job training, especially as wide-ranging construction experience can give prospective cost estimators an advantage. Since a deep knowledge of mathematics and finance is required, an individual lacking background in these fields should enroll in relevant and reputable academic programs.

Experienced cost estimators may eventually rise to managerial positions in construction or manufacturing or become independent consultants.

Professional Certification and Licensure

Certification is used to show experience, knowledge, and competence in the cost-estimating profession for both new and experienced estimators. Some employers require a cost estimator to be certified before being hired. Even if an employer does not require certification, an individual who voluntarily seeks out certification will more easily find employment and advance in the field.

Additional Requirements

Cost estimators must have a strong background in mathematics and finance as well as knowledge of the construction and manufacturing processes. They need to be able to analyze data thoroughly, use their conclusions to forecast a project's budget accurately, exercise good judgment, and manage time well. They must be extremely detail oriented and great problem solvers. They also need to possess strong communication and collaboration skills in order to negotiate costs and ensure a project is completed in time and on budget. As the technology and methods of the construction and manufacturing industries progress, a cost estimator also needs to stay informed about changes in his or her field and be open to learning about these developments.

Fun Fact

The top ten languages spoken in the U.S. besides English are German, French, Tagalog, Arabic, French Creole, Spanish, Russian, Korean, Chinese and Vietnamese.

Source: http://www.census.gov/prod/2013pubs/acs-22.pdf.

EARNINGS AND ADVANCEMENT

Earnings depend on the individual's education, experience, and amount of responsibility, and the type, size and geographic location of the employer. Some cost estimators are paid a commission on sales. Median annual earnings of cost estimators were $59,460 in 2013. The lowest ten percent earned less than $35,000, and the highest ten percent earned more than $98,000.

Cost estimators may receive paid vacations, holidays, and sick days; life and health insurance; and retirement benefits. These are usually paid by the employer. Some cost estimators also have a savings and stock investment plan. Some also receive cost-of-living allowances.

Metropolitan Areas with the Highest Employment Level in This Occupation

Metropolitan area	Employment[1]	Employment per thousand jobs	Hourly mean wage
New York-White Plains-Wayne, NY-NJ	5,120	0.98	$39.92
Los Angeles-Long Beach-Glendale, CA	4,830	1.22	$32.27
Houston-Sugar Land-Baytown, TX	4,380	1.59	$33.47
Washington-Arlington-Alexandria, DC-VA-MD-WV	4,360	1.84	$35.03
Chicago-Joliet-Naperville, IL	3,970	1.07	$33.60
Philadelphia, PA	3,580	1.94	$31.16
Atlanta-Sandy Springs-Marietta, GA	3,530	1.53	$30.54
Phoenix-Mesa-Glendale, AZ	3,360	1.89	$31.64
Dallas-Plano-Irving, TX	2,990	1.39	$32.58
Denver-Aurora-Broomfield, CO	2,950	2.30	$30.49

[1] Does not include self-employed. Source: Bureau of Labor Statistics

EMPLOYMENT AND OUTLOOK

Cost estimators held about 200,000 jobs nationally in 2012, primarily in construction industries. Employment is expected to grow much faster than the average for all occupations through the year 2022, which means employment is projected to increase 25 percent or more. Employment growth in the construction industry, in which about two-thirds of all cost estimators are employed, will be the driving force behind the demand for these workers. Construction and repair of highways, streets, and bridges, and construction of more subway systems, airports, water and sewage systems and electric power plants and transmission lines will also stimulate demand for many more cost estimators.

Job prospects in construction should be best for those workers with a degree in construction management or construction science, engineering, or architectural drafting, or those who have experience in various phases of construction or a specialty craft area.

Employment Trend, Projected 2012–22

Cost Estimators: 15%

Business Operations Specialists: 15%

Total, All Occupations: 15%

Note: "All Occupations" includes all occupations in the U.S. Economy. Source: U.S. Bureau of Labor Statistics, Employment Projections Program.

Related Occupations

- Automotive Service Advisor
- Budget Analyst
- Industrial Engineer
- Personal Financial Advisor
- Production Coordinator
- Purchasing Agent
- Sales Engineer

Conversation With . . .
CHRISTIAN AMORELLO

Cost Estimator & Project Manager
J Cougler Inc., West Harwich MA
General Contracting, 18 years

1. **What was your individual career path in terms of education/training, entry-level job, or other significant opportunity?**

In both high school and college, I played sports and took a lot of classes in studio art, math and science. I decided to get my bachelor's in architectural studies. When I was 16 and had just gotten my drivers license, I started as a "Go For" with a construction crew on a sewer rehabilitation project. It was my job to get whatever the pipe layers in the trench needed and drop it down to them. I was always going to get fittings, tools, pipe lubricant, chains and, of course, coffee. Eventually, they started sending me around the county to pick up materials. I got good at making lists, learning what route to take to get everything in the shortest drive, and, eventually, who to get it from. This was my logistics training, most of which was before cell phones. I eventually started managing a crew.

The company I started with primarily did underground utility work like sewers and water mains. After college I realized I wanted to work above ground and preferred the construction end of architecture. I started working in residential construction in New York City. There I focused on project management, contracting with subcontractors, and estimating $10 million projects for competitive bids.

2. **What are the most important skills and/or qualities for someone in your profession?**

Accountability is a quality that people expect in any profession; project management and cost estimating are no different.

Additional to that is the skill to appraise a situation, evaluate variables, assess risk, determine steps to work through the situation and communicate these steps. I traveled around the world for a few years after college and relied heavily on my ability to size things up and willingness to ask questions. Estimating for construction is similar. You won't know everything about construction, so you must be willing to ask a lot of questions

3. **What do you wish you had known going into this profession?**

I wish I had learned to speak a few languages. A construction job site is usually a culturally diverse place.

4. **Are there many job opportunities in your profession? In what specific areas?**

Yes, there are a lot of opportunities as a cost estimator. Estimating is not limited to construction; it can be applied to any project. Businesses are always looking for someone who can recognize the steps required to accomplish something and estimate the cost of those steps.

5. **How do you see your profession changing in the next five years, what role will technology play in those changes, and what skills will be required?**

The math and geometry required for estimating I don't think will ever change. What has changed is the means by which we acquire data and perform calculations. Estimating used to be blueprints, a scale, a calculator and a pad of paper. With the use of digital design such as AutoCAD by architects and engineers, we get construction documents in digital form. There are estimating programs that scan a PDF and calculate the linear feet, square footage, and cubic yards and come up with a control estimate. Using websites like Google maps and its "street view" we may not even need to visit the site. We can see the topography and site access online.

In the next five years, I see the biggest impact being a shift to a more technologically savvy work force. There are plenty of contractors who have embraced email and smart phones and estimating software, but they are not the majority. I spend a considerable amount of time helping subcontractors embrace technology. Right now you can say, "I'll email it to you" to a group of contractors and someone in the group will reply, "Can you fax it to me?"

6. **What do you like most about your job? What do you like least about your job?**

You are always moving onto the next project at the next location, and most every project is unique. What I enjoy least is working on a project for someone whose goals don't align with the reality of what the project is.

7. **Can you suggest a valuable "try this" for students considering a career in your profession?**

I worked as a line cook in New York City while I was in college. I found it to be invaluable. I learned how to make a deadline every five minutes; meet someone else's standards over and over again; comprehend and follow a process for assembly (a recipe); accept criticism and (hopefully) praise; and get along with lots of different people in hot, cramped areas.

Without experience, it isn't easy to get a job in construction, but restaurant kitchens are always hiring.

SELECTED SCHOOLS

Many colleges and universities, especially those with business
schools, offer programs in business operations and finance, including
instruction in cost estimation. Some institutions with architecture
and building programs sometimes also offer this. The student can also
gain initial training at a technical or community college. For some of
the more prominent institutions in this field, see the list of selected
schools in the "Operations Manager" chapter.

MORE INFORMATION

AACE International
1265 Suncrest Towne Centre Drive
Morgantown, WV 26505-1876
304.296.8444
www.aacei.org

**American Society of Professional
Estimators**
2525 Perimeter Place Drive
Suite 103
Nashville, TN 37214
888.378.6283
www.aspenational.org

**International Cost Estimating &
Analysis Association**
8221 Old Courthouse Road, Suite 106
Vienna, VA 22182
703.938.5090
www.iceaaonline.org

**Professional Construction
Estimators Association**
P.O. Box 680336
Charlotte, NC 28216
877.521.7232
www.pcea.org

Patrick Cooper/Editor

Credit & Loan Officer

Snapshot

Career Cluster: Banking & Finance; Business Administration

Interests: Financial trends, organizing information, mathematics, customer service, sales

Earnings (Yearly Average): $36,050

Employment & Outlook: Average Growth Expected

OVERVIEW

Sphere of Work

Credit and loan officers are responsible for the credit and loan activities of financial institutions. Credit and loan officers interact directly with loan and credit applicants and interview them about their personal and financial histories. Credit and loan officers also review and process loan and credit applications, participate in credit and loan fraud investigations, send out loan and credit approval or denial notices, respond to inquiries from loan and credit applicants, and notify customers of delinquent loans or credit accounts. They generally

work under the direct supervision of credit and loan managers, who review and authorize all final loan and credit decisions.

Work Environment

Credit and loan officers generally work in offices and call centers at commercial banks, credit card companies, mortgage companies, savings and loan associations, and credit unions. Credit and loan officers frequently travel from their offices at financial institutions to client homes or businesses to negotiate loan agreements. Most credit and loan officers work regular forty-hour weeks, although overtime may be required during periods of peak business.

Profile

Working Conditions: Work Indoors
Physical Strength: Light Work
Education Needs: High School Diploma or G.E.D., Technical/Community College
Licensure/Certification: Required
Physical Abilities Not Required: No Heavy Labor
Opportunities For Experience: Part-Time Work
Holland Interest Score*: CES, CSE

* See Appendix A

Occupation Interest

Individuals attracted to the loan and credit field tend to be organized and detail-oriented people who find satisfaction in tracking financial trends and assessing risk. Those who excel in loan and credit jobs demonstrate financial and mathematical acumen, focus, responsibility, and effective time management. Credit and loan officers should be knowledgeable about finance, exhibit good judgment, and have a background in customer service. Credit and loan officers who are persuasive and have experience in sales may enjoy greater success in this field as they frequently receive a commission or bonus for the loans they close.

A Day in the Life—Duties and Responsibilities

Loan clerks perform the background research necessary to determine an applicant's eligibility for credit or a loan. They first interview loan and credit applicants about their financial history, including contact information, employer, education, debts, income, and assets. They also verify the identity of any loan co-signers, request credit ratings from credit bureaus and associations, and confirm the value of collateral (property used to ensure repayment of a loan). Once applications have been reviewed, loan clerks may be asked to send out loan and credit approval or denial notices. When a loan application is approved, the loan clerk must prepare and gather documents for the loan closing, record all related transactions, and provide repayment information to the client.

Credit and loan officers perform more sophisticated and complex tasks in the loan application process. Depending on the size and type of the organization, they may personally interview clients and thoroughly investigate their credit histories, as a loan clerk does. Credit and loan officers are additionally responsible for educating loan applicants about various loan and credit options, comparing credit histories of prospective borrowers, analyzing client financial statements, and reviewing and processing loan and credit applications. Under the guidance of the credit manager and institutional loan policies, the credit and loan officer decides whether loans or credit should be extended to applicants. Once applications have been reviewed, credit and loan officers may notify clients of loan and credit approval or denial. When a loan is approved, the loan officer calculates repayment schedules, negotiates terms, and finalizes loan transactions. Credit and loan officers may also investigate credit fraud, prepare credit and loan history reports, create loan request summary reports for managers, and report delinquent accounts to credit agencies. Some specialize in personal or commercial loans or mortgages.

Credit authorizers determine credit eligibility and perform credit-related tasks. They receive notification of charges from vendors and keep records of customer credit and loan payments. Using this information and predefined guidelines, they determine whether a client is eligible for credit. As needed, they also prepare credit card charge plates for business and send charge statements and overdue notices to clients.

Duties and Responsibilities

- Conducting personal interviews with applicants
- Contacting credit references and other sources of credit history
- Filling out reports and credit applications
- Referring to credit records to approve lines of credit or credit card purchases
- Keeping abreast of financial trends regarding loan types, interest rates, etc.

OCCUPATION SPECIALTIES

Credit Checkers

Credit Checkers verify information of credit applicants by contacting credit reporting agencies, previous employers, and other credit services.

Loan Interviewers

Loan Interviewers, also called Loan Processors, interview applicants and others to get and verify personal and financial information needed to complete loan applications. They also prepare the documents that go to the appraiser and are issued at the closing of a loan.

Credit Authorizers

Credit Authorizers evaluate customers' computerized credit records and payment histories to decide, based on predetermined standards, whether to approve new credit.

WORK ENVIRONMENT

Physical Environment

Credit and loan officers generally work in office environments in commercial banks, credit card companies, mortgage companies, savings and loan associations, and credit unions. The work of a credit and loan officer requires sitting at a desk and using computers for long periods each day. Credit and loan officers are employed in similar office settings but often travel locally to work with clients.

Human Environment

Credit and loan officers interact with loan applicants, business owners, colleagues, and supervisors. They should be comfortable discussing financial data with clients, and must also be able to inform and instruct clients about loan procedures and options.

Relevant Skills and Abilities

Communication Skills
- Editing written information
- Listening attentively
- Speaking effectively
- Writing concisely

Interpersonal/Social Skills
- Being friendly
- Listening attentively

Organization & Management Skills
- Paying attention to and handling details
- Performing routine work

Research & Planning Skills
- Gathering information

Technological Environment

Credit and loan officers use computers, telephones, and Internet tools for communication. Financial analysis software and spreadsheets are other basic tools they use to complete their work. Credit and loan officers may use scanners, smart phones, and accounting and management software in addition to basic office equipment

EDUCATION, TRAINING, AND ADVANCEMENT

High School/Secondary

High school students interested in pursuing a career as a credit and loan officer should prepare themselves by building good study habits and by developing strong mathematical skills. High school courses in bookkeeping and mathematics will provide a solid foundation for work as a credit and loan officer or college-level study in the field. High school students interested in this career path may benefit from seeking internships or part-time work with financial organizations that will familiarize them with credit procedures. Those who wish to become loan interviewers or credit checkers may find employment directly after high school, while those who intend to become credit authorizers should apply to college or university programs.

Suggested High School Subjects
- Accounting
- Applied Communication
- Business
- Business & Computer Technology
- Business Data Processing
- Business Law
- English
- Keyboarding
- Mathematics

Famous First

The first credit card to be honored nationally was the Diners Club card, established in 1950 by credit company official, Frank McNamara, and attorney Ralph Scheider. Diners Club card holders could use the card at a variety of restaurants, department stores, and retail chains.

College/Postsecondary

Postsecondary students interested in becoming loan interviewers or credit checkers should consider completing finance and credit analysis training at vocational schools or community colleges. Those who intend to become loan authorizers should pursue a bachelor's degree in economics, mathematics, accounting, or business. Classes in computer science, political science, and ethics may also prove useful in their future work. Postsecondary students can gain work experience and a competitive advantage in future job searches by securing internships or part-time employment with local businesses or financial organizations.

Related College Majors
- Banking & Financial Support Services
- Business Administration
- Financial Operations

Adult Job Seekers

AAdults seeking credit and loan officer jobs have generally earned at least a high school diploma. Prospective loan authorizers usually have a bachelor's degree and, in some cases, a master's of business administration (MBA). Most employers also provide some job training. Adult job seekers may benefit from joining professional finance or accounting associations as a means of networking. Professional finance associations, such as the Risk Management Association, the Financial Managers Society, and the National Association of Credit Management, maintain job lists advertising open positions.

Professional Certification and Licensure

Certification and licensure is not legally required for credit and loan officers but may be required as a condition of employment or promotion. Mortgage loan officers must obtain licensure, a process that involves education, testing, background checks, and continuing education for renewal. Options for voluntary certification in the loan and credit fields include the Risk Management Association's Credit Risk Certified (CRC) designation and the National Association of Credit Management's Certified Credit Executive (CCE), Credit Business Fellow (CBF), and Credit Business Associate (CBA) designations. These voluntary certifications have education, experience, testing, recertification, and continuing education requirements.

Additional Requirements

Successful credit and loan officers take the time to become knowledgeable about the profession's requirements, responsibilities, and opportunities. Integrity and professional ethics are essential qualities in credit and loan officers since they have access to confidential financial information. Membership in professional finance associations can help create a sense of professional community among all credit and loan officers. Credit and loan officers must follow trends and developments in the field so they can best meet the loan and credit needs of their clients.

EARNINGS AND ADVANCEMENT

With experience, credit and loan officers may rise to management positions and be in charge of overseeing credit authorizations and training new employees. Median annual earnings of credit and loan officers were $36,050 in 2013. The lowest ten percent earned less than $24,000, and the highest ten percent earned more than $51,000.

Full-time credit and loan officers may receive paid vacations, holidays, and sick days; life and health insurance; and retirement benefits. These are usually paid by the employer. Part-time employees usually do not receive these benefits.

Metropolitan Areas with the Highest Employment Level in This Occupation

Metropolitan area	Employment[1]	Employment per thousand jobs	Hourly mean wage
Dallas-Plano-Irving, TX	10,890	5.06	$19.55
Chicago-Joliet-Naperville, IL	7,090	1.91	$19.09
Phoenix-Mesa-Glendale, AZ	7,030	3.95	$18.61
New York-White Plains-Wayne, NY-NJ	6,670	1.27	$19.39
Houston-Sugar Land-Baytown, TX	4,390	1.59	$19.30
Minneapolis-St. Paul-Bloomington, MN-WI	4,190	2.34	$18.62
Los Angeles-Long Beach-Glendale, CA	4,090	1.03	$20.68
St. Louis, MO-IL	3,680	2.85	$18.78
Santa Ana-Anaheim-Irvine, CA	3,430	2.36	$21.50
Tampa-St. Petersburg-Clearwater, FL	3,030	2.63	$17.36

[1] Does not include self-employed. Source: Bureau of Labor Statistics

EMPLOYMENT AND OUTLOOK

Credit and loan officers held about 250,000 jobs nationally in 2012. Employment is expected to grow about as fast as the average for all occupations through the year 2022, which means employment is projected to increase 9 percent to 14 percent. Despite a projected increase in the number of credit applications, online services and other technological innovations will allow these applications to be processed, checked and authorized by fewer workers than were required in the past.

Related Occupations

- Bill and Account Collector
- Credit Manager

Conversation With . . .
PAUL WALSH

Mortgage Officer
Mortgage Financial, Inc.
Lending profession, 24 years

1. What was your individual career path in terms of education/training, entry-level job, or other significant opportunity?

I was actually a real estate broker for five years before going into lending. The experience of buying my first home made me decide to switch careers. (I actually, in a previous life, worked in high tech). When I bought my house, my financing experience was horrendous. After I closed on the house, I kept thinking about this for two or three years. Finally, I just made the change and left the world of high tech. So, it was both the personal experience I had and the opportunity I saw that led me to get into real estate and then lending. Also, I had my bachelor's degree and to move to the next level in the world of high tech would have required a master's degree. I had a family and it just wasn't in me to pursue a master's. There's really no training required of loan officers, which has to change, it just has to. But we are licensed and required to pass two exams.

2. What are the most important skills and/or qualities for someone in your profession?

Truly, right now it's understanding exactly what the consumer wants or needs and, to some extent, protecting them from themselves. If someone wants to buy a $450,000 house and just cannot afford it, part of the job is reeling them in with realistic expectations. You have to be able to place people in the right loan program. I may get compensated more if I put someone in an FHA loan versus a Fannie Mae, but is that the best thing for them? Or the loan with the lowest interest rate may not be the least expensive. So you just really have to know what you're doing—that sounds ridiculous, but you'd be amazed how many people in this field don't know what they're doing, even with a license. You have to have good ethics. You will be required to have a criminal background check, be fingerprinted by the FBI, and submit a credit report

3.   What do you wish you had known going into this profession?

I wish I had known the importance of having a team and working as a team. No one person can really do the entire loan process alone. For instance, I no longer do reverse mortgages. I now know my skill set. I wish I had known that I can't be all things to all people. Right from the start, I would have chosen a specialty and stuck to it.

4. Are there many job opportunities in your profession? In what specific areas?

Being a mortgage officer is really a sales job. You're selling a product, and those skills will always be in demand. But the future of this business is in the world of mortgage compliance, because the government is taking mortgage compliance very, very seriously. If sales isn't your thing, I would suggest compliance.

5. How do you see your profession changing in the next five years, what role will technology play in those changes, and what skills will be required?

Technology is huge. I'm very old school and like to meet person to person. I'm a pen and paper guy. But many mortgage officers or loan officers and their clients nowadays never meet. They rarely even talk. You just go online and submit everything electronically. e-Mortgages and e-financing is really where this business is going. I consider that unfortunate.

6. What do you like most about your job? What do you like least about your job?

For me, it's always the people, and first-time homebuyers in particular. What I enjoy most is the personal interaction, and basically solving problems for people. The economy hasn't been great. If someone has excessive credit card debt or other financial problems — if they have a mortgage and a home — you can use that equity to structure things and really come up with a solution to help people out of unfortunate situations.

What I enjoy least is dealing with all the regulations, though I agree wholeheartedly with it. The compliance part is very, very difficult, and the inconsistencies from lender to lender and the multitude of product guidelines or "overlays" gets complicated.

7. Can you suggest a valuable "try this" for students considering a career in your profession?

Team up with someone who does what I do and work with them for a summer. You'll learn things like how to look at assets and recognize risk profiles. Even with an inside position, where you're sending out verification of employment forms, you'll learn the ropes and learn industry guidelines. Over the course of a summer, someone could learn a tremendous amount about this business.

SELECTED SCHOOLS

Many colleges and universities, especially those with business schools, offer programs in finance and business administration. The student can also gain initial training at a technical or community college. For some of the more prominent institutions in this field, see the list of selected schools in the "Financial Manager" chapter.

MORE INFORMATION

Financial Managers Society
100 W. Monroe Street, Suite 1700
Chicago, IL 60603
312.578.1300
www.fmsinc.org

National Association of Credit Management
Education Department
8840 Columbia 100 Parkway
Columbia, MD 21045
410.740.5560
www.nacm.org

Risk Management Association
1801 Market Street, Suite 300
Philadelphia, PA 19103-1628
215.446.4000
www.rmahq.org

Simone Isadora Flynn/Editor

Credit Manager

Snapshot

Career Cluster: Banking & Finance; Business Administration
Interests: Financial trends, risk assessment, mathematics, research
Earnings (Yearly Average): $64,030
Employment & Outlook: Slower Than Average Growth Expected

OVERVIEW

Sphere of Work

Credit managers, also referred to as credit analysts, credit administrators, and risk analysts, are responsible for the credit operations of businesses, corporations, nonprofit organizations, and government agencies. They provide diverse financial services, which may include developing credit-rating evaluation systems, collecting debt, setting credit ceilings, and reviewing applicant credit eligibility. Credit managers conduct financial research and present their findings in financial risk reports reviewed by stockholders and stakeholders and used for organizational decision-making.

Work Environment

Credit managers work in offices, particularly in commercial banks, mortgage companies, savings and loan associations, and credit unions. Depending on employer and particular job description, a credit manager may telecommute from a home office, visit client offices as a contractor, or work on a full-time basis in an employer's office. A credit manager may work as a full-time member of a finance team or as a term-of-project contractor.

Profile

Working Conditions: Work Indoors
Physical Strength: Light Work
Education Needs: Bachelor's Degree
Licensure/Certification: Usually Not Required
Physical Abilities Not Required: No Heavy Labor
Opportunities For Experience: Part-Time Work
Holland Interest Score*: CES

* See Appendix A

Occupation Interest

Individuals attracted to the credit management profession tend to be ambitious, organized, and detail-oriented people who find satisfaction in tracking financial trends and assessing risk. Those who excel as credit managers exhibit financial and mathematical acumen, intense focus, responsibility, and effective time management. Credit managers should enjoy finance and have a background in risk assessment.

A Day in the Life—Duties and Responsibilities

The daily duties and responsibilities of credit managers vary with job specialty and employer. Areas of credit management specialization include developing credit-rating evaluation systems, collecting debt, setting credit ceilings, and determining who is eligible for credit. Credit managers in commercial banks, mortgage companies, savings and loan associations, and credit unions are required to satisfy different constituents and meet different financial goals.

Credit managers perform or supervise a variety of credit-related operations for their employers. They analyze customer or client financial statements, assess the risk levels and outcomes associated with credit lending, write credit analysis reports, and draft credit or lending risk reports for chief financial officers, finance managers, and stockholders to use in making lending decisions. They are responsible for the processing of loan applications. This may involve requesting credit ratings from credit bureaus and associations, reviewing and approving or denying loan requests using expected return data based on credit histories of prospective borrowers, negotiating loan terms, and finalizing loan transactions. Credit managers must also manage loan portfolios and create loan request summary reports for financial and investment managers. They ensure collection of outstanding debts from borrowers, oversee investigations of loan or credit fraud, report delinquent accounts to credit agencies, and set credit limits on credit cards or lines of credit. Credit managers may also consult on the development of technologies designed to prevent credit fraud. Those employed in smaller institutions are more likely to perform some or all of these tasks themselves.

In addition, organizations may require credit managers to select, implement, and troubleshoot financial software systems, as well as stay up to date with regulatory and ethical issues and news in finance by reading finance industry journals and participating in industry associations. Credit managers employed by learning institutions also participate in ongoing discussions of work teams, workflows, dynamics, and best practices

Duties and Responsibilities

- **Formulating credit policies**
- **Establishing financial standards for borrowers**
- **Reviewing and evaluating results of investigations of credit requests**
- **Assessing risks to the company in issuing credit**
- **Supervising the collection of bad accounts**
- **Monitoring for evidence of any credit fraud**
- **Overseeing credit and loan officers and other staff**

OCCUPATION SPECIALTIES

Financial Institution Managers

Financial Institution Managers manage banks, credit unions, or finance companies. They direct and coordinate activities to implement policies, procedures, and practices concerning granting or extending lines of credit and loans.

Loan Officers

Loan Officers handle credit applications and work with clients to obtain their personal and financial histories. They send out approval or denial notices, respond to inquiries from loan and credit applicants, and notify customers of delinquent loans or credit accounts.

Risk Managers

Risk Managers control financial risk by using hedging and other strategies to limit or offset the probability of a financial loss or a company's exposure to financial uncertainty. Among the risks they try to limit are those due to currency or commodity price changes.

WORK ENVIRONMENT

Physical Environment

Credit managers generally work in pleasant office environments. The work of a credit manager requires sitting at a desk and using computers for long periods each day.

Human Environment

Credit managers interact with loan applicants, business owners, colleagues, and stockholders. They should be comfortable attending meetings, giving frequent speeches, and supervising and directing other financial employees, such as loan clerks and loan officers.

Relevant Skills and Abilities

Analytical Skills
- Analyzing data

Communication Skills
- Speaking effectively
- Writing concisely

Interpersonal/Social Skills
- Cooperating with others
- Having good judgment
- Working as a member of a team

Organization & Management Skills
- Coordinating tasks
- Making decisions
- Managing people/groups

Technical Skills
- Performing mathematical and technical work

Technological Environment

Credit managers communicate using computers, telephones, and Internet communication tools. They rely on financial analysis software and spreadsheets to generate analyses and reports.

EDUCATION, TRAINING, AND ADVANCEMENT

High School/Secondary

High school students interested in pursuing a career as a credit manager should prepare themselves by building good study habits and by developing an ease with numbers and mathematical functions. High school coursework in bookkeeping and mathematics will provide a strong foundation for college-level study in the field. Due to the diversity of credit manager responsibilities, high school students interested in this career path may benefit from internships or part-time work with financial organizations.

Suggested High School Subjects
- Accounting
- Applied Communication
- Bookkeeping

- Business Data Processing
- Business Math
- College Preparatory
- Economics
- English
- Mathematics
- Psychology

Famous First

The first federal credit union was the Morris Shepard Federal Credit Union of Texarcana, Texas, launched in 1934 and named after the sponsor of the act that authorized federal credit unions. Its purpose was "to make more available to people of small means credit for provident purposes through a ... system of cooperative credit."

College/Postsecondary

Postsecondary students interested in becoming credit managers should earn a bachelor's degree in economics, mathematics, accounting, or business. Classes in computer science, political science, and ethics may also prove useful in their future work. Postsecondary students can gain work experience and potential advantage in their future job searches through internships or part-time employment with local businesses or financial organizations.

Related College Majors
- Business Administration
- Finance

Adult Job Seekers

Adults seeking employment in credit management have generally a bachelor's degree in finance or a related field and, in some cases, a master's degree in business administration (MBA). Qualified adult job seekers may benefit from joining professional finance or accounting associations as a means of professional networking. Professional finance associations, such as the Risk Management Association, the Financial Managers Society and the National Association of Credit Management, generally maintain job lists advertising open accounting positions.

Professional Certification and Licensure

Certification and licensure is not legally required for general credit managers but may be required as a condition of employment or promotion. Options for voluntary credit manager certification include the Credit Risk Certified (CRC) designation from the Risk Management Association and the Certified Credit Executive (CCE), Credit Business Fellow (CBF), and Credit Business Associate (CBA) designations from the National Association of Credit Management. These voluntary certifications have education, experience, testing, recertification, and continuing education requirements. Professional certification conveys proficiency in credit concepts, management, accounting, finance, and law.

Additional Requirements

Successful credit managers will be knowledgeable about the profession's requirements, responsibilities, and opportunities. Credit managers must adhere to ethical and professional standards because they routinely access and evaluate confidential financial information. Membership in professional finance associations is encouraged among all credit managers as a means of building professional community

EARNINGS AND ADVANCEMENT

Earnings of credit managers vary according to the experience and background of the individual and the geographic location and size of the employer. Salaries are likely to be higher in large organizations and cities.

Median annual earnings of credit managers were $64,030 in 2013. The lowest ten percent earned less than $39,000, and the highest ten percent earned more than $119,000. Many credit managers in private industry received additional compensation in the form of bonuses. Credit managers may receive paid vacations, holidays, and sick days; life and health insurance; and retirement benefits. These are usually paid by the employer

Metropolitan Areas with the Highest Employment Level in This Occupation

Metropolitan area	Employment[1]	Employment per thousand jobs	Hourly mean wage
New York-White Plains-Wayne, NY-NJ	4,470	0.85	$56.06
Chicago-Joliet-Naperville, IL	2,450	0.66	$37.48
Dallas-Plano-Irving, TX	2,370	1.10	$36.39
Atlanta-Sandy Springs-Marietta, GA	1,970	0.85	$33.31
Los Angeles-Long Beach-Glendale, CA	1,880	0.47	$35.52
Minneapolis-St. Paul-Bloomington, MN-WI	1,760	0.98	$31.14
Charlotte-Gastonia-Rock Hill, NC-SC	1,740	1.98	$40.74
Boston-Cambridge-Quincy, MA	1,370	0.78	$38.67
Wilmington, DE-MD-NJ	1,290	3.95	$29.22
Santa Ana-Anaheim-Irvine, CA	1,110	0.77	$36.80

[1] Does not include self-employed. Source: Bureau of Labor Statistics.

EMPLOYMENT AND OUTLOOK

Financial managers, of which credit managers are a part, held about 532,000 jobs in 2012. Although these managers are found in virtually every industry, about one-third were employed by insurance and finance institutions, such as banks, savings institutions, finance companies, credit unions, insurance carriers and securities dealers. Employment is expected to grow somewhat slower than the average for all occupations through the year 2022, which means employment is projected to increase 3 percent to 9 percent.

Employment Trend, Projected 2012–22

Total, All Occupations: 11%

Financial Managers: 9%

Credit Managers: 7%

Note: "All Occupations" includes all occupations in the U.S. Economy. Source: U.S. Bureau of Labor Statistics, Employment Projections Program.

Related Occupations
- Accountant
- Auditor
- Bill & Account Collector
- Financial Manager
- Loan Clerk & Credit Authorizer

Conversation With . . .
LEEZA PATEL-MALINOWSKI

Isle of Capri Casino, Lake Charles, LA
Credit Manager, 15 years

1. What was your individual career path in terms of education/training, entry-level job, or other significant opportunity?

The casino industry is vivacious and can employ many different kinds of talents. My personal academic background started in fashion merchandising with courses at the Fashion Institute of Technology (FIT). Later, I studied technology at Fairleigh Dickinson University in New Jersey. I've also taken classes independently in algebra and accounting. I can honestly say I have been able to apply some of things from each of the areas I have studied to various parts of the — curriculum from merchandising and fashion can be applied to marketing and design. I was able to twist the basic mechanics. Of course, education in technology is applicable almost universally.

Back in 2003, I started as a customer care representative at a casino in Atlantic City and worked my way up to credit representative, and eventually credit manager.

2. What are the most important skills and/or qualities for someone in your profession?

Openness—since the entire casino industry is going through a tailspin, along with the global economy, one has to be open to move—to move into new positions, different departments, and different locations.

3. What do you wish you had known going into this profession?

Although I am typically not retrospective, looking back I wish I had taken formal training in table games. Without that formal training, it took a long time to learn these games. This knowledge is such a critical component in issuing gaming-related credit.

4. Are there many job opportunities in your profession? In what specific areas?

Generally, credit jobs in casinos are far and few between because these are well-paid, revenue-generating positions and people rarely leave these jobs.

5. How do you see your profession changing in the next five years, what role will technology play in those changes, and what skills will be required?

Casino credit departments used to be organized under Casino Operations or Finance. However, the most recent trend is to classify credit departments under marketing since it can be largely a marketing tool. I definitely see that casino marketing professionals with casino credit knowledge are considered more valuable.

Technology is playing a huge role by making the majority of processes electronic, proactive, and streamlined. This has improved accuracy by eliminating the majority of touch points that originally were prone to human error

6. What do you like most about your job? What do you like least about your job?

I enjoy meeting new people and developing relationships. I also like the fact that, with casinos open in so many states, there is an opportunity to relocate and explore different parts of the country—surely a plus for anyone who does not mind relocating every once a while.

The least favorable part of this—and any other job in a casino—is the schedule, and not being able to have holidays and weekends off.

7. Can you suggest a valuable "try this" for students considering a career in your profession?

If one is trying to get into the casino business, the best area to start in—as well as move up in—are games and marketing. Next time you are in a casino, you can ask to be connected to a casino host and observe what they do. That should give a real perspective of what goes in and what can be expected out of these positions.

SELECTED SCHOOLS

Many colleges and universities, especially those with business schools, offer programs in finance and business administration. The student can also gain initial training at a technical or community college. For some of the more prominent institutions in this field, see list of selected schools in the "Financial Manager" chapter.

MORE INFORMATION

Association for Financial Professionals
4520 East-West Highway
Suite 750
Bethesda, MD 30814
301.907.2862
www.afponline.org

Financial Managers Society
100 W. Monroe Street
Suite 1700
Chicago, IL 60603
312.578.1300
www.fmsinc.org

National Association of Credit Management
Education Department
8840 Columbia 100 Parkway
Columbia, MD 21045
410.740.5560
www.nacm.org

Risk Management Association
1801 Market Street, Suite 300
Philadelphia, PA 19103-1628
800.677.7621
www.rmahq.org

Simone Isadora Flynn/Editor

Customer Service Representative

Snapshot

Career Cluster: Business Administration; Communications & Media; Sales & Marketing

Interests: Talking on the telephone, interacting with people, handling conflict

Earnings (Yearly Average): $30,870

Employment & Outlook: Average Growth Expected

OVERVIEW

Sphere of Work

Customer service representatives provide a wide range of support to customers and serve as the primary point of contact between a company and its customer base. They spend the work day responding accurately to customer questions and inquiries, solving customer problems, and handling customer complaints. Customer service representatives are found in a very broad range of industries and in any context where an organization provides product or service support to its customers. For this reason, customer service representatives are usually well-trained in their company's products and services and

policies and procedures. Many also perform administrative tasks such as placing orders and processing invoices and returns.

Work Environment

Customer service representatives generally work in office environments. Most work in call centers, but many will also work in retail and other commercial environments. Customer service representatives interact constantly with customers. In most cases, this involves phone calls, but it may also involve writing or assisting customers in person. This may include other customer service representatives and supervisors, as well as people from other departments. Customer service representatives engaged in full-time work may expect to work approximately forty hours per week, but work hours may vary significantly depending on the employer and industry. Extended customer service hours usually mean that a customer service representative will work some evening or weekend shifts. Part-time roles are also available.

Profile

Working Conditions: Work Indoors
Physical Strength: Light Work
Education Needs: On-The-Job Training
High School Diploma or G.E.D.
Licensure/Certification: Usually Not
  Required
Physical Abilities Not Required: No
  Heavy Labor
Opportunities For Experience: Part-
  Time Work
Holland Interest Score*: CES

* See Appendix A

Occupation Interest

This occupation suits people who enjoy interacting with other people on a daily basis. Those attracted to customer service roles generally have good communication skills and find satisfaction in interacting with people. They should be able to demonstrate patience and empathy when dealing with customer complaints or questions. In some cases, customer service representatives may also be required to be highly proficient or knowledgeable in a certain technical field (for example, customer service representatives who provide computing helpdesk support).

A Day in the Life—Duties and Responsibilities

TA customer service representative's work involves assisting and supporting customers with their inquiries. This may include answering questions, providing technical help and advice, processing orders, taking payment information, responding to complaints, forwarding customers to supervisors for difficult inquiries, and performing other tasks as needed.

This is a role which requires patience, empathy, and tact, especially when dealing with customer complaints. It also requires the ability to solve problems. In many instances, customer service representatives must be able to deal with a large volume of customer inquiries, especially if they are employed in call centers or similar environments.

Customer interactions may occur in person, on the telephone, and/or via email and instant messaging. In the course of resolving customer inquiries they may be searching for and entering information into databases, preparing letters and emails, and using the Internet.

Customer service representatives may expect to communicate and collaborate with a variety of colleagues and/or third party vendors. Interorganizational coordination may be required among a variety of departments and the customer service representative may be required to attend meetings or regularly liaise with other individuals and groups. They may have to attend periodic training to familiarize themselves with new company products and policies

Duties and Responsibilities

- Taking customer calls
- Informing customers and potential customers of company services
- Demonstrating company goodwill
- Tracing through complicated billing or shipping problems
- Investigating service difficulties and providing solutions
- Solving customer problems

WORK ENVIRONMENT

Physical Environment

Office settings predominate. Many industries employ customer service representatives, and the specific physical environment will be influenced by the size and type of employer. There is a trend among some national and global companies to consolidate their customer support services at a single location. These work environments are often call centers.

Relevant Skills and Abilities

Communication Skills
- Listening attentively
- Speaking effectively

Interpersonal/Social Skills
- Being able to work independently
- Cooperating with others
- Working as a member of a team

Organization & Management Skills
- Managing conflict

Human Environment

Customer service representative roles demand strong communication skills. This job involves almost constant interaction with people, so patience, courtesy, and attention to detail are highly regarded. Some customer service representative roles include face-to-face contact with customers while others may involve only telephone or Internet-mediated contact.

Technological Environment

Daily operations will demand the use of standard office technologies, including telephone, e-mail, photocopiers, and Internet. Customer service representatives are usually also required to use computers and software, including word processing programs, spreadsheets, and specialist databases. Keyboarding skills are an advantage

EDUCATION, TRAINING, AND ADVANCEMENT

High School/Secondary

High school students can best prepare for a career as a customer service representative by taking courses in business and communications. Foreign languages may be advantageous as an increasing number of employers work in cross-cultural contexts and extend into global markets. Studies in mathematics and accounting provide a foundation for the numerical requirements of the role. Likewise, computing and keyboarding would be beneficial. Psychology and cultural studies may help candidates to develop empathetic relationship skills and to gain insight into creative problem solving. Becoming involved in part-time customer service work while still in high school (e.g. afterschool or weekend work in administration, hospitality, or retail) is an excellent way to gain entry-level experience into the customer service profession.

Suggested High School Subjects
- Business & Computer Technology
- English
- Foreign Languages
- Keyboarding
- Mathematics
- Psychology
- Speech

Famous First

The first "truth-in-advertising" law was enacted by New York State in 1898. The law was designed to prevent "misleading and dishonest representations" regarding merchandise for sale. Specifically, it made it a misdemeanor to present any advertisement that had "the appearance of an advantageous offer, which is untrue or calculated to mislead."

Postsecondary

The customer service representative profession generally requires no formal postsecondary educational qualifications, although an associate's or bachelor's degree in psychology, communications, or a related discipline may be attractive to employers. On-the-job experience in customer service support and delivery is usually considered more important than formal qualifications. Many employers will provide extensive induction and on-the-job training to ensure that their customer service representatives become experts in the products and services they represent.

Related College Majors
- Administrative Assistant/Secretarial Science
- General Retailing & Wholesaling Operations & Skills
- General Selling Skills & Sales Operations
- Receptionist Training

Adult Job Seekers

Adults seeking a career transition into or return to a customer service representative position are advised to refresh their skills and update their resume. Entry-level opportunities may exist as part-time, full-time, after-hours or weekend roles, as well as temporary or contract jobs. Aspiring customer service representatives may first obtain experience in the same company at a lower level and then progress to the customer service representative position. Opportunities for career advancement will depend largely on the size and type of organization in which the candidate works and their breadth of experience. Larger organizations may provide a tiered promotional system which ties the customer service representative's position title and wages to their level of experience and/or length of service. Customer service representatives seeking promotion may consider opportunities in supervisory or management roles.

Professional Certification and Licensure

There is no professional certification or licensure required for customer service representatives.

Additional Requirements

High quality customer service is increasingly recognized by business leaders and managers as a major driver of business success, since it helps consumers distinguish between organizations that provide similar goods and services. This is slowly helping to transition the perception of customer service from a basic business support role to a more highly valued profession and career. Those individuals who achieve proficiency in a foreign language may have an advantage over other candidates. Customer service representatives should be skilled at remaining courteous even when conversing with rude customers. Effective, professional conflict resolution is extremely valuable in this position

Fun Fact

A dissatisfied customer will tell between 9-15 people about their experience, and happy customers who get their issue resolved tell about 4-6 people about their experience.
Source: Return on Behavior Magazine, http://returnonbehavior.com/2010/10/50-facts-about-customer-experience-for-2011/.

59% of a company's customers stop doing business with that company due to poor customer service.
Source: https://blog.kissmetrics.com/happy-campers/

EARNINGS AND ADVANCEMENT

Advancement may mean becoming head of customer service or, in a small to medium sized firm, becoming an office manager. Median annual earnings of customer service representatives were $30,870 in 2013. The lowest ten percent earned less than $20,000, and the highest ten percent earned more than $50,000.

Customer service representatives may receive paid vacations, holidays, and sick days; life and health insurance; and retirement benefits. These are usually paid by the employer.

Metropolitan Areas with the Highest Employment Level in This Occupation

Metropolitan area	Employment[1]	Employment per thousand jobs	Hourly mean wage
New York-White Plains-Wayne, NY-NJ	82,040	15.65	$19.36
Chicago-Joliet-Naperville, IL	74,600	20.16	$18.06
Atlanta-Sandy Springs-Marietta, GA	60,350	26.15	$17.13
Los Angeles-Long Beach-Glendale, CA	57,910	14.57	$18.28
Dallas-Plano-Irving, TX	52,640	24.49	$16.35
Phoenix-Mesa-Glendale, AZ	51,440	28.88	$15.62
Houston-Sugar Land-Baytown, TX	50,750	18.40	$15.01
Tampa-St. Petersburg-Clearwater, FL	37,490	32.55	$14.90
Minneapolis-St. Paul-Bloomington, MN-WI	37,030	20.67	$18.18
Philadelphia, PA	36,150	19.65	$18.11

[1] Does not include self-employed. Source: Bureau of Labor Statistics.

EMPLOYMENT AND OUTLOOK

Customer service representatives held about 2.4 million jobs nationally in 2013. Although they were found in a variety of industries, the largest numbers were employed by call centers (customer contact, or sales solicitation, centers), insurance agencies, retailers, and financial institutions. Employment is expected to grow about as fast as the average for all occupations through the year 2022, which means employment is projected to increase 10 percent to 15 percent. Customer service is critical to the success of any organization that deals with customers, and strong customer service can build sales and visibility as companies try to distinguish themselves from competitors. In many industries, the need to gain a competitive edge and retain customers will become increasingly important over the next decade, and this will result in strong job growth for customer service representatives.

Employment Trend, Projected 2012–22

Customer Service Representatives: 13%

Total, All Occupations: 11%

Office and Administrative Support Occupations: 7%

Note: "All Occupations" includes all occupations in the U.S. Economy. Source: U.S. Bureau of Labor Statistics, Employment Projections Program.

Related Occupations
- Administrative Assistant
- Computer Support Specialist
- Online Merchant
- Receptionist & Information Clerk
- Retail Salesperson
- Secretary

Conversation With . . .
NATALIE SNIDER

Inside Sales and Customer Support for
learning company's online products, 10 years
Isla Mujeres, MX

1. What was your individual career path in terms of education/training, entry-level job, or other significant opportunity?

I was one term short of my nursing degree when a private school contacted me to come work for them. I taught grammar school and middle school for 12 years, and got my undergraduate degree in history through continuing education. I was hired away from teaching by my present employer. They were looking for my teaching experience.

My job is to handle some brief online training. I do webinars for teachers learning to use the product, and I make sure the product works for individual teachers and their students. I also contact people through phone or email to check on how the product is working and to help them with their renewals.

The product is differentiated instruction and diagnostic assessment. So, a student will log on, take an hour-long assessment in reading, and at the end the product will show the student's grade level, why they are where they are, and then give tools to the educator to boost the student's weak skills. We also provide differentiated instruction that aligns with the assessment to provide the student with a virtual one-on-one tutor.

The reason teaching has helped me in this job is that I understand the world of education, how busy teachers' lives are, and what they really need to get started. I can talk to them on an educational level, rather than a technical or business level.

As a practical matter, the thing I do most is walk people through any trouble they are having with their account. I troubleshoot and help them connect with others in our company if I cannot help them. Sometimes it involves taking over their computer and doing remote work for them.

I had this job for two years before my husband and I moved to Isla Mujeres. I talked with my boss about it, and he said, "If you can work remotely and maintain your availability, fine."

2. What are the most important skills and/or qualities for someone in your profession?

You need to be very punctual. You need to keep up with the changing elements of education and our products through continuing education and be self-motivated to do so. You need good conversational skills, and you need to be good at directing people.

3. What do you wish you had known going into this profession?

I wish I had known more small business management terminology that's used within the company. For instance, the first time I heard "IEP" — individualized education program — that term was unfamiliar to me. As an educator in the classroom, I didn't know that acronym

4. Are there many job opportunities in your profession? In what specific areas?

There are probably a lot of opportunities to work remotely. Within this part of the education profession, I don't know. I have a specialized title within my company, and there aren't a lot of people like me.

5. How do you see your profession changing in the next five years, what role will technology play in those changes, and what skills will be required?

You need to stay up on what's new in terms of technology since you need to communicate remotely, as well as to conduct webinars and essentially go into the classroom. Within my company, there are people who to travel but more and more that's changing.

6. What do you like most about your job? What do you like least about your job?

The best thing is that I get to work remotely. I set my own hours for the most part and I like the people I work with.

I least like relying on the internet. If it's down or there's a problem, I have to head off to an internet cafe. Also, working remotely has a downside: I never get a vacation and am almost always available.

7. Can you suggest a valuable "try this" for students considering a career in your profession?

I would suggest taking an online class so that you start connecting yourself with people that way, as well as learning to be accountable for your time.

SELECTED SCHOOLS

For those interested in training beyond high school, most technical
and community colleges offer programs in business administration,
including sales, marketing, and customer service. Interested students
are advised to consult with their school guidance counselor or to
research area postsecondary schools and training programs.

MORE INFORMATION

**International Customer
Management Association**
121 South Tejon Street, Suite 1100
Colorado Springs, CO 80903
719.955.8149
www.icmi.com

**International Customer Service
Association**
1110 South Avenue, Suite 50
Staten Island, NY 10314
347.273.1303
www.icsatoday.org

**National Customer Service
Association**
1714 Pfitzer Road
Normal, IL 61761
309.452.8831
www.nationalcsa.com

Kylie Hughes/Editor

Executive Secretary

Snapshot

Career Cluster: Business Administration

Interests: Communicating with others, being supportive of others, organizing information

Earnings (Yearly Average): $49,290

Employment & Outlook: Average Growth Expected

OVERVIEW

Sphere of Work

Executive secretaries assist executives to achieve more, communicate better with employees, and improve personal and organizational efficiency. They achieve this by providing high-level administrative, clerical, and secretarial support to one or more members of an organization's executive management team. The scope of their responsibilities exceeds that of regular secretarial work because they provide services to top-level management. They may be required to arrange appointments, coordinate with important people, and plan high priority meetings, events, and projects. They also research and prepare documents and reports, direct or forward confidential communications, and use tact and good judgment at all times.

Work Environment

Executive secretaries usually work in office environments, in close proximity to the executive staff they support. They interact with a team of clerical and administrative personnel, which may be comprised of administrative assistants, clerks, and receptionists. Their daily responsibilities require strong interpersonal, collaborative, and communication skills. Executive secretaries must communicate confidently and appropriately with people at all levels within their organization and from a wide variety of backgrounds outside of their organization. Executive secretaries usually work approximately forty hours per week during normal office hours, but many are called on to work longer hours. Executive secretaries are generally expected to work similar hours to the executive staff they support. Travel may be required in some circumstances. Because executives are ultimately responsible for meeting organizational goals, their secretaries experience job-related stress as project deadlines approach.

Profile

Working Conditions: Work Indoors
Physical Strength: Light Work
Education Needs: High School Diploma or G.E.D., Technical/Community College
Licensure/Certification: Recommended
Physical Abilities Not Required: No Heavy Labor
Opportunities For Experience: Volunteer Work, Part-Time Work
Holland Interest Score*: ESA

* See Appendix A

Occupation Interest

This occupation attracts those who possess advanced administrative and organizational capabilities along with excellent written and oral communication skills. Sophisticated analytical abilities, high-level communications skills, and excellent people skills must complement solid secretarial skills. Individuals attracted to an executive secretary career generally enjoy working in administrative support roles but wish to be involved at a strategic level. They must be trustworthy enough to keep sensitive information confidential. Their behavior should reflect the level of professionalism demonstrated by the executive staff they support.

A Day in the Life—Duties and Responsibilities

The tasks an executive secretary performs on any given day tend to be determined by the priorities of the executive staff they support. Most days involve a mixture of basic and more sophisticated secretarial duties. Basic secretarial duties may include answering the telephone, organizing appointments, managing a calendar, writing and sending e-mails, typing written communications, photocopying, filing records, making travel arrangements, and taking notes. An executive secretary's day is likely to be divided between deskwork and meetings.

The more complex duties of an executive secretary include supervising other secretaries and administrative staff, training groups and individuals, hosting or shadowing high priority visitors, and coordinating projects, events, and people. He or she also prepares reports, papers, and budgets.

Executive secretaries are expected to demonstrate an excellent understanding of their organization's operations, aims, principles, and priorities. They must apply this knowledge when they are researching, organizing, and distilling information to pass along to management. They may be expected to analyze information and make recommendations.

Many of an executive secretary's daily responsibilities demand diplomacy and good judgment. The executive secretary often acts as a gatekeeper by screening calls and other communications to protect executive staff from unnecessary distractions. He or she responds to communications on behalf of the staff they support, works with important people, and attends meetings or events as a representative of the organization's executive. An executive secretary must also have an eye for detail and accuracy. They may be expected to proofread and pre-screen legal and other important documents prior to obtaining the executive's signature

Duties and Responsibilities

- Answering phones and taking messages
- Scheduling appointments and updating calendars
- Reviewing incoming documents and handling as appropriate
- Drafting memos and preparing or assisting with reports
- Maintaining files and databases
- Meeting and greeting visitors
- Arranging meetings and taking meeting notes

WORK ENVIRONMENT

Physical Environment

Office settings predominate. Executive secretaries usually work in close proximity to the executive staff they support. The specific physical environment is influenced by the size and type of the employer and industry.

Relevant Skills and Abilities

Communication Skills
- Speaking effectively
- Writing concisely

Interpersonal/Social Skills
- Being able to work independently
- Being patient
- Having good judgment

Organization & Management Skills
- Organizing information or materials
- Paying attention to and handling details

Unclassified Skills
- Having a good sense of humor

Human Environment

Executive secretarial work demands strong teamwork and collaborative skills. Executive secretaries interact on a daily basis with a wide range of people within and outside of their place of employment. They are likely to interact with people at all levels and from diverse backgrounds. The role demands excellent oral and written communication skills, including fluency, empathy, diplomacy, and good judgment.

Technological Environment

Standard office technologies include computers, telephones, e-mail, photocopiers, fax machines, and the Internet. Executive secretaries are required to be competent in the use of word processing programs, contact management software, spreadsheets, and presentation programs. They also need to use specialized systems, such as databases and enterprise-wide resource platforms. Fast, accurate typing skills are essential

EDUCATION, TRAINING, AND ADVANCEMENT

High School/Secondary

High school students can best prepare for a career as an executive secretary by taking courses in English language and composition and applied communication subjects, such as business writing. Foreign languages may also be advantageous as an increasing number of employers work in cross-cultural contexts. Studies in applied mathematics and accounting would provide a foundation for the statistical and analytical requirements of the role. Computer courses are highly beneficial, as are shorthand skills.

Involvement in part-time administrative or clerical work while still in high school is an excellent way to gain entry-level experience in the secretarial profession

Suggested High School Subjects
- Applied Communication
- Business & Computer Technology
- Business English
- Composition
- English
- Keyboarding
- Shorthand
- Speech

Famous First

The first copy machine to achieve commercial success was the Haloid 914, which was manufactured in Rochester, New York, and introduced in 1950 by the Haloid company who manufactured photographic paper and equipment. They named the process "xerography," Greek for "dry writing." So successful was the new product that in 1961 Haloid changed its name to Xerox Corporation

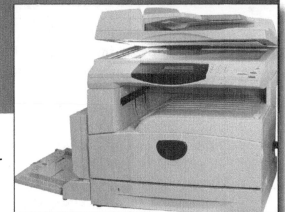

Postsecondary

Historically, executive secretarial work has not required formal postsecondary educational qualifications. However, an increasing number of employers now expect executive secretaries to possess an associate's degree or, in some cases, a bachelor's degree in business administration or other relevant field. On-the-job experience, along with relevant industry knowledge, is also very important.

Opportunities for career advancement depend largely on the size and type of organization in which the candidate works and their accumulated experience. Larger organizations are likely to provide more scope for growth and greater compensation

Related College Majors
- Administrative Assistant/Secretarial Science
- Business Administration & Management
- Office Supervision & Management

Adult Job Seekers

Adults seeking a career transition to an executive secretary position are advised to refresh their skills and update their resume. Emphasis should be placed on solid secretarial skills, which are complemented by advanced administrative abilities, analytical competency, and experience supporting managers at an executive level. Experience in relevant industries or with certain employers should also be highlighted in the candidate's resume and application letter.

Networking, job searching, and interviewing are critical. Aspiring executive secretaries should also consider similar roles, such as secretary, administrator, and office manager. A return to study may also be beneficial. In addition to universities, technical, and community colleges, the International Association of Administrative Professionals (IAAP) and Association of Executive and Administrative Professionals (AEAP) offer accredited and non-accredited training options for aspiring office professionals.

Professional Certification and Licensure

There are no formal professional certifications or licensure requirements for executive secretaries, but gaining recognition as a Certified Professional Secretary or Certified Administrative Professional may improve one's job prospects. These certifications are awarded by the International Association of Administrative Professionals. Those interested in becoming certified should consult credible professional associations within the field and follow professional debate as to the relevancy and value of any certification program.

Additional Requirements

This is a position in which having an even-tempered, capable, highly organized personality is an asset. Executive secretaries are expected to embody a level of professionalism appropriate to the executive staff they support. Deportment, confidence, public speaking and presentation skills, a good sense of humor, and a positive attitude are all important qualities in an executive secretary.

Fun Fact

Administrative office staff – once known only as secretaries – are finding new job titles such as Chief Executive Administrator, Director of First Impressions, Administrative Chief of Staff, Director of Administration, and Administrative Services Manager, according to a recent survey by OfficeTeam and the International Association of Administrative Professionals (IAAP). These professionals have found themselves undertaking a variety of odd jobs such as getting a snake out of the women's bathroom, organizing a hula-hoop competition for executive staff, and writing a skit about hand-washing.

Source: http://www.iaap-hq.org/blog/robert-hosking/evolving-administrative-job-descriptions-and-job-titles

EARNINGS AND ADVANCEMENT

Earnings of executive secretaries depend on the place of employment and the individual's experience and skill. Median annual earnings of executive secretaries were $49,290 in 2013. The lowest ten percent earned less than $32,000, and the highest ten percent earned more than $74,000.

Executive secretaries may receive paid vacations, holidays, and sick days; life and health insurance; and retirement benefits. These are usually paid by the employer.

Metropolitan Areas with the Highest
Employment Level in This Occupation

Metropolitan area	Employment[1]	Employment per thousand jobs	Hourly mean wage
New York-White Plains-Wayne, NY-NJ	50,680	9.67	$32.54
Los Angeles-Long Beach-Glendale, CA	29,140	7.33	$27.70
Chicago-Joliet-Naperville, IL	28,430	7.68	$24.96
Washington-Arlington-Alexandria, DC-VA-MD-WV	21,400	9.04	$29.28
Houston-Sugar Land-Baytown, TX	17,530	6.36	$26.14
Boston-Cambridge-Quincy, MA	16,260	9.30	$27.69
Atlanta-Sandy Springs-Marietta, GA	15,350	6.65	$24.80
Minneapolis-St. Paul-Bloomington, MN-WI	15,100	8.43	$24.25
Dallas-Plano-Irving, TX	13,970	6.50	$25.86
Santa Ana-Anaheim-Irvine, CA	11,420	7.86	$27.47

[1] Does not include self-employed. Source: Bureau of Labor Statistics.

EMPLOYMENT AND OUTLOOK

Executive secretaries held about 875,000 jobs nationally in 2012. Employment is expected to grow about as fast as the average for all occupations through the year 2022, which means employment is projected to increase 9 percent to 16 percent. Highly qualified executive secretaries skilled in new technologies will have the best job prospects.

Employment Trend, Projected 2012–22

Secretaries and Administrative Assistants (All): 12%

Total, All Occupations: 11%

Office and Administrative Support Occupations: 7%

Note: "All Occupations" includes all occupations in the U.S. Economy. Source: U.S. Bureau of Labor Statistics, Employment Projections Program.

Related Occupations

- Administrative Assistant
- Administrative Support Supervisor
- Legal Secretary
- Medical Assistant
- Medical Transcriptionist
- Receptionist & Information Clerk
- Secretary

Conversation With . . .
JUDY HEATH

Executive Assistant to the President, 12 years
Anne Arundel Community College, Arnold, MD
Executive Secretary, 22 years

1. **What was your individual career path in terms of education/training, entry-level job, or other significant opportunity?**

   I originally wanted to be a teacher, but wasn't able to finish my first semester of college due to family issues. I held low-level jobs, then went on to raise my children for 18 years. At the time I needed to go into the workforce, I used my skills of being able to type, write, and organize. I had done public speaking for my church, written newsletters for my family because we were missionaries, and had edited newsletters.

   I began working at Columbia International University in South Carolina as a data entry person. Because I was in my 40s, I had maturity and was promoted until I was secretary to the provost. Because the wages were not high, I decided to look for employment outside higher education. I got a job as executive secretary to the head of one of the larger law firms in Columbia. They were looking to hire someone into a legal secretary position. Although I lacked legal experience, I had maturity, people skills, am well-spoken, and a quick learner. I worked at three different law firms over five years, and each time I made a move I earned more money.

   My family moved to Annapolis, MD in 1998 and I went to the largest law firm in the city at that time and got a job. But I was working in medical malpractice, which I didn't like. So I landed a job for a large firm in Washington, D.C., where I stayed for 2 1/2 years. If the commute hadn't been so brutal, I might have stayed.

   My husband is the financial aid director at Anne Arundel Community College and I had seen the college president speak before and was impressed. I happened to see that she was looking for an executive assistant and that's how I came to be here."

2. **What are the most important skills and/or qualities for someone in your profession?**

   I see two sides to this question. In my position as assistant to the highest-level person in the organization, discretion, discernment, integrity and people skills are key. On a more practical side are the skills of typing, organization, or knowledge of technology. I have to be willing to learn and keep learning.

3. What do you wish you had known going into this profession?

I have not learned shorthand. I know that sounds crazy because it's old-fashioned, but I go in with a pad to meet with my boss who says, I want you to do this, this, and this...shorthand would make it so easy to take notes.

4. Are there many job opportunities in your profession? In what specific areas?

There are a lot of big firms in my area, and there's a tremendous need. Sometimes you have to put in time as a lower-level administrative assistant, but I think there are a lot of opportunities. Everyone needs assistance.

It's important to network. You have to engage yourself in these circles so people get to know you.

5. What do you like most about your job? What do you like least about your job?

I have always been in the position of working for the final decision-maker in an organization. I like the responsibility that goes with that, and being able to really get things done. There's not a lot that I don't enjoy. I love people, I love helping the president, I like knowing who to go to, I like being a go-to person, I like the ever-changing environment. For instance, we got a call today, which is a Thursday, from a senator's office, who wants to do a round-table discussion on campus on Monday.

I'm fortunate because I have a part-time assistant who handles many of the more mundane tasks

6. Can you suggest a valuable "try this" for students considering a career in your profession?

Shadow somebody in an office, do some filing, and learn about office protocols. You could volunteer at your church office, or for another organization, and help them with organization and technology. There are a lot of opportunities to volunteer and be exposed to this kind of work.

SELECTED SCHOOLS

For those interested in training beyond high school, most technical and community colleges offer programs in business administration, including office administration and/or secretarial science. Interested students are advised to consult with their school guidance counselor or to research area postsecondary schools and training programs.

MORE INFORMATION

Association of Executive and Administrative Professionals
900 S. Washington Street
Suite G-13
Falls Church, VA 22046
703.237.8616
www.theaeap.com

International Association of Administrative Professionals
P.O. Box 20404
Kansas City, MO 64195-0404
816.891.6600
www.iaap-hq.org

Kylie Hughes/Editor

Financial Manager

Snapshot

Career Cluster: Banking & Finance; Business Administration; Government & Public Administration

Interests: Mathematics, accounting, financial trends, business operations

Earnings (Yearly Average): $112,700

Employment & Outlook: Slightly Slower Than Average Growth Expected

OVERVIEW

Sphere of Work

Financial managers are responsible for directing, monitoring, safeguarding, and ensuring the profitability of the financial operations of businesses, corporations, nonprofit organizations, and government entities. They provide diverse financial services, including financial report preparation and review, budget analysis, investment guidance, and long-term financial goal development. Financial managers develop financial strategies and plans to implement and evaluate the strategies.

Work Environment

Financial managers work in offices and are often required to travel to annual meetings and stockholder meetings. Depending on employer and job specialization, a financial manager may telecommute from a home office, visit client offices as a contractor, or work on a full-time basis in an employer's office. A financial manager may be hired as a full-time leader of a finance team or as a term-of-project contractor. A financial manager's work environment is based around technology, including computers and accounting software programs.

Profile

Working Conditions: Work Indoors
Physical Strength: Light Work
Education Needs: Bachelor's Degree, Master's Degree
Licensure/Certification: Recommended
Physical Abilities Not Required: No Heavy Labor
Opportunities For Experience: Internship, Part-Time Work
Holland Interest Score*: ESR

* See Appendix A

Occupation Interest

Individuals attracted to the financial management profession tend to be ambitious, organized, analytical, outgoing, and detail-oriented people who find satisfaction in tracking financial trends and in learning new technologies and methods. Those who excel as financial managers continually educate themselves about and respond to regulatory change. Prospective financial managers may find satisfaction in developing investment plans and goals as well as staying up to date on financial best practices and ethical and legal matters in finance.

A Day in the Life—Duties and Responsibilities

Financial managers generally work within or in concert with management and accounting departments. Most businesses have a single financial manager to direct financial operations. In financial institutions, such as commercial banks, mortgage companies, savings and loan associations, and credit unions, multiple financial managers direct the internal financial operations and those of clients, investors, and customers.

The daily duties and responsibilities of financial managers vary by job specialization. Areas of financial management specialization include controller, treasurer, credit manager, cash manager, risk manager, insurance manager, and banking manager. Financial managers working as controllers in accounting and auditing departments are responsible for drafting financial reports, such as anticipated future earnings, expenses, and income, required for regulatory compliance, stakeholder review, and tax purposes. Treasurers develop budgets that align with organizational goals, oversee mergers and acquisitions, raise capital, and supervise investment funds. Credit managers oversee all credit-related operations, including debt collection, setting credit limits, and deciding how and when to offer credit. Cash managers oversee all cash transactions. Risk managers minimize the risks associated with financial operations by purchasing insurance and limiting exposure to currency changes. Branch managers at banks oversee all bank branch operations, including loan approval, hiring, and community relations.

Organizations may also require financial managers to select, implement, and troubleshoot financial software systems, as well as stay up to date with regulatory and ethical issues and news in finance by reading finance industry journals and participating in industry associations. Financial managers employed by some organizations also participate in ongoing discussions of work teams, workflows, dynamics, and best practices.

Duties and Responsibilities

- Preparing financial statements and business forecasts
- Controlling assets, records, collateral and securities held by the institution
- Reviewing company financial data and identifying ways to reduce costs and increase profitability
- Analyzing market trends and identifying business opportunities
- Establishing corporate policies and procedures regarding financial operations
- Directing the activities of finance staff
- Advising top management in the making of business decisions

OCCUPATION SPECIALTIES

Financial Institution Managers

Financial Institution Managers are often known by the type of institution they manage, such as bank branch managers, trust company managers or savings and loan association managers. They may also be designated according to the type of loan made, such as consumer credit managers.

Treasurers and Controllers

Treasurers direct financial planning as well as obtain and invest funds for a local government. Controllers direct the preparation of financial reports that summarize and forecast an organization's financial position, including income statements, balance sheets, and future earnings projections.

Cash Managers

Cash Managers monitor and control the flow of cash that comes in and goes out of the company to meet the company's business and investment needs.

Credit Managers

Credit Managers oversee their firm's credit business. They set credit-rating criteria, determine credit ceilings, and monitor the collections of past-due accounts.

Risk Managers

Risk Managers control financial risk by using hedging and other strategies to limit or offset the probability of a financial loss or a company's exposure to financial uncertainty. Among the risks they try to limit are those due to currency or commodity price changes.

WORK ENVIRONMENT

Physical Environment

Financial managers generally work in pleasant office environments. The work of a financial manager requires sitting at a desk and using computers for long periods each day.

Relevant Skills and Abilities

Analytical Skills
- Analyzing data

Communication Skills
- Speaking effectively
- Writing concisely

Interpersonal/Social Skills
- Leading others
- Working as a member of a team

Organization & Management Skills
- Coordinating tasks
- Having good judgment
- Making decisions
- Managing people/groups

Human Environment

Financial managers interact with managers, business owners, employees, and stockholders. Financial managers should be comfortable attending meetings, giving frequent speeches, and supervising and directing employees.

Technological Environment

Financial managers communicate using computers, telephones, and Internet communication tools. They rely on financial analysis software and spreadsheets for analyses and reports

EDUCATION, TRAINING, AND ADVANCEMENT

High School/Secondary

High school students interested in pursuing a career as a financial manager should prepare themselves by building good study habits and by developing an ease with numbers and mathematical functions. High school-level study of bookkeeping and mathematics can provide a strong foundation for college-level study in the field of financial management. Due to the diversity of financial manager responsibilities, high school students interested in this career path may benefit from seeking internships or part-time work with financial organizations.

Suggested High School Subjects
- Accounting
- Algebra
- Applied Communication
- Bookkeeping
- Business
- Business Law
- College Preparatory
- Composition
- Economics
- English
- Government
- Merchandising
- Political Science
- Social Studies
- Statistics

Famous First

A General Mills stockholders' meeting was the first of its kind to be televised coast-to-coast simultaneously, on October 29, 1959, in New York City, Minneapolis, Chicago and Los Angeles. A closed-circuit television system allowed stockholders in the various locations to ask questions of chairman Gerald Kennedy, and president Charles Heffelfinger.

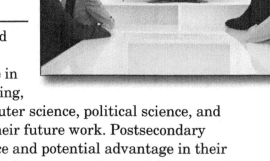

College/Postsecondary

Postsecondary students interested in becoming financial managers should earn the bachelor's degree in economics, mathematics, accounting, or business. Coursework in computer science, political science, and ethics may also prove useful in their future work. Postsecondary students can gain work experience and potential advantage in their future job searches through internships or part-time employment with local businesses or financial organizations. For advanced positions, a master's degree is usually expected.

Related College Majors
- Business/Managerial Economics
- Finance

Adult Job Seekers

Adults seeking financial management jobs generally have a bachelor's degree and, in some cases, a master's of business administration (MBA). Adult job seekers may benefit from joining professional finance or accounting associations as a means of networking. Professional finance and accounting associations, such as the Association for Investment Management and Research and the Society of Financial Service Professionals, often maintain job lists advertising open accounting positions.

Professional Certification and Licensure

Financial managers who work in accounting departments may be required to become a Certified Public Accountant (CPA) as a condition of employment. The American Institute of Certified Public Accountants administers the national CPA examination in four discrete parts that must be completed within two years. Financial managers working in specialized fields may choose to pursue voluntary certifications, such as the Chartered Financial Analyst, the Certified Treasury Professional, the Certified Management Accountant, Certified Government Financial Manager, the Certified Financial Risk Manager, and the Certified Healthcare Financial Manager designations. These certifications require at least a bachelor's degree and some work experience in the field, and are available through the Institute of Management Accountants, the Association for Financial Professionals, and the CFA Institute.

Additional Requirements

Successful financial managers will be knowledgeable about the profession's requirements, responsibilities, and opportunities. Professionals in this role have access to confidential financial information and must adhere to strict ethical standards. Membership in professional finance and accounting associations is encouraged among all financial managers as a means of building professional community

Fun Fact

Before he was a disciple, Matthew was a tax collector for the Romans. Today, St. Matthew is the Roman Catholic patron saint of a multitude of financial professionals: accountants, tax collectors, bookkeepers, stock brokers and bankers.

Source: http://catholicherald.com/stories/A-Patron-Saint-for-Bankers-and-Accountants,1953

EARNINGS AND ADVANCEMENT

Earnings of financial managers depend on the individual's abilities and position and the type and size of the employer. Median annual earnings of financial managers were $112,700 in 2013. The lowest ten percent earned less than $61,000, and the highest ten percent earned more than $180,000.

Financial managers may receive paid vacations, holidays, and sick days; life and health insurance; retirement benefits; educational assistance; and yearly bonuses.

Metropolitan Areas with the Highest Employment Level in This Occupation

Metropolitan area	Employment[1]	Employment per thousand jobs	Hourly mean wage
New York-White Plains-Wayne, NY-NJ	31,310	5.97	$87.96
Chicago-Joliet-Naperville, IL	21,350	5.77	$63.80
Los Angeles-Long Beach-Glendale, CA	19,860	5.00	$70.50
Boston-Cambridge-Quincy, MA	14,620	8.36	$64.39
Washington-Arlington-Alexandria, DC-VA-MD-WV	14,610	6.17	$69.14
Minneapolis-St. Paul-Bloomington, MN-WI	11,290	6.30	$60.96
Atlanta-Sandy Springs-Marietta, GA	10,240	4.44	$61.89
Houston-Sugar Land-Baytown, TX	8,690	3.15	$68.99
Dallas-Plano-Irving, TX	7,890	3.67	$65.14
Santa Ana-Anaheim-Irvine, CA	7,770	5.35	$70.19

[1] Does not include self-employed. Source: Bureau of Labor Statistics.

EMPLOYMENT AND OUTLOOK

Financial managers held about 532,000 jobs nationally in 2012. Employment is expected to grow slightly slower than the average for all occupations through the year 2022, which means employment is projected to increase 5 percent to 11 percent. The increasing need for financial expertise as a result of regulatory reforms and the expansion of the economy will drive job growth over the next decade. As the economy expands, both the growth of established companies and the creation of new businesses will spur demand for financial managers. However, mergers, acquisitions, and corporate downsizing are likely to restrict the employment growth to some extent.

Employment Trend, Projected 2012–22

Total, All Occupations: 11%

Financial Managers: 9%

Management Occupations: 7%

Note: "All Occupations" includes all occupations in the U.S. Economy. Source: U.S. Bureau of Labor Statistics, Employment Projections Program.

Related Occupations

- Accountant
- Actuary
- Auditor
- City Manager
- Court Administrator
- Credit Manager
- Financial Analyst
- General Manager & Top Executive
- Online Merchant
- Personal Financial Advisor
- Public Administrator

Conversation With . . .
JOSEPH NATIVO

CFO, 26 years
Kumon, Teaneck, NJ

1. What was your individual career path in terms of education/training, entry-level job, or other significant opportunity?

I worked as an apprentice for a small CPA firm during college. I learned how to prepare bank reconciliations, payroll tax returns, and income tax returns. Back then, we prepared tax returns by hand. Looking back, preparing the returns manually was the best experience I could have ever received. It gave me a solid foundation and made the eventual switch to tax software a cinch. After graduating from Rutgers University with a bachelor's in Accounting and earning my CPA license, I spent several years working for a mid-sized firm. Although I enjoyed working in public accounting tremendously, I wanted to experience the private industry. I accepted an accounting manager position at Kumon North America Inc., a franchisor of after-school math and reading centers. The U.S. operations were quite small when I joined the company back in 1992. Today, Kumon is the market leader with nearly 1,500 locations and over 275,000 students in the U.S.

2. What are the most important skills and/or qualities for someone in your profession?

Today's CFOs are expected to wear multiple hats. You have to be adaptable and exhibit a willingness to take on new challenges. Having a thorough understanding of the business operations is just as important as knowing the financial side because with this knowledge, the CFO can support executive management in strategic planning. Strong interpersonal skills and the ability to manage at all levels are paramount. A CFO must possess strong problem-solving skills and make decisions based on accurate and timely analyses. Finally, a high level of integrity, a strong sense of urgency, and being results-oriented are core qualities of a CFO.

3. What do you wish you had known going into this profession?

 Unique corporate cultures exist at every organization. Learning how to work within the culture isn't something taught while attending university. Strong interpersonal skills and adaptability come with time and experience. Therefore, don't be afraid to ask questions. Pick the brains of others in your organization and absorb as much as possible.

4. **Are there many job opportunities in your profession? In what specific areas?**

Demand for accounting positions is at an all-time high. According to the U.S. Bureau of Labor Statistics, a growth rate of 13 percent is projected through 2022. The unemployment rate for accountants is much lower when compared to the national average. U.S. News and World Report's 2014 Best Jobs issue ranked Accounting as the 3rd best career.

Positions are available in public accounting, private industry, government, and not-for-profit organizations. Many higher level positions will require a CPA or MBA as well.

5. **How do you see your profession changing in the next five years? What role will technology play in those changes, and what skills will be required?**

Cloud, mobile, social media, and Big Data are the emerging technologies with the most impact on the accounting profession, according to a survey of more than 400 U.S. accountants released by software provider CCH, a Wolters Kluwer business. These technologies allow professionals to provide financial data more effectively to end-users. As the automation of data collection continues to increase, accounting professionals will be able to shift focus from crunching numbers to analyzing data and advising key stakeholders

6. **What do you like most about your job? What do you like least about your job?**

I really believe in Kumon's corporate mission. We help children unlock their potential through self-learning with the aim to foster sound, capable individuals who can contribute to the global community. I've always taken pride in the fact that we make a difference in the lives of children worldwide. Also, my role is not limited to debits and credits. I like being involved with different areas of the operations and enjoy being a resource for my colleagues. If I can offer information that allows them to perform better and contribute to company goals, then I will continue to find my work meaningful and fruitful.

As in most professions, the hours can be long and the pressure can be high. Therefore, work-life balance is very important. I always remind my staff to use their paid vacation time whenever possible. We have to allow ourselves to recharge our batteries from time to time.

7. Can you suggest a valuable "try this" for students considering a career in your profession?

Seek an internship as early as possible. Don't wait until your senior year. The point is to get your feet wet and gain real world experience. The knowledge acquired will be invaluable after you graduate. Hopefully, an internship will lead to a full-time position. Regardless, any experience you gain will shed insight on how public or private firms operate. It will also help you figure out which path to seek in the business world. An accounting degree with a CPA and/or MBA will open many doors.

SELECTED SCHOOLS

Many colleges and universities, especially those with business schools, offer programs in finance and business administration. The student can also gain initial training through enrollment at a technical or community college. For advanced positions, a master's of business administration (MBA) with a concentration in finance is usually expected. Below are listed some of the more prominent institutions in this field.

Carnegie Mellon University
Tepper School of Business
500 Forbes Avenue
Pittsburgh, PA 15213
412.268.2268
tepper.cmu.edu

Indiana University—
Bloomington
Kelley School of Business
1309 E. 10th Street
Bloomington, IN 47405
812.855.8100
kelley.iu.edu

Massachusetts Institute of
Technology
Sloan School of Management
50 Memorial Drive
Cambridge, MA 02142
617.253.2659
mitsloan.mit.edu

New York University
Stern School of Business
665 Broadway, 11th Floor
New York, NY 10012
212.998.4500
www.stern.nyu.edu

University of California—
Berkeley
Haas School of Business
S450 Student Services Building
#1900
Berkeley, CA 94720
510.642.1421
haas.berkeley.edu

University of Michigan—
Ann Arbor
Ross School of Business
701 Tappan Avenue
Ann Arbor, MI 48109
734.763.5796
michiganross.umich.edu

University of North Carolina—
Chapel Hill
Kenan-Flagler Business School
Campus Box 3490, McColl Building
Chapel Hill, NC 27599
919.962.3235
www.kenan-flagler.unc.edu

University of Pennsylvania
The Wharton School
1 College Hall
Philadelphia, PA 19104
215.898.6376
www.whatron.upenn.edu

University of Texas—Austin
McCombs School of Business
1 University Station, B6000
Austin, TX 78712
512.471.5921
www.mccombs.utexas.edu

University of Virginia
Darden School of Business
PO Box 6550
Charlottseville, VA 22906
434.924.3900
www.darden.virginia.edu

MORE INFORMATION

AAssociation for Financial Professionals
4520 East-West Highway, Suite 750
Bethesda, MD 30814
301.907.2862
www.afponline.org

CFA Institute
560 Ray C. Hunt Drive
Charlottesville, VA 22903-2981
800.247.8132
www.cfainstitute.org

Financial Management Association Int'l.
University of South Florida
College of Business Administration
Tampa, FL 33620
813.974.2084
www.fma.org

Financial Managers Society
100 W. Monroe Street, Suite 1700
Chicago, IL 60603
312.578.1300
www.fmsinc.org

Institute of Internal Auditors
247 Maitland Avenue
Altamonte Springs, FL 32701
407.937.1111
www.theiia.org

Society of Financial Service Professionals
19 Campus Boulevard, Suite 100
Newtown Square, PA 19073-3239
610.526.2500
www.financialpro.org

Simone Isadora Flynn/Editor

Human Resources Manager

Snapshot

Career Cluster: Business Administration; Human Services

Interests: Organizations, human behavior, working life, solving problems, resolving conflict

Earnings (Yearly Average): $100,800

Employment & Outlook: Faster Than Average Growth Expected

OVERVIEW

Sphere of Work

Human resources managers, also referred to as human resources professionals or benefits specialists, provide job training and job placement support services to individuals and companies, recruit new workers, conduct job interviews, refer clients for jobs, or supervise the hiring process. Human resources managers may also provide training for employees and staff on benefits-related issues such as health benefits, paid time off, educational benefits, insurance and retirement benefits, and taxes.

Work Environment

Human resources managers spend their workdays seeing clients in a wide variety of settings, including corporate human resources or staffing departments, job counseling and placement agencies, and college and university career counseling offices. Human resources managers have a fixed office where they see clients but may also travel to see potential job candidates or attend job fairs. Given the diverse demands of human resources work, human resources managers may need to work days, evenings, and weekends to meet client, department, or company needs.

Profile

Working Conditions: Work Indoors
Physical Strength: Light Work
Education Needs: Bachelor's Degree, Master's Degree
Licensure/Certification: Recommended
Physical Abilities Not Required: No Heavy Labor
Opportunities For Experience: Internship, Apprenticeship, Military Service, Volunteer Work
Part-Time Work
Holland Interest Score*: ESR

* See Appendix A

Occupation Interest

Individuals drawn to the human resources profession tend to be intelligent and have the ability to quickly assess situations and people, find resources, resolve conflicts, and solve problems. Those most successful at the job of human resources manager display traits such as time management, knowledge of human behavior, computer skills, and business savvy. Human resources managers should enjoy spending time with a wide range of people, including those from diverse cultural, social, and educational backgrounds.

A Day in the Life—Duties and Responsibilities

The daily occupational duties and responsibilities of human resources managers will be determined by the individual's area of job specialization and work environment. Specialties of human resources managers include recruiting, vocational assessment, staffing, interviewing, job training, job placement, and benefits training.

Human resources managers may recruit job candidates, interview possible job candidates, visit job fairs at colleges and universities, and conduct job candidate evaluations to assess vocational aptitude, work history, and job readiness. They make hiring recommendations, conduct background checks, and may coordinate drug tests for new hires. Human resources managers also review job listings and forums to stay informed about available jobs within their business and industry, and they must develop connections and familiarity with local employment agencies. Supervising a staff of human resources specialists or assistants also falls under the purview of this job.

Human resources managers must keep up to date on current best practices in their field. They may be expected to write or update an employee handbook describing company policies such as dress, work relationships, email standards, and paid time off. They must take time to stay informed about current labor laws, trends, and regulations. They are responsible for conducting benefits workshops and training seminars for employees and staff on benefits-related issues such as health benefits, paid time off policies, educational benefits, life insurance and retirement benefits, and taxes. Human resources managers also direct human resources employees and the human resources department at large.

In addition, all human resources managers are responsible for completing employee records and required documentation, such as job referral forms, on a daily basis

Duties and Responsibilities

- Recruiting, testing and orientating new employees
- Investigating and resolving questions of equal employment
- Preparing job descriptions
- Reporting on the effects of industry trends on workers
- Promoting the use of public employment programs
- Devising ways of assuring fair compensation
- Designing and administering benefits programs
- Planning and implementing employee training programs
- Promoting occupational safety and health
- Negotiating agreements to disputes involving a company
- Supporting management in labor negotiations
- Advising both labor and management to resolve disputes
- Deciding disputes to bind both labor and management to contracts

OCCUPATION SPECIALTIES

Occupational Analysts

Occupational Analysts do research to classify jobs and describe the effects of trends on workers.

Labor Relations Specialists

Industrial Relations Directors formulate policy, oversee labor relations and negotiate agreements involving unions.

Benefits Managers

Benefits Managers specialize in handling a company's employee benefits, especially health insurance and pensions.

Education and Training Managers

Education and Training Managers supervise employees in skill development, learning and morale.

Recruiting Managers

Recruiting Managers oversee the recruiting and hiring responsibilities of the human resources department.

Payroll Specialists

Payroll Specialists handle the operations of an organization's payroll department, ensuring that all aspects of payroll are processed correctly and on time

WORK ENVIRONMENT

Physical Environment

The immediate physical environment of human resources managers varies according to their company size, geographical location, and job specialization. Human resources managers involved in job placement and benefits training spend their workdays seeing clients in corporate human resources and staffing departments while human resources managers involved in employee recruitment spend their workdays visiting job training and placement programs and college and university career counseling offices.

Relevant Skills and Abilities

Communication Skills
- Persuading others
- Speaking effectively

Interpersonal/Social Skills
- Being patient
- Cooperating with others
- Understanding conflict

Organization & Management Skills
- Coordinating tasks
- Managing people/groups
- Managing time
- Meeting goals and deadlines
- Performing duties that change frequently

Research & Planning Skills
- Developing evaluation strategies
- Solving problems

Technical Skills
- Working with both people and data

Human Environment

Human resources managers work with a wide variety of people. They should be comfortable meeting with potential job candidates, colleagues, staff, supervisors, college and university students, and unemployed people.

Technological Environment

Human resources managers use computers, cell phones, cars, and Internet communication tools to perform their job. They should be comfortable using computers to access employee records as well as post available positions online

EDUCATION, TRAINING, AND ADVANCEMENT

High School/Secondary

High school students interested in pursuing a career in human resources should prepare themselves by developing good study habits. High school courses in foreign languages, psychology, and writing will provide a strong foundation for work as a human resources specialist and manager or college-level work in the field. Due to the range of human resources job requirements, high school students interested in this career path will benefit from seeking internships or part-time work that expose the students to managerial roles and diverse professions.

Suggested High School Subjects

- Business
- College Preparatory
- English
- Humanities
- Mathematics
- Psychology
- Social Studies
- Statistics

Famous First

The first pension plan was offered by American Express Company to its employees in 1875. The plan included employees 60 years of age or older with at least 20 years of employment. Approved beneficiaries received 50 percent of the average salary they had earned over the preceding 10 years, with a cap of $500.

College/Postsecondary

Postsecondary students interested in becoming human resources specialists or managers should work towards the bachelor's degree in human resource management or a related field. Classes in psychology, business administration, and foreign languages may also prove useful in their future work. Advanced positions in this field often require a master's degree in human resources development. Postsecondary students can gain work experience and potential advantage in their future job searches by obtaining internships or part-time employment in career placement or job training programs.

Related College Majors
- Business Administration
- Human Resources Management
- Labor/Personnel Relations & Studies
- Management

Adult Job Seekers

Adults seeking employment as human resources managers should have earned, at a minimum, a bachelor's degree in human resource management or a related field, such as business administration, personnel administration, or labor relations. Employers may require human resources managers to have a master's degree and related national certification. Adult job seekers should educate themselves about the educational and professional license requirements of their home states and the organizations where they seek employment. They may also benefit from joining professional associations, such as the Society for Human Resource Management and the National Employment Counseling Association, which generally offer help with networking and job searching.

Professional Certification and Licensure

Certification for human resources managers is voluntary but often recommended or requested by employers. The main human resources specialist and manager certifications are the Professional in Human Resources (PHR) designation, the Senior Professional in Human Resources (SPHR) designation, and the Global Professional in Human Resources (GPHR) designation offered by the Human Resources Certification Institute. The PHR, SPHR, and the GPHR certifications are earned by passing a national examination testing knowledge of human resources practices and federal employment rules and regulations including affirmative action and the American with Disabilities Act. Continuing education coursework is a condition of ongoing certification.

Additional Requirements

Successful human resources managers engage in ongoing professional development to maintain their certifications. Because human resources managers have access to personal information and hiring or job placement influence, they must adhere to strict codes of professional ethics. Membership in professional human resources associations is encouraged among all human resources managers as a means of building professional community and networking

Fun Fact

The National Cash Register Company, known today as NCR, established the first personnel management department in the aftermath of a 1901 strike and lockout. Other factories followed in an effort to deal with grievances, safety, wages, and other issues that are handled by today's Human Resources departments.

Source: http://www.brighthubpm.com/resource-management/77387-a-history-of-human-resource-management/

EARNINGS AND ADVANCEMENT

According to a salary survey by the National Association of Colleges and Employers, individuals with a bachelor's degree in human resources were offered starting salaries of $49,359 in 2012.

Median annual earnings of human resources managers were $100,800 in 2013. The lowest ten percent earned less than $59,000, and the highest ten percent earned more than $177.000. The annual earnings of non-managerial human resources specialists averaged $61,560 in 2013.

Human resources managers may receive paid vacations, holidays, and sick days; life and health insurance; and retirement benefits. These are usually paid by the employer

Metropolitan Areas with the Highest Employment Level in This Occupation

Metropolitan area	Employment[1]	Employment per thousand jobs	Hourly mean wage
New York-White Plains-Wayne, NY-NJ	7,230	1.38	$65.61
Chicago-Joliet-Naperville, IL	4,000	1.08	$49.54
Los Angeles-Long Beach-Glendale, CA	3,750	0.94	$55.69
Washington-Arlington-Alexandria, DC-VA-MD-WV	3,340	1.41	$65.02
Minneapolis-St. Paul-Bloomington, MN-WI	2,860	1.60	$55.08
Atlanta-Sandy Springs-Marietta, GA	2,610	1.13	$55.36
Boston-Cambridge-Quincy, MA	2,460	1.40	$59.93
Houston-Sugar Land-Baytown, TX	2,130	0.77	$59.26
Seattle-Bellevue-Everett, WA	2,010	1.39	$56.80
Phoenix-Mesa-Glendale, AZ	1,860	1.05	$47.73

[1] Does not include self-employed. Source: Bureau of Labor Statistics.

EMPLOYMENT AND OUTLOOK

Human resources managers held about 102,000 jobs nationally in 2012; human resources specialists, on the other hand, held about 418,000 jobs in 2012. The private sector accounted for nearly 90 percent of jobs, primarily in the services industry in the areas of administrative and support services; professional, scientific and technical services; manufacturing; health care and social assistance; and finance and insurance.

Employment of human resources managers is expected to grow about as fast as the average for all occupations through the year 2022, which means employment is projected to increase 9 percent to 16 percent. Legislation and court rulings setting standards in various areas, such as occupational safety and health, equal employment opportunity, wages, health care, pensions, and family leave will increase demand for human resources managers. In addition, employers are expected to devote greater resources to job-specific training programs in response to the increasing complexity of many jobs, the aging of the workforce, and technological advances that can leave employees with obsolete skills

Employment Trend, Projected 2012–22

Human Resources Managers: 13%

Total, All Occupations: 11%

Management Occupations: 7%

Note: "All Occupations" includes all occupations in the U.S. Economy. Source: U.S. Bureau of Labor Statistics, Employment Projections Program.

Related Occupations

- Court Administrator
- Employment Specialist
- General Manager & Top Executive
- Lawyer
- Management Analyst & Consultant
- Psychologist

Related Military Occupations

- Emergency Management Officer
- Personnel Manager
- Recruiting Manager
- Teacher & Instructor
- Training & Education Director

Conversation With . . .
KAREN STONE MICKOOL

Executive Director, Stone Associates,
Human Resource Consulting Firm, 5 years
Santa Fe, NM

1. What was your individual career path in terms of education/training, entry-level job, or other significant opportunity?

Before moving into traditional human resources, I spent many years training and developing leaders — first college students, then corporate executives. My Master's Degree is in higher education administration and counseling; my undergraduate degree is in special education. I worked my way up the ranks in higher education working in student life departments, where I focused on student leadership. When I took a position as a management development specialist with the Bank of New York, Delaware, my focus shifted to leadership development for mid-level executives. Over time, I held several leadership training positions with major companies and have had interesting assignments such as helping to run a global management development program for an engineering firm with state-of-the-art training facilities.

After that employer started struggling financially and I was laid off, a headhunter called to see if I'd be interested in a human resources job. I told him that I wasn't qualified! He called back to say his client still wanted to talk to me because they felt I had the ability to sit with senior leadership and help guide an organization. I was hired because they felt they could train me to manage HR functions like payroll and benefits.

In 2009, I moved to Santa Fe, NM for personal reasons and was able to start my own consulting practice. My company specializes in partnering with small businesses. We manage the full employment cycle of an employee from hiring to orienting and training, to developing the employee, to, sometimes, exiting the employee if that's the appropriate thing to do.

Business needs change quickly and layoffs are common. But you can reinvent yourself, and ultimately benefit from that change. Be conscientious about maintaining your professional network because those contacts will help you through transitions and job changes. I have been laid off three times in my career and every time I landed back on my feet with a better job with more responsibility and a better compensation package.

2. What are the most important skills and/or qualities for someone in your profession?

Discretion. You must be ethical and trustworthy. You are in a position to know highly sensitive information and maintaining confidentiality is key. You won't succeed if you cant keep a lot of secrets.

To be effective you must keep up with what's going on in employment law. Unfortunately we live in a litigious society, and these issues come into play on a daily basis. There's a fine line here—we don't give legal advice, but we need to know when legal advice is needed.

Finally, it's critical that you go into an organization and learn about the business: how the organization works, how they make money, what the key business propositions are and how they affect the company's goals and outcomes. The only way to be a credible voice is to show that you understand the business

3. What do you wish you had known going into this profession?

I wish I'd had more background with basics like payroll and benefits early on. But, I had invaluable opportunities at a very senior level that most HR people don't get until much later in their careers.

4. Are there many job opportunities in your profession? In what specific areas?

There are always going to be jobs, and they're always going to be competitive.

5. How do you see your profession changing in the next five years? What role will technology play in those changes, and what skills will be required?

Today's HR leaders are truly involved in setting a company's strategy and direction. To sit at the table with business leaders, it's not enough to understand human resources; you need a good business foundation.

6. What do you like most about your job? What do you like least about your job?

Every day is different. I coach senior level executives and small business owners, and I'm truly helping people better themselves and build their businesses. I also fill the role of HR manager for some clients, handling daily responsibilities like helping to fill job vacancies.

It's hard to make difficult decisions. Sometimes, what's in the best interest of the business is not in the best interest of the employee and you have to find a way to reconcile that.

7. Can you suggest a valuable "try this" for students considering a career in your profession?

Get an internship, and become involved with the professional organization, SHRM, the Society for Human Resource Management (www.shrm.org.) Many colleges have student chapters which give you the opportunity to get involved early in your career.

SELECTED SCHOOLS

Many colleges and universities, especially those with business schools, offer programs human resources development. The student can also gain initial training at a technical or community college. For advanced positions in large firms a master's degree (MBA) is often required. Below are listed some of the more prominent graduate institutions in this field.

Michigan State University
Eli Broad College of Business
632 Bogue Street
East Lansing, MI 48824
517.355.8377
broad.msu.edu

Northwestern University
Kellogg School of Management
2169 Campus Drive
Evanston, IL 60208
847.467.7000
www.kellogg.northwestern.edu

Purdue University
Krannert School of Management
403 W. State Street
West Lafayette, IN 47907
765.496.4343
www.krannert.purdue.edu

Stanford University
Stanford Graduate School of
Business
655 Knight Way
Stanford, CA 94305
650.723.2146
www.gsb.stanford.edu

**University of California—
Berkeley**
Haas School of Business
S450 Student Services Building
#1900
Berkeley, CA 94720
510.642.1421
haas.berkeley.edu

University of Chicago
Booth School of Business
5807 S. Woodlawn Avenue
Chicago, IL 60637
773.702.7743
www.chicagobooth.edu

**University of Michigan—
Ann Arbor**
Ross School of Business
701 Tappan Avenue
Ann Arbor, MI 48109
734.763.5796
michiganross.umich.edu

**University of Southern
California**
Marshall School of Business
3670 Trousdale Parkway
Los Angeles, CA 90089
213.740.8674
www.marshall.usc.edu

University of Wisconsin— Madison
Wisconsin School of Business
Grainger Hall
975 University Avenue
Madison, WI 53706
608.262.1550
bus.wisc.edu

Vanderbilt University
Owen Graduate School of
Management
401 21st Avenue South
Nashville, TN 37203
615.322.2534
www.owen.vanderbilt.edu

MORE INFORMATION

American Management Association
1601 Broadway
New York, NY 10019
212.568.8100
www.amanet.org

American Society for Training and Development
Fulfillment Department
1640 King Street, Box 1443
Alexandria, VA 22313-2043
800.628.2783
www.astd.org

American Staffing Association
277 South Washington St., Suite 200
Alexandria, VA 22314
703.253.2020
www.staffingtoday.net

Human Resources Certification Institute
1800 Duke Street
Alexandria, VA 22314
www.hrci.org

International Association of Workforce Professionals
1801 Louisville Road
Frankfort, KY 40601
888.898.9960
www.iawponline.org

International Foundation of Employee Benefit Plans
P.O. Box 69
Brookfield, WI 53008-0069
888.334.3327
www.ifebp.org

International Public Management Association for Human Resources
1617 Duke Street
Alexandria, VA 22314
703.549.7100
www.ipma-hr.org

National Association of Personnel Service
131 Prominence Lane, Suite 130
Dawsonville, GA 30534
706.531.0060
www.naps360.org

National Employment Counseling Association
6836 Bee Cave Road, Suite 260
Austin, TX 78746
www.employmentcounseling.org

Society for Human Resource Management
1800 Duke Street
Alexandria, VA 22314
800.283.7476
www.shrm.org

World at Work
14040 N. Northsight Boulevard
Scottsdale, AZ 85260
877.951.9191
www.worldatwork.org

Simone Isadora Flynn/Editor

Management Consultant

Snapshot

Career Cluster: Business Administration; Government & Public Administration

Interests: Organizational studies, investigating ideas, solving problems, communicating with others

Earnings (Yearly Average): $79,870

Employment & Outlook: Faster Than Average Growth Expected

OVERVIEW

Sphere of Work

Management consultants, also known as management analysts, conduct independent reviews of managerial bodies within organizations, businesses, and government and offer insight, analysis, and suggestions for improvement. Input from management consultants traditionally focuses on improving productivity through adaptations in communication strategy, leadership style, or operations procedures. Management consultants also review documentation and internal communication procedures and suggest improvements.

Work Environment

Management consultants traditionally observe and document a particular firm's management staff in their work environment, whatever it may be. While office settings predominate, management consultants are also often required to make observations in the field, which can mean exposure to any number of various work environments, from manufacturing facilities to retail locations, to mining, agricultural, and construction sites.

Profile

Working Conditions: Work Indoors
Physical Strength: Light Work
Education Needs: Bachelor's Degree, Master's Degree
Licensure/Certification: Recommended
Physical Abilities Not Required: No Heavy Labor
Opportunities For Experience: Internship, Military Service
Holland Interest Score*: ICR

* See Appendix A

Occupation Interest

Management consultants are traditionally creative thinkers who enjoy investigation and developing enterprising solutions to complex problems. The field traditionally attracts professionals who have a dedicated interest to the function of organizations. Management consultants are commonly highly organized individuals who avoid redundancy and pride themselves on their ability to offer effective solutions to situational and organizational problems.

A Day in the Life—Duties and Responsibilities

Management consultants begin their analysis of organizations and companies through both live and documentary research. They intricately review decision-making processes, productivity, and employee satisfaction. Many conduct interviews with management staff and their subordinates in order to attain a firm grasp of the company's production process and organizational hierarchy. This process can take several weeks according to the particular size of the firm and the scope of the investigation.

Management consultants analyze accrued data and attempt to make interpretations with regard to potential improvements to productivity, efficiency, communication, and other processes. Management consultants suggest a variety of approaches to common organizational problems, often in the form of technology updates, changes in leadership style, staffing changes, and disciplinary methods.

Consultants present their analysis to the management team or executive board of the company they are consulting. They convey their findings through both written analysis and presentations.

The post-analysis role of management consultants entails assisting companies in their attempts to make suggested changes, examining their progress and ensuring that past issues in communication and production have been successfully resolved.

Duties and Responsibilities

- Gathering and organizing information on organizational procedures and problems
- Analyzing statistics and other data
- Interviewing employees
- Submitting written recommendations to clients
- Making oral presentations

WORK ENVIRONMENT

Physical Environment

Office settings predominate, although immediate physical environments can vary from project to project across all realms of business and industry.

Human Environment

Management consulting requires extensive interaction with both members of outside organizations and with fellow analysts.

Relevant Skills and Abilities

Analytical Skills
- Analyzing information

Communication Skills
- Listening attentively
- Persuading others

Interpersonal/Social Skills
- Cooperating with others
- Working as a member of a team

Organization & Management Skills
- Coordinating tasks
- Making decisions
- Managing people/groups
- Performing duties that change frequently

Research & Planning Skills
- Developing evaluation strategies
- Solving problems

Technical Skills
- Working with data or numbers

Work Environment Skills
- Traveling

Technological Environment

Management consultants utilize a variety of technologies, ranging from analytical software to resource planning, presentation, and project management tools.

EDUCATION, TRAINING, AND ADVANCEMENT

High School/Secondary

High school students can best prepare for a career as a management consultant by taking courses in algebra, calculus, communications, public speaking, business, and computer science. Extra-curricular activities such as sports and student government can provide students with the enterprising skills beneficial to a future career involving leadership and decision making. Internships with a consulting firm can also provide high school students with an important introduction to the basics of the field.

Suggested High School Subjects
- Business Administration
- College Preparatory
- English

Famous First

The first management consultant of note was Austrian-born Peter Drucker (1909-2005). He moved to the United States in the early 1930s and became a professor of politics and philosophy before specializing in management. His first consulting job was at General Motors in the 1940s. His first major book, *The Concept of the Corporation* discusses "management by objectives," and the laying out of specific courses of action to meet one's objectives.

College/Postsecondary

While several colleges in the United States offer postsecondary coursework related to management analysis, specific degree programs in the field are relatively scarce. College students interested in a career in consulting usually begin by completing a bachelor's degree program in business administration. Students in business administration complete coursework in basic accounting, finance, human resource management, and organizational philosophy. They also survey coursework in statistics, business law, critical thinking, and business leadership.

Many management analysis professionals also have advanced degrees in business administration. Graduate business students learn to apply the strategies and theories they have learned in the classroom to real-life business problems through participation in professional development programs and the completion of capstone projects.

Related College Majors

- Business Administration & Management
- Enterprise Management & Operation
- International Business
- Labor/Personnel Relations & Studies
- Management Science
- Operations Management & Supervision

Adult Job Seekers

Management consulting is not a common field for adult job seekers. This is largely due to the considerable amount of business training and professional experience required to execute the role of management analyst. The majority of management consultants are career management professionals who enter the field after several years of success as business executives or management professionals. Individuals with no background in a related field should enroll in a college or vocational school that offers a program in business administration.

Professional Certification and Licensure

No specific professional licensure or certification is required for a career as a management analyst, though several national and international organizations exist for professionals to share knowledge, learn of immersion trends in the field, and set up professional contacts.

Additional Requirements

Successful management consultants are sound analytical thinkers with the ability to see complex problems through to completion. Management consultants possess the organizational skills to see how the individual facets of an organization interact with each other. They are also diplomatic and sympathetic communicators who can suggest changes in communication and leadership structure in a pro-active and respectful manner.

Fun Fact

By the year 2020, 85% of the buyer-seller interaction will happen online through social media and video.

Source: TeleSmart Communications via http://sales.linkedin.com/blog/sales-strategy-23-facts-about-buyers-and-purchasing/

EARNINGS AND ADVANCEMENT

Earnings for management consultants vary widely by the type, size and location of the employer and the education and experience of the employee. Median annual earnings of management consultants were $79,870 in 2013. The lowest ten percent earned less than $45,000, and the highest ten percent earned more than $145,000.

Management consultants may receive paid vacations, holidays, and sick days; life and health insurance; and retirement benefits. These are usually paid by the employer. Travel expenses are usually reimbursed by employers. The self-employed must handle benefits for themselves.

Metropolitan Areas with the Highest
Employment Level in This Occupation

Metropolitan area	Employment[1]	Employment per thousand jobs	Hourly mean wage
Washington-Arlington-Alexandria, DC-VA-MD-WV	56,730	23.96	$47.60
New York-White Plains-Wayne, NY-NJ	30,110	5.74	$51.73
Atlanta-Sandy Springs-Marietta, GA	21,260	9.21	$43.90
Chicago-Joliet-Naperville, IL	20,300	5.49	$51.24
Los Angeles-Long Beach-Glendale, CA	17,250	4.34	$43.29
Boston-Cambridge-Quincy, MA	16,710	9.55	$50.37
Seattle-Bellevue-Everett, WA	10,520	7.26	$48.49
San Francisco-San Mateo-Redwood City, CA	9,600	9.18	$57.13
Dallas-Plano-Irving, TX	8,820	4.10	$45.93
Baltimore-Towson, MD	8,700	6.79	$48.34

[1] Does not include self-employed. Source: Bureau of Labor Statistics.

EMPLOYMENT AND OUTLOOK

Nationally, there were about 719,000 management consultants employed in 2012. About one-fourth were self-employed. Most other management analysts and consultants worked for management, scientific and technical consulting firms; computer systems design and related services firms; and for federal, state and local governments.

Employment is expected to grow faster than the average for all occupations through the year 2022, which means employment is projected to increase 20 percent or more. This is a result of industry and government continuing to rely on outside expertise to improve the performance of their organizations and cut costs. Growth is expected in large consulting firms, but also in smaller niche consulting firms whose consultants specialize in specific areas of expertise, such as biotechnology, healthcare, information technology, human resources, engineering and marketing. The best opportunities will be for those with graduate degrees or industry experience.

Employment Trend, Projected 2012–22

Management Consultants: 19%

Business and Financial Operations Occupations: 13%

Total, All Occupations: 11%

Note: "All Occupations" includes all occupations in the U.S. Economy. Source: U.S. Bureau of Labor Statistics, Employment Projections Program.

Related Occupations

- Actuary
- City Manager
- Computer Systems Analyst
- Economist
- General Manager & Top Executive
- Human Resources Specialist/ Manager
- Operations Research Analyst
- Statistician

Related Occupations

- Industrial Engineer
- Management Analyst

Conversation With . . .
TOM KENNEDY

Management consultant, 15 years
The Kennedy Group
Boston, MA

1. What was your individual career path in terms of education/training, entry-level job, or other significant opportunity?

I founded The Kennedy Group about 15 years ago. We focus on communications skills: presentation skills, public speaking, media skills. I had spent 20 years in broadcast news, doing television news, radio talk; I was a program director. In the mid-90s, I was doing talk at WBZ radio in Boston when it went all news and I had to reinvent myself. A dear friend said, "You should do what I'm doing—coach business executives." From my years in broadcast, I had the communication skills, but not the business acumen. I spent time in the mid-1990s building a business consultancy. Coincidentally, my wife was get-ting her MBA and I, vicariously through her, studied business. I'm also involved with the Institute of Management Consultants, which is a national organization. Most of our members are independent consultants."

2. What are the most important skills and/or qualities for someone in your profession?

Interpersonal skills are the essential skill of any management consultant practice because you're selling something intangible—you're selling strategy. You have to make clients comfortable in the belief that you're acting in their best interest. Consultancy is in a very real sense a fiduciary role. Your goal is always your client's success.

The ability to help clients identify the problem is also an important skill. The problem that clients bring to a consultant is rarely the actual problem. They may say the problem is that revenues are down or they're having a problem finding the right people. But if revenues are down, it's because there's something broken. If they can't attract good people, something's wrong with the corporate culture. You need to ask the right questions and listen. Until we truly understand the underlying issues, we can't get to the crux of the problem.

We all bring different communication styles to the table. In my business, the communication business, bridging those styles is essential

3. **What do you wish you had known going into this profession?**

    That I was becoming a sales person. You have to go out there and sell yourself, get clients and get business. A lot of people, especially the more technical people, are not comfortable with that at all.

4. **Are there many job opportunities in your profession? In what specific areas?**

    The beauty of consulting is there are consultants in every conceivable area of business.

    Independent management consultants, by virtue of the fact that they're independent, do very little hiring. The big guys, the McKinsey & Companys, the Deloittes, usually hire MBAs, which is a good opportunity for a younger person to get to know the business—if they go in with the idea that they are there to learn, not to teach. They are the fact finders, they bring the data to the "gray hairs," so to speak. Many management consultants try to be all things to all people. My advice is pick a niche and be the best there is at it and you'll succeed.

5. **How do you see your profession changing in the next five years? What role will technology play in those changes, and what skills will be required?**

    Technology of course changes everything. There's something new every 18 months or two years. Marketing is the best example. Social media has really changed the field of marketing. Why anyone would buy a TV spot again, when most people DVR and fast forward through commercials?

    You have to be video-confident—camera-ready, I call it—in business today. In all areas of management consulting, technology will drive innovation, but it will never replace the people who have been there, done that. Technology is just a tool to leverage the wisdom, the knowledge and the benefit that the consultant brings

6. **What do you like most about your job? What do you like least about your job?**

    What I enjoy most are the brilliant people I work with on the cutting edge of business and law and technology. That's the fun part, meeting cutting-edge people doing fascinating things, changing the world, literally changing the world. I learn more from my clients than they do from me.

    What I enjoy least is very minor. It's stuff like paperwork. I hate doing the invoicing, the record-keeping, the financial stuff, so I farm that out. If there's anything substantial that anyone hates about their job, they're in the wrong job.

7. Can you suggest a valuable "try this" for students considering a career in your profession?

An internship at a consulting firm is certainly worth considering. Go out to client consultancies and taken it all in. Have a plan, but be prepared to thorow the plan away. Have a mentor. Have a person whose opinion you can trust.

SELECTED SCHOOLS

Many colleges and universities, especially those with business schools, offer programs in business administration and management. The student can also gain initial training through a technical or community college. For advanced positions, a master's of business administration (MBA) with a concentration in management is usually expected. Below are listed some of the more prominent graduate institutions in this field.

Columbia University
Columbia Business School
3022 Broadway
Manhattan, NY 10027
212.854.5553
www8.gsb.columbia.edu

Dartmouth College
Tuck School of Business
100 Tuck Hall
Hanover, NH 03755
603.646.8825
www.tuck.dartmouth.edu

Harvard University
Harvard Business School
Soldiers Field
Boston, MA 02163
617.495.6000
www.hbs.edu

Massachusetts Institute of Technology
Sloan School of Management
50 Memorial Drive
Cambridge, MA 02142
617.253.2659
mitsloan.mit.edu

Northwestern University
Kellogg School of Management
2169 Campus Drive
Evanston, IL 60208
847.467.7000
www.kellogg.northwestern.edu

Stanford University
Stanford Graduate School of Business
655 Knight Way
Stanford, CA 94305
650.723.2146
www.gsb.stanford.edu

University of California—Berkeley
Haas School of Business
S450 Student Services Building #1900
Berkeley, CA 94720
510.642.1421
haas.berkeley.edu

University of Michigan—Ann Arbor
Ross School of Business
701 Tappan Avenue
Ann Arbor, MI 48109
734.763.5796
michiganross.umich.edu

University of Pennsylvania
The Wharton School
1 College Hall
Philadelphia, PA 19104
215.898.6376
www.whatron.upenn.edu

University of Virginia
Darden School of Business
PO Box 6550
Charlottseville, VA 22906
434.924.3900
www.darden.virginia.edu

MORE INFORMATION

American Management Association
1601 Broadway
New York, NY 10019
212.568.8100
www.amanet.org

Association of Management Consulting Firms
370 Lexington Avenue, Suite 2209
New York, NY 10017
212.262.3055
www.amcf.org

Global Management Analysts Association
108 West 13th Street
Wilmington, DE 19081
www.gmaaweb.org

Institute of Management
Consultants USA
2025 M Street, NW, Suite 800
Washington, DC 20036
202.367.1134
www.imcusa.org

Office of Personnel Management
1900 E Street, NW
Washington, DC 20415-0001
202.606.1800
www.opm.gov

John Pritchard/Editor

Market Researcher

Snapshot

Career Cluster: Business Administration; Sales & Service

Interests: Marketing, advertising, analyzing data, communicating with others, sales

Earnings (Yearly Average): $60,800

Employment & Outlook: Faster Than Average Growth Expected

OVERVIEW

Sphere of Work

Market researchers, also known as market research analysts, collect and interpret information about consumers, sales, employee satisfaction, and other facets of the business market. Their findings and analyses are used by clients to target specialized markets, develop brand allegiance, determine profitability and pricing, and prepare marketing and advertising campaigns.

Market researchers are skilled communicators who interact with consumers in a variety of ways. Analysts obtain consumer or employee data through one-on-one interviews, focus group meetings, questionnaires, and polls. Market researchers are also skilled in numerical data analysis and mathematical problem solving. One of their primary tasks is to present large quantities of complex data in a clear and cohesive manner.

Work Environment

Market researchers work primarily in professional environments, either as independent consultants or as employees of consulting firms, corporations, or government organizations. Data collection may take place in any number of locations depending on the company or product being analyzed, and fieldwork is often required to establish direct contact with consumers.

Profile

Working Conditions: Work Indoors
Physical Strength: Light Work
Education Needs: Bachelor's Degree
Licensure/Certification: Usually Not Required
Physical Abilities Not Required: No Heavy Labor
Opportunities For Experience: Internship
Holland Interest Score*: ISC

* See Appendix A

Occupation Interest

Market research is a diverse field encompassing a variety of disciplines. As such, the field attracts scholars and professionals with academic and work experience in marketing, advertising, analytics, computer science, communication, public relations, business, and sales.

Some researchers come to the field after lengthy careers in sales and marketing. Conversely, many young professionals spend an early portion of their careers as market researchers to build a foundation for future work in advertising, sales, or public relations.

A Day in the Life—Duties and Responsibilities

The day-to-day duties of market researchers are traditionally divided into three major areas of concentration: data collection, data interpretation, and presentation of results.

The data collection tasks of market researchers vary from product to product and company to company. Some market researchers collect consumer or employee data from fieldwork, one-on-one interviews, or focus groups. Other tactics include disseminating survey questionnaires, cold-calling, or conducting public opinion polls.

When the desired data has been collected, market researchers must next interpret the study's findings. Analysts break down data and use reports and visual aids in order to identify particular consumer opinions, product demand, and potential avenues for improvement in product development, internal operations, design, and marketing strategy.

The information acquired by researchers is then presented to clients and businesses in the form of a written report, an oral presentation with accompanying graphics, or a combination of the two. Many market research firms also use their data to forecast future customer opinion, sales trends, and market fluctuation. These predictions are often crucial to the development of new marketing programs and sales strategies

Duties and Responsibilities

- Designing research tools to collect customer opinions and data
- Gathering data through personal, telephone, or other survey means
- Analyzing information from customers and other sources
- Consulting records, journals, reports, financial publications, and industry statistics
- Preparing reports and presenting findings
- Making recommendations based on findings

WORK ENVIRONMENT

Physical Environment

Market researchers primarily work in office settings. Data collection work may entail field surveys and direct interaction with consumers. Market researchers may also work in retail locations, at public venues and events, and on university campuses. Researchers traditionally work regular business hours, though survey and research projects may require extended hours and weekend work.

Relevant Skills and Abilities

Analytical Skills
- Analyzing information

Communication Skills
- Speaking effectively
- Writing concisely

Interpersonal/Social Skills
- Being objective
- Cooperating with others
- Working as a member of a team

Organization & Management Skills
- Making decisions
- Paying attention to and handling details

Research & Planning Skills
- Creating ideas
- Laying out plans
- Solving problems

Human Environment

Focused interaction with other people is one of the most important aspects of market research. The job entails asking extensive questions regarding personal habits, spending, and consumer beliefs. Excellent communication skills are paramount.

Technological Environment

Market researchers use telephones, computers, web conferencing applications, databases, presentation software, and analytic software to organize and present data and relevant findings.

EDUCATION, TRAINING, AND ADVANCEMENT

High School/Secondary

High school students can prepare to enter the field of market research analysis with courses in algebra, calculus, public speaking, and computer science. English and writing courses are also important, as they hone written presentation skills.

Internships and summer volunteer work can provide students with experience and knowledge about the field. Marketing interns are often charged with disseminating surveys, collecting and keying data, or distributing information to focus groups and target markets at public events.

Suggested High School Subjects
- Algebra
- Applied Math
- Business Law
- Calculus
- College Preparatory
- Computer Science
- Economics
- English
- Mathematics
- Psychology
- Social Studies
- Sociology
- Statistics

Famous First

The first marketing and sales campaign based on sex appeal was the 1911 campaign for Woodbury Soap, developed by the J. Walter Thompson Agency of New York. A quarter-page ad in *Ladies' Home Journal* showed a woman in an open-neck dress being embraced by a tuxedo-clad gentleman, with the caption, "You too can have 'A skin you love to touch.'"

College/Postsecondary

Postsecondary education is traditionally a prerequisite for job openings in market research. Employees enter the field from a variety of postsecondary fields of study, including communications, advertising, marketing, public relations, social science, statistics, finance, and business management.

Undergraduate courses in research methodology, rhetorical communication, statistics, psychology, and sociology are all effective building blocks for a career in market research. Students should also complete coursework focused on traditional marketing strategies, including global market segmentation, response modeling, and marketing ethics. Advanced mathematical coursework helps students record and interpret patterns in data, while coursework in marketing instructs students in putting such findings to use in a commercial environment. Landmark marketing research and key historical developments in the field are also traditionally surveyed.

Some colleges and universities in the United States offer graduate-level programs specializing in market research. Admission into such programs is difficult. Graduate students study advanced analysis methods ranging from perceptual mapping, customer loyalty development, data mining, and website traffic metrics. Graduate work in market research allows students to gain hands-on experience in marketing analysis research, interpretation, and presentation and to develop contacts and relationships that can provide an important foundation for a career in the field

Related College Majors
- Applied & Resource Economics
- Business Marketing/Marketing Management
- Econometrics & Quantitative Economics
- Economics, General
- Marketing Research

Adult Job Seekers

Transitioning to a career in market research analysis can be difficult for adults seeking new opportunities or new career paths, given the amount of academic and professional experience that is often required. Transitioning is easier for experienced professionals transferring to the field from similar or relevant professional realms such as advertising, marketing, or media. Advanced degrees in market research, marketing, business management, statistics, or other related fields can give market researchers a competitive edge when seeking higher level positions.

Professional Certification and Licensure

No professional certification or licensure is required for market researchers, but many nationwide professional organizations, such as the American Marketing Association and the Marketing Research Association, offer voluntary certifications to their members. These certifications typically require a specified amount of experience in the field, completion of a written exam, and ongoing coursework for certification renewal.

Additional Requirements

In addition to the analytical and mathematical prowess inherent to the role, excellent conversation skills, amicability, and patience are qualities that help professionals excel at market research. Market researchers must be able to form trusting relationships with consumers in order to acquire honest information about their thoughts, opinions, and buying habits, much of which can be considered personal information

Fun Fact

The first market research was conducted in the streets, questioning people about magazines they had read and ads they had noticed. In the late 1980s, with the development of call centers, research shifted to the telephone. Today, it's often conducted in real time. At the Cincinnati Zoo, for instance, members swipe their cards at various exhibits and food stands, resulting in tailored promotions sent to their cell phones.

Source: http://www.marketresearchworld.net/content/view/3754/49/ and www.visioncritical.com/blog/3-trends-of-future-market-research#sthash.WS5qjh2O.dpuf

EARNINGS AND ADVANCEMENT

Graduate training increasingly is required for many market researcher jobs and for advancement to more responsible positions. In government, industry, research organizations and consulting firms, market researchers who have a graduate degree can usually qualify for more responsible research and administrative positions.

Median annual earnings of market researchers were $60,800 in 2013. The lowest ten percent earned less than $34,000, and the highest ten percent earned more than $114,000.

Market researchers entering careers in higher education may receive benefits such as summer research money, computer access, money for student research assistants, and secretarial support. Those who work in the private sector may receive paid vacations, holidays, and sick days; life and health insurance; and retirement benefits. These are usually paid by the employer.

Metropolitan Areas with the Highest
Employment Level in This Occupation

Metropolitan area	Employment[1]	Employment per thousand jobs	Hourly mean wage
New York-White Plains-Wayne, NY-NJ	31,810	6.07	$36.25
Los Angeles-Long Beach-Glendale, CA	18,840	4.74	$33.75
Washington-Arlington-Alexandria, DC-VA-MD-WV	17,090	7.22	$36.14
Chicago-Joliet-Naperville, IL	11,950	3.23	$31.02
Seattle-Bellevue-Everett, WA	10,910	7.53	$40.35
San Francisco-San Mateo-Redwood City, CA	10,830	10.36	$41.69
Boston-Cambridge-Quincy, MA	10,750	6.14	$34.39
Atlanta-Sandy Springs-Marietta, GA	10,620	4.60	$31.30
Philadelphia, PA	10,220	5.55	$34.40
Minneapolis-St. Paul-Bloomington, MN-WI	10,110	5.65	$32.43

[1] Does not include self-employed. Source: Bureau of Labor Statistics.

EMPLOYMENT AND OUTLOOK

Market researchers and marketing specialists held about 416,000 jobs nationally in 2012. Because of the applicability of market research to many industries, market researchers are employed throughout the economy. Employment is expected to grow much faster than the average for all occupations through the year 2022, which means employment is projected to increase 29 percent or more. This is due primarily to the increasingly competitive economy. Marketing research provides organizations with valuable feedback from purchasers, allowing companies to evaluate customer satisfaction and plan for the future. Job openings are also likely to result from the need to replace experienced workers who transfer to other occupations or retire

Employment Trend, Projected 2012–22

Market Researchers: 32%

Business Operations Specialists: 13%

Total, All Occupations: 11%

Note: "All Occupations" includes all occupations in the U.S. Economy. Source: U.S. Bureau of Labor Statistics, Employment Projections Program.

Related Occupations

- Economist
- Electronic Commerce Specialist
- Online Merchant
- Sociologist
- Urban & Regional Planner

Conversation With . . .
TED DONNELLY

Mnaging Director
Baltimore Research, 16 years
Baltimore, MD

1. What was your individual career path in terms of education/training, entry-level job, or other significant opportunity?

I completed my undergraduate degree in psychology with minors in sociology and business at Penn State. In my consumer behavior classes, I enjoyed the crossover of social, cognitive and behavior psychology with marketing. I also always enjoyed conducting primary research. Consequently, I did a master's in business with a focus on marketing research and a PhD in consumer behavior and advertising research at the University of Edinburgh in Scotland.

Once I completed my doctorate, I accepted a job at Baltimore Research, a small firm in Towson, MD. Traditionally, the firm only offered focus group space, recruiting of participants and field services. I came on as director of research to bring full-service research consulting capabilities and analysis. I've been the managing director since 2007, overseeing all company operations, strategic planning, finance, marketing, etc. I still do research consulting as well.

I have Professional Researcher Certification (PRC) and am heavily involved in our professional association, the Marketing Research Association (MRA). The value of volunteering with a professional or trade association should not be underestimated as an outlet for professional development. It has had a significant impact on my career.

2. What are the most important skills and/or qualities for someone in your profession?

Certainly an innate curiosity helps. As you help solve business problems, you begin to learn a lot about business models across a variety of industries. You need to be a quick study to jump from consumer packaged goods to pharmaceuticals to financial services, education, entertainment or whatever else comes your way. Whether you're a consultant, a project manager or in data collection, strong people skills are imperative. It's not just all number crunching.

3. What do you wish you had known going into this profession?

The career path is quite a bit different for corporate researchers—individuals working in the research departments of companies such as Proctor & Gamble or Bank of America (known as the buyer side) versus people working at market research firms (the supplier side). Corporate researchers obviously have a more singular focus on whatever it is that their company sells. I was always interested in working as a corporate researcher at some point to gain experience from that perspective. I had assumed you start out on the supplier side and naturally graduate to the corporate side. Now most of jobs on the corporate side would be a step back for me, but probably would be interesting work. In retrospect, it may have made sense to try that out earlier in my career.

4. Are there many job opportunities in your profession? In what specific areas?

There definitely are. The industry is growing, with lots of innovative offerings in the mix. It's getting much more competitive. But while there more companies competing for business, that means opportunities for job seekers.

5. How do you see your profession changing in the next five years? What role will technology play in those changes, and what skills will be required?

Marketing research traditionally has been slow to adapt and change. However, the last five years have seen an incredible amount of change largely due to technology. Researchers are trying to get a deeper understanding of their target audience and that leads to more in the moment research methods. Mobile will continue to evolve and play a role, where consumers can record consumption behaviors as they occur and provide feedback and insight. Geofencing technology is allowing questions to be pushed to consumers as they walk into a store or out of a restaurant, and social media analytics are allowing us to make sense of consumers' attitudes within their natural conversations outside a research engagement. At the same time, traditional methods offer distinct advantages for certain applications and I don't see the entire industry relying exclusively on catchy tools. Those who will thrive will have an intuitive ability to make sense out of this explosive access to information.

6. What do you like most about your job? What do you like least about your job?

What I enjoy most is solving business problems. I really enjoy getting to counsel clients through challenges. I also love the people in this field. It's a relatively small, tight-knit community.

What I enjoy least is probably the deadline-driven nature of it. While it can be exciting, we operate under tight timelines and there are a lot of unknowns and curve balls that can be thrown your way when collecting information from very specific consumer segments. There are challenges to the business model as well from government regulation, increased competition and the commoditization of information

7. Can you suggest a valuable "try this" for students considering a career in your profession?

We regularly hire interns, and I imagine other firms do as well. Certainly, if you have the opportunity to participate in a focus group or some sort of research study, it will give you a glimpse into the field.

SELECTED SCHOOLS

Many colleges and universities, especially those with business schools, offer programs in marketing and market research. The student can also gain initial training at a technical or community college. For some of the more prominent institutions in this field, see the "Advertising & Marketing Manager" chapter.

MORE INFORMATION

American Marketing Association
311 S. Wacker Drive, Suite 5800
Chicago, IL 60606
800.262.1150
www.ama.org

**Council of American Survey
Research Organizations**
170 North Country Road, Suite 4
Port Jefferson, NY 11777
631.928.6954
www.casro.org

Marketing Research Association
1156 15th Street NW, Suite 302
Washington, DC 20005
202.800.2545
marketingresearch.org

John Pritchard/Editor

Network & Computer Systems Administrator

Snapshot

Career Cluster: Business Administration; Information Technology

Interests: Computer programming, computer science, software development

Earnings (Yearly Average): $74,000

Employment & Outlook: Faster Than Average Growth Expected

OVERVIEW

Sphere of Work

Network and computer systems administrators design, build, and maintain computer networks and systems for businesses and organizations. In addition to constructing local area networks and wide area networks, systems administrators also support and maintain organizational Internet systems and related infrastructure. Any computer problems or computer-related questions posed

by employees of a company are traditionally handled by system administrators or their staff.

Network and computer systems administrators work closely with computer security professionals and other senior administrative staff to ensure that the computing needs of a business or organization are in place and are functioning properly. They also assist fellow employees with computer-related projects and routine maintenance.

Work Environment

Network and computer systems administrators work predominantly in business, administrative, and office settings. They are employed by large companies often have their own workspaces adjacent to facilities that house computer servers and other hardware relevant to network systems. Network and computer systems administrators are often required to strike a balance between work conducted on their own and collaborative work with other staff members, which can include system maintenance, demonstrations of hardware and software capabilities, or developing and implementing new technologies with fellow staff.

Profile

Working Conditions: Work Indoors
Physical Strength: Light Work
Education Needs: Bachelor's Degree
Licensure/Certification:
Recommended
Physical Abilities Not Required: No
Heavy Labor
Opportunities For Experience:
Military Service,Volunteer Work, Part-
Time Work
Holland Interest Score*: IRC

* See Appendix A

Occupation Interest

The field of computer administration traditionally attracts professionals with technological skills who have a lengthy history of involvement with and demonstrated passion for computing, be it through academic study, personal interest, or professional development. Most network and computer systems administrators develop an interest in working with and around computers at a young age and are intricately familiar with modern developments in personal and business computing. They may also enter the discipline through previous exposure to programming, software development, or any one of numerous disciplines related to computer science.

A Day in the Life—Duties and Responsibilities

Network and computer systems administrators divide their time between monitoring and maintaining existing computer systems, devising new computer and network technologies with other staff, and assisting different departments and fellow employees with their computing and networking needs through maintenance, troubleshooting, and conducting training seminars.

Network and computer system administrators are traditionally the primary individuals responsible for the configuration and maintenance of network e-mail systems. In addition to monitoring archival systems and implementing virus prevention programs, they are also called upon to set up network and mobile e-mail accounts for new employees or vendors.

In addition to e-mail systems, network and computer system administrators also maintain computer systems related to inventories, financial records, meeting logs, and other relevant data. They build, maintain, and monitor backup systems for archival data. They often work in concert with organizational computer security specialists to ensure that data can be recovered in the event of an unforeseen system failure.

Network and computer system administrators also spend a great deal of time troubleshooting and installing new programs on network computers, making updates to employee machines so productivity is not interrupted, or routing out any viruses or system malfunctions that are preventing them from accessing projects. They are traditionally in charge of the master computer and network systems from which all company computers are connected. They may be called upon to supervise access to particular network locations

Duties and Responsibilities

- Managing and maintaining an organization's computer network and systems, including hardware and software
- Diagnosing and solving system problems
- Performing functions related to data security, virus protection and disaster recovery
- Monitoring system performance to determine current and future adjustments that need to be made
- Communicating with system users to understand and correct issues

OCCUPATION SPECIALTIES

Computer and Information Systems Managers

Computer and Information Systems Managers, often called IT managers, plan, coordinate, and direct computer-related activities in an organization. They help determine the information technology goals of an organization and are responsible for implementing computer systems to meet those goals.

Computer Network Architects

Computer Network Architects design and build data communication networks, including local area networks (LANs), wide area networks (WANs), and intranets. These networks range from a small connection between two offices to a multinational series of globally distributed communications systems.

Computer Systems Analysts

Computer Systems Analysts study an organization's current computer systems and procedures and design information systems solutions to help the organization operate more efficiently and effectively. They bring business and information technology (IT) together by understanding the needs and limitations of both.

Information Security Specialists

Information Security Specialists plan and carry out security measures to protect an organization's computer networks and systems. Their responsibilities are continually expanding as the number of cyberattacks increase.

Database Administrators

Database Administrators (DBAs) use specialized software to store and organize data, such as financial information and customer shipping records. They make sure that data are available to users and are secure from unauthorized access.

WORK ENVIRONMENT

Physical Environment

Network and computer systems administrators work primarily in computer labs and office settings. They balance a workload that is performed at their own individual workstation and the workstations of other employees.

Network and computer systems administrators work in nearly every type of industry and organization, including local, state and federal governments; construction; medical research; publishing; education; and media.

Human Environment

Systems administration requires patience and collaboration and explanatory skills. Network and computer systems administrators normally interact with colleagues across various departments on a daily basis, including engineers, technicians, managers, directors, and executive staff.

Relevant Skills and Abilities

Analytical Skills

- Analyzing information and/or data

Communication Skills

- Speaking effectively
- Writing concisely
- Listening attentively
- Reading well

Interpersonal/Social Skills

- Being able to work both independently and as a member of a team

Organization & Management Skills

- Paying attention to and handling details
- Performing duties that change frequently
- Managing time
- Managing equipment/materials
- Coordinating tasks
- Making decisions
- Handling challenging situations

Research & Planning Skills

- Identifying problems
- Determining alternatives
- Gathering information
- Solving problems
- Defining needs
- Developing evaluation strategies

Technical Skills

- Performing scientific, mathematical and technical work
- Working with machines, tools or other objects
- Using technology to process information
- Understanding which technology is appropriate for a task
- Applying the technology to a task
- Maintaining and repairing technology

Technological Environment

Network and computer systems administrators must be well versed in the entire gamut of contemporary computer systems technologies, ranging from circuitry, processors, and programming languages, and all computer hardware and software relevant to their industry of expertise, including applications and database platforms.

EDUCATION, TRAINING, AND ADVANCEMENT

High School/Secondary

High school students can best prepare for a career in network and computer systems administration by completing coursework in algebra, calculus, geometry, trigonometry, introductory computer science, and programming. Specialized seminars or advanced placement coursework related to computer topics are also recommended.

Many high school students supplement their course load by participating in volunteer programs and summer internships in which they can work directly with system administration fundamentals and its importance in the professional world.

Suggested High School Subjects
- Algebra
- Applied Communication
- Applied Math
- Business & Computer Technology
- Business Data Processing
- Calculus
- College Preparatory
- Computer Programming
- Computer Science
- English
- Geometry
- Keyboarding
- Mathematics
- Statistics
- Trigonometry

Famous First

The first large commercial computer network was the SABRE (Semi-Automated Business Research Environment) airline reservation system, developed for American Airlines by IBM in 1964. The system went online via AOL in 1990, and in 2000 it split off from American Airlines. Today SABRE Holdings operates the Travelocity online travel agency, which allows customers to book reservations with airlines, hotels, car rental companies, tour operators, railways, and other travel services.

College/Postsecondary

Systems administration has evolved from a niche field to an academic and professional specialty widely studied across post-secondary institutions in the United States. Requirements for specific academic training in the field often vary from position to position and industry to industry, though a bachelor's degree in a related field is commonplace for most entry-level positions. Several certificate-level and undergraduate programs are available nationwide.

While graduate programs specifically related to systems administration are rare, applicants with master's-level accreditation in fields such as programming, computer science, and networking are often prime candidates for senior management positions related to network and systems administration in major companies, research institutes, and universities. Basic bachelor's degree coursework in systems administration programs includes topics such as system administration, network infrastructures, UNIX, business telecommunications, and information security.

Related College Majors
- Computer Installation & Repair
- Computer Maintenance Technology
- Computer Programming
- Computer Science

- Data Processing Technology
- Information Sciences & Systems
- Management Information Systems & Business Data Processing

Adult Job Seekers

Network and computer systems administrators are often employed by businesses and organizations of all size and scope. Senior-level positions at large organizations and companies are usually the domain of professionals with extensive academic and professional experience in computing. However, adult job seekers interested in a career change to the field can, with requisite training, acquire the skills necessary to become eligible for systems administrator positions at smaller organizations. Network and computer systems administrators traditionally work regular business hours.

Professional Certification and Licensure

The number of available and required certifications for network and computer systems administrators is complex and varied. Examples include Microsoft Certified IT Professional certification, Linux certification, and Accredited Systems Engineer certification.'

Additional Requirements

Network and computer systems administrators must possess a constant desire to stay up to date with emerging developments in digital technology, networking, and database systems. Organizations rely on network and computer systems administrators to help their firms stay in tune with the technologies that can expand their production and profitability

Fun Fact

We all know that keeping in instant touch is easy in the digital age, but imagine what it was like to watch your loved one blast off into space before email. That all changed in 1991, when the crew of *STS-43 Atlantis* sent an email back to earth.

Source: http://mashable.com/2011/01/26/e-mail-facts/

EARNINGS AND ADVANCEMENT

Median annual earnings of network and computer system administrators were $74,000 in 2013. The lowest ten percent earned less than $45,000, and the highest ten percent earned more than $117,000.

Network and computer system administrators may receive paid vacations, holidays and sick days; life and health insurance; and retirement benefits. These are usually paid by the employer

Metropolitan Areas with the Highest Employment Level in This Occupation

Metropolitan area	Employment[1]	Employment per thousand jobs	Hourly mean wage
Washington-Arlington-Alexandria, DC-VA-MD-WV	18,170	7.68	$45.90
New York-White Plains-Wayne, NY-NJ	14,840	2.83	$43.97
Chicago-Joliet-Naperville, IL	9,960	2.69	$38.14
Dallas-Plano-Irving, TX	9,950	4.63	$40.41
Los Angeles-Long Beach-Glendale, CA	9,950	2.50	$39.16
Houston-Sugar Land-Baytown, TX	9,080	3.29	$44.47
Atlanta-Sandy Springs-Marietta, GA	8,350	3.62	$39.34
Denver-Aurora-Broomfield, CO	6,590	5.14	$38.90
Minneapolis-St. Paul-Bloomington, MN-WI	6,520	3.64	$37.77
Boston-Cambridge-Quincy, MA	6,290	3.60	$40.09

[1] Does not include self-employed. Source: Bureau of Labor Statistics.

EMPLOYMENT AND OUTLOOK

Network and computer system administrators held about 366,000 jobs nationally in 2012. Employment of network and computer system administrators is expected to grow as fast as the average for all occupations through the year 2022, which means employment is projected to increase 9 percent to 16 percent. Almost every organization in today's workforce needs to keep a computer network running smoothly and secure from hackers, viruses and other attacks. The growth of security as a main concern for organizations will help to fuel the growth of network and computer system administrators.

In addition, the demand for organizations to have newer, faster and more mobile networks; the growth of the use of information technology in the healthcare field; and the growth of e-commerce will continue to create new jobs for network and computer systems administrators. This growth demands workers who can help their organizations use the Internet and other technologies to communicate with employees, clients and customers

Employment Trend, Projected 2012–22

Computer Occupations: 18%

Network and Computer Systems Administrators: 12%

Total, All Occupations: 11%

Note: "All Occupations" includes all occupations in the U.S. Economy. Source: U.S. Bureau of Labor Statistics, Employment Projections Program.

Related Occupations
- Computer & Information Systems Manager
- Computer Engineer
- Computer Network Architect

- Computer Programmer
- Computer Support Specialist
- Computer Systems Analyst
- Database Administrator
- Information Security Analyst
- Software Developer
- Web Administrator
- Web Developer

Related Military Occupations

- Computer Programmer
- Computer Systems Officer
- Computer Systems Specialist

Conversation With . . .
PATRICIA A. VEON

Second-tier Technical Service Support
Frederick MD Country Schools, 9 years
Tech Services field, 25 years

1. **What was your individual career path in terms of education/training, entry-level job, or other significant opportunity?**

I came from a large family with limited resources, so higher education was not something I ever envisioned that I would be able to achieve. In high school, I took classes that would lead to basic employment, such as typing, shorthand and bookkeeping.

My first job in high school was working as a cashier. This led to a bookkeeping position.

When I lost the bookkeeping job as a young, newly-separated mother, due to sexual harassment, I realized, as I looked for work, that I could not identify my profession. Time was moving ahead, but,with only a high school education, I was falling behind.

I applied to numerous places for work, without success. Finally, at a job interview with a friend of my mother, she told me to get some training and come back. So I did.

I was very good at math, and I knew I had a talent for fixing things and solving problems. I needed to find how to make a living doing this. At the time, the government had a program to train people while they were on unemployment. I went to the job training agency in my hometown, and they gave me a test to determine my strengths and weaknesses. Sure enough, I was good at working with people and solving problems.

They helped me find a school that offered a one-year, full time, intense electronic education. By the end of the school year, I had seven job offers.

After I went to work as an electronics tech — and then as a technical writer — I started taking classes to fill in my degree. Working full-time and raising my three children, it took more than five years to complete an AA degree in Electronics from Frederick Community College in Maryland.

I learned most of my computer and network skills on the job or by studying and taking classes. I worked for Packard BioScience Company, who sent me to many classes to learn how to be a trainer. I did technical training for eight years for all of their service engineers and customers.

I moved to doing tech support in a school — even though it paid about a third of what I was making — because I was traveling all over the country and the world doing training and I wanted to get off the road. Now, I have a territory of nine schools. When the school-based tech runs into a problem they don't know how to fix, they call me. I do some network work, a lot of software work and training

2. **What are the most important skills and/or qualities for someone in your profession?**

You need an inherent ability to figure things out. If you're not curious about how things work, I don't think you'll make it.

Communication is vital — the most important part of my job — whether I am talking to a user to explain something on their level, or documenting a process.

Also, the tech field is always changing, making it challenging to stay up with everything. But it is never boring. If you're in the tech field, you can't stop learning. It's a job with homework.

3. **What do you wish you had known going into this profession?**

I wish I had known that having a higher education degree would have made me much more marketable. I also wish I had realized that I could make a living at something that I enjoyed at an earlier age. I wasted many years just making a living.

4. **Are there many job opportunities in your profession? In what specific areas?**

Job opportunities abound in the tech field. There is always a need for people who can set up and run networks for companies and government agencies.

5. **How do you see your profession changing in the next five years? What role will technology play in those changes, and what skills will be required?**

Network security is the biggest area of growth right now. If you can work in network security, you can name your price.

6. **What do you like most about your job? What do you like least about your job?**

I enjoy the people. I don't enjoy the office politics.

7. Can you suggest a valuable "try this" for students considering a career in your profession?

You need to find a problem and try to figure it out. I can fix anything: give me a toaster and I can either fix it, or find out how.

SELECTED SCHOOLS

Most colleges and universities offer programs in computer science, sometimes with a concentration in network and systems administration. The student can also gain initial training at a technical or community college. For advanced positions, a master's degree is often expected. Below are listed some of the more prominent institutions in this field.

California Institute of Technology
1200 East California Boulevard
Pasadena, CA 91125
626.395.6811
www.caltech.edu

Carnegie Mellon University
5000 Forbes Avenue
Pittsburgh, PA 15213
412.268.2000
www.cmu.edu

Cornell University
410 Thurston Avenue
Ithaca, NY 14850
607.255.5241
www.cornell.edu

Georgia Institute of Technology
North Avenue NW
Atlanta, GA 30332
404.894.2000
www.gatech.edu

Massachusetts Institute of Technology
77 Massachusetts Avenue
Cambridge, MA 02139
617.253.1000
web.mit.edu

Stanford University
450 Serra Mall
Stanford, CA 94305
650.723.2300
www.stanford.edu

University of California— Berkeley
103 Sproul Hall
Berkeley, CA 94720
510.642.3175
berkeley.edu

University of Illinois— Urbana-Champaign
901 West Illinois Street
Urbana, IL 61801
217.333.0302
illinois.edu

University of Michigan— Ann Arbor
515 E. Jefferson Street
Ann Arbor, MI 48109
734.764.7433
umich.edu

University of Texas— Austin
1823 Red River Station
PO Box 8058
Austin, TX 78701
512.475.7440
www.utexas.edu

MORE INFORMATION

**League of Professional System
Administrators**
P.O. Box 5161
Trenton, NJ 08638-0161
202.567.7201
lopsa.org

**National Association of System
Administrators**
3305 South IL Rte. 31
Crystal Lake, IL 60012
800.724.9692
www.nasasupport.com

**Network Professional
Association**
4891 Pacific Highway, Suite 115
San Diego, CA 92110
888.672.6720
www.npa.org

_____
John Pritchard/Editor

Operations Director

Snapshot

Career Cluster: Business Administration; Government & Public Service

Interests: Business operations, management, logistics, supervising others

Earnings (Yearly Average): $96,430

Employment & Outlook: Average Growth Expected

OVERVIEW

Sphere of Work

Operations directors are responsible for making strategic business decisions to ensure that their organizations run smoothly and profitably. They occupy the top tier of management and, as such, bear responsibility toward the owners and stakeholders for the organization's performance. Significantly compensated, they are expected to provide a corresponding level of leadership and direction to other managers, as well as to formulate and communicate high-level policy. In the non-profit and government sectors, they may have job titles such as chief or superintendent.

Work Environment

Operations directors usually spend most of their work day in office environments. Typically, they have their own office or office suite close to other members of an organization's top management team. Operations directors can expect to spend a fair amount of time traveling away from home if their organization is national or multinational. They are frequently expected to put in as many hours as required to fulfill their duties. As a result, many operations directors work sixty or more hours a week, including evenings, weekends, and holidays.

Profile

Working Conditions: Work Indoors
Physical Strength: Light Work
Education Needs: Bachelor's Degree, Master's Degree
Licensure/Certification: Usually Not Required
Physical Abilities Not Required: No Heavy Labor
Opportunities For Experience: Military Service, Part-Time Work
Holland Interest Score*: ESR

* See Appendix A

Occupation Interest

This occupation suits people who combine technical knowledge and abilities relevant to the industry they work in with sophisticated business and leadership skills and the desire and commitment needed to effectively run an organization. They must have the experience, foresight, and ability to develop an organization's strategic direction by taking into account the competitive environment, market opportunities and challenges, micro- and macroeconomics, sociopolitical factors, resource requirements, and operations. Strong analytical abilities and the capacity to set goals for short- and long-term planning are a must in this profession. This job usually requires long hours and a level of responsibility that may cause stress.

A Day in the Life—Duties and Responsibilities

An operations director's day may be dedicated to dealing with one issue or a wide variety of issues. It is likely, however, that a significant proportion of the day will be spent communicating with others, either one-on-one or in group meetings. The operations director is likely to schedule regular meetings with key staff and committees about issues such as budgets, financial results, sales forecasts, and special projects. He or she will meet regularly with the key staff who report to them. This may include, for example, the chief financial officer, human resources director, sales and marketing directors, and any other key staff. The operations director is likely to delegate duties as needed to his or her support staff, as well as task them with special projects, research, and analysis. Individuals in this position are additionally responsible for developing lower-level employees into future managers.

The organization's executives and directors may also be involved at a strategic level in special projects and initiatives. Depending on the type of organization, this may include, for example, crisis and reputation management, new product development and launches, mergers and acquisitions, site openings and closures, strategic operational and logistic changes, and policy development.

The operations director is responsible for reporting to the company's board of directors, owners, and investors. In the case of publicly listed companies, this includes shareholders. The operations director is responsible for ensuring that the company fulfills its legal and fiduciary responsibilities. In doing so, the operations director makes a personal guarantee to the company's board and shareholders that the information provided in official legal and financial reports is accurate and reliable

Duties and Responsibilities

- Setting general goals and policies in collaboration with other top executives and the board of directors
- Meeting with business and government leaders to discuss policy-related matters
- Directing the operations of firms and agencies
- Overseeing department managers and junior executives
- Achieving organizational goals quickly and economically

WORK ENVIRONMENT

Physical Environment

Operations directors usually work from their own office, which tends to be pleasant and well-appointed. The operations director's physical environment will be influenced by the size and type of employer and the industry in which he or she operates.

Relevant Skills and Abilities

Communication Skills
- Speaking effectively
- Writing concisely

Interpersonal/Social Skills
- Asserting oneself
- Cooperating with others
- Motivating others

Organization & Management Skills
- Demonstrating leadership
- Making decisions

Research & Planning Skills
- Developing evaluation strategies
- Solving problems

Work Environment Skills
- Traveling

Human Environment

This role involves a great amount of interaction with others. Operations directors must possess advanced oral and written communication skills, including the ability to collaborate, negotiate, and resolve conflict. They must be able to conduct themselves with diplomacy and tact and interact confidently with powerful people.

Technological Environment

Daily operations may demand the use of standard office technologies, including computers, telephones, e-mail, photocopiers, and the Internet. Operations directors are usually supported by an executive secretary or administrative team who completes much of the more routine paperwork and requests. The technology used by someone in this position can vary depending on the industry the organization occupies

EDUCATION, TRAINING, AND ADVANCEMENT

High School/Secondary

High school students can best prepare for a career as an operations director by taking courses in applied communication subjects such as business writing as well as computer science. Foreign languages may also be beneficial. Courses that develop general business skills may include accounting, entrepreneurship, bookkeeping, business management, and applied mathematics. Administrative skills may be developed by taking subjects such as business computing and typing. Becoming involved in part-time administrative or clerical work after school or during the weekends builds people skills and is a helpful way to begin learning about business operations and management. Leadership experience can be developed through taking part in extracurricular activities.

Suggested High School Subjects
- Applied Communication
- College Preparatory
- Composition
- Computer Science
- English
- Entrepreneurship

Famous First

The first containerized shipping operation was launched in 1956 by Malcolm McLean of Maxton, North Carolina who developed a large shipping container that could be loaded with goods at the factory, carried by truck to a port facility, and then placed on a ship for transport. McLean's first container, Ideal X, left the port of Newark, New Jersey in April 1956. Today, containerized shipping is the industry standard worldwide and a multi-billion dollar business.

College/Postsecondary

In keeping with the level of responsibility of the position, most employers expect their operations directors to possess postsecondary qualifications. The minimum requirement is considered to be a bachelor's degree in business or another relevant field. A master's degree in business administration (MBA) is sometimes, but not always, considered to be a requirement. Because this position is extremely results-oriented, some individuals earn more advanced degrees or certifications, while others advance as a result of proving their abilities through on-the-job experience.

Related College Majors
- Business Administration & Management
- Enterprise Management & Operation
- Entrepreneurship
- Finance
- Non-Profit Management & Operation
- Retailing & Wholesaling Operations

Adult Job Seekers

Adults seeking a career as an operations director should emphasize any prior management experience or advanced knowledge of the core competencies of business management, such as financial management, human resource management, operations, and sales and marketing. Adult job seekers may need to supplement their current skill set by taking classes in relevant areas. Candidates should keep in mind that many companies promote their existing managers into top executive positions. Networking, job searching, and interviewing are, therefore, critical, and this should include registering with executive recruitment agencies.

Professional Certification and Licensure

There are no formal professional certifications or licensing requirements for operations directors, but professional associations offer operations directors certifications and some industry authorities require staff to hold special licenses. The American Management Association (AMA) and National Management Association (NMA) provide certificate programs in a range of specialty areas, as well as general management.

Additional Requirements

The workload and pressures placed on operations directors are often relentless or intense, so these individuals should be highly motivated, confident, and able to thrive under pressure. Work/life balance may be difficult to achieve or maintain in such a demanding and responsible role, which often requires a great commitment of time and energy.

According to a salary survey by the National Association of Colleges and Employers, individuals with a bachelor's degree in human resources were offered starting salaries of $49,359 in 2012.

Fun Fact

To move or not to move for a job: are you willing? Many careers have been advanced by a move but it's important to make sure that moving is for you. That's because moving was found to be more stressful than having a baby or getting a new job.

Source: Nov. 30, 2012 My Move Consumer Insights Study by MyMove.com.

EARNINGS AND ADVANCEMENT

Operations directors' earnings depend on the level of managerial responsibility, length of service, and type, size and geographic location of the firm. Salaries in manufacturing and finance are generally higher than in state and local government.

Median annual earnings of operations directors were $96,430 in 2013. The lowest ten percent earned less than $50,000, and the highest ten percent earned well over $175,000.

Operations directors are paid vacations, holidays, and sick days; life and health insurance; and retirement benefits. These are paid by the employer. They may also receive the use of company aircraft and cars, expense allowances and stock options.

Metropolitan Areas with the Highest
Employment Level in This Occupation

Metropolitan area	Employment	Employment per thousand jobs	Hourly mean wage
New York-White Plains-Wayne, NY-NJ	81,500	15.55	$77.74
Los Angeles-Long Beach-Glendale, CA	69,290	17.43	$61.50
Chicago-Joliet-Naperville, IL	63,250	17.09	$52.40
Washington-Arlington-Alexandria, DC-VA-MD-WV	51,760	21.86	$68.59
Atlanta-Sandy Springs-Marietta, GA	50,480	21.87	$57.36
Houston-Sugar Land-Baytown, TX	47,220	17.12	$63.07
Dallas-Plano-Irving, TX	37,270	17.34	$63.07
Boston-Cambridge-Quincy, MA	34,020	19.45	$67.32
Phoenix-Mesa-Glendale, AZ	28,210	15.83	$52.02
Santa Ana-Anaheim-Irvine, CA	28,000	19.28	$62.99

Source: Bureau of Labor Statistics.

EMPLOYMENT AND OUTLOOK

Operations directors held about 2 million jobs nationally in 2012. Employment is most concentrated in business services, retail stores, financial institutions, educational institutions, hospitals and the government. Employment is expected to grow as fast as the average for all occupations through the year 2022, which means employment is projected to increase 9 percent to 15 percent. Demand for jobs is expected to increase in the financial services and health services industry but expected to decline in many manufacturing industries.

Employment Trend, Projected 2012–22

Operations Directors and General Managers: 12%

Total, All Occupations: 11%

Top Executives: 11%

Note: "All Occupations" includes all occupations in the U.S. Economy. Source: U.S. Bureau of Labor Statistics, Employment Projections Program.

Related Occupations

- City Manager
- Computer & Information Systems Manager
- Education Administrator
- Financial Manager
- Human Resources Specialist/ Manager
- Information Technology Project Manager
- Management Consultant
- Medical & Health Services Manager
- Public Administrator
- Public Relations Specialist
- Retail Store Sales Manager

Related Military Occupations

- Executive Officer
- Operations Officer

Conversation With . . .
MIKE KARR

Vice President of Operations
SEKISUI SPI, 2 years
Operations Manager field, 15 years

1. What was your individual career path in terms of education/training, entry-level job, or other significant opportunity?

I never dreamed of "working in a factory" when I left high school but after a few years of working odd jobs and attending community college classes, I needed money. A friend got me into his company that made automotive aftermarket products. Planning to only stay the summer, I was there 13.5 years. I started looking around and determined better ways to do some of the processes. Management recognized this and asked me to go back to school and move into a supervisor role. From there I kept moving up while earning an Associate's Degree in Business Administration. Over time, the combination of knowing production and office operations opened up opportunity. I continued to move up and earned a BBA through an accelerated college program. As my network grew, I gained other opportunities that included running an aerosol packaging plant and doing sales for another company. I am now the VP of Operations for this company and responsible for two facilities, one in Bloomsburg, Pennsylvania and the other in Holland, Michigan.

2. What are the most important skills and/or qualities for someone in your profession?

The ability to provide accurate and timely information along with solutions has been the key to my success. That and the ability to deal with all the challenges that managing people brings by staying consistent, fair, and direct. Like any success in business, keeping current, studying and understanding you scope of responsibility, and acting decisively are keys. I've always been able to look at processes and systems and ask "Is there a better way to do that?" to make decisions when others did not want the responsibility, to develop employees and teams and keep them focused on our goals, and to maintain a strong focus on the "numbers," sometimes called Key Performance Indicators, or KPIs.

I've also been willing to move to take on new challenges, and to counter my shortfalls by hiring experts in the areas where my skills are weak.

3.   What do you wish you had known going into this profession?

You will work long hours. The more responsibility you take on, the more you never really get away from the job. If you run a 24/7 plant, there is no true down time because you have to be able to deal with emergencies — or at least put the systems in place to deal with emergencies — and that's critical when it comes to employee safety. Somebody getting hurt or worse is the worst position an Operations Manager can be in, both personally and professionally. You are responsible for all that goes on, and you have to embrace that responsibility or else get out of this profession.

4. Are there many job opportunities in your profession? In what specific areas?

Opportunities for Operations Managers are often in service industries, and often low paying. Opportunities to run large manufacturing plants are not plentiful, and you need a good network and much experience to succeed. However, I strongly believe that if you want to do this and put the time in to learn, you will find a company that needs your skills.

5. How do you see your profession changing in the next five years? What role will technology play in those changes, and what skills will be required?

Like many positions, technology — including social media — requires a person to constantly evolve. How you train, how you buy equipment, types and changes in equipment, utilities, asset management, trucking and overall logistics are just some of the areas that change quickly. Something like 3D printing could change an industry within a couple of years. An Operations Manager always has to look ahead or be blind-sided by market and technology changes.

6. What do you like most about your job? What do you like least about your job?

I enjoy setting direction and being involved with employees on attaining goals. I enjoy when people are making a living because everyone has success. I like shaping the strategy and the planning involved. The least enjoyable part of my job is my constant concern about employee safety. I train constantly and try to limit risks; my goal has always been to send everyone home intact, the same way they came in. When that does not happen, it can make the job miserable

7. **Can you suggest a valuable "try this" for students considering a career in your profession?**

Work in a factory for a summer and see the processes. Also, I would think most any Operations Manager would be willing to sit with you and explain the path needed to gain the required knowledge and experience. It is not a job someone could do right out of college. You should have some level of college, even just basic business management, and then work in production, shipping, scheduling, quality, HR, and maybe even customer service. Use what you learn to grow your skills and experience.

SELECTED SCHOOLS

Many colleges and universities, especially those with business schools, offer programs in business administration and operations management. The student can also gain initial training through a technical or community college. For advanced positions, a master's of business administration (MBA) with a concentration in operations is usually expected. Below are listed some of the more prominent graduate institutions in this field.

Carnegie Mellon University
Tepper School of Business
500 Forbes Avenue
Pittsburgh, PA 15213
412.268.2268
tepper.cmu.edu

Columbia University
Columbia Business School
3022 Broadway
Manhattan, NY 10027
212.854.5553
www8.gsb.columbia.edu

Harvard University
Harvard Business School
Soldiers Field
Boston, MA 02163
617.495.6000
www.hbs.edu

Indiana University–Bloomington
Kelley School of Business
1309 E. 10th Street
Bloomington, IN 47405
812.855.8100
kelley.iu.edu

Massachusetts Institute of Technology
Sloan School of Management
50 Memorial Drive
Cambridge, MA 02142
617.253.2659
mitsloan.mit.edu

Northwestern University
Kellogg School of Management
2169 Campus Drive
Evanston, IL 60208
847.467.7000
www.kellogg.northwestern.edu

Purdue University
Krannert School of Management
403 W. State Street
West Lafayette, IN 47907
765.496.4343
www.krannert.purdue.edu

Stanford University
Stanford Graduate School of Business
655 Knight Way
Stanford, CA 94305
650.723.2146
www.gsb.stanford.edu

University of Michigan–Ann Arbor
Ross School of Business
701 Tappan Avenue
Ann Arbor, MI 48109
734.763.5796
michiganross.umich.edu

University of Pennsylvania
The Wharton School
1 College Hall
Philadelphia, PA 19104
215.898.6376
www.whatron.upenn.edu

MORE INFORMATION

American Management Association
1601 Broadway
New York, NY 10019
212.568.8100
www.amanet.org

Business and Professional Women's Foundation
1718 M Street NW, #148
Washington, DC 20036
202.293.1100
www.bpwfoundation.org

National Management Association
2210 Arbor Boulevard
Dayton, OH 45439
937.294.0421
www.nma1.org

Kylie Hughes/Editor

Payroll Administrator

Snapshot

Career Cluster(s): Business Administration

Interests: Bookkeeping, accounting, business administration, data processing, finance

Earnings (Yearly Average): $38,670

Employment & Outlook: Average Growth Expected

OVERVIEW

Sphere of Work

Payroll administrators implement all stages of the payroll process for their organization. In particular, payroll administrators are timekeepers who track employee hours and time worked as well as employee commissions and benefits. They must also process paychecks on a regular basis. Payroll administrators are knowledgeable about and help implement changes to insurance deductibles and payments as well as social security and taxes. Payroll administrators often work alongside benefits specialists and certified public accountants in payroll, personnel, or accounting departments.

Work Environment

Payroll administrators work in offices in organizations such as businesses, hospitals, insurance companies, educational institutions, government agencies, and various branches of the military. Depending on employer and particular job description, a payroll clerk may telecommute from a home-office, visit client offices as a contractor, or work on a full-time basis in an employer's office. Payroll administrators may be hired as full-time members of payroll teams or as term-of-project contractors. Most payroll administrators work forty-hour weeks, but overtime may be necessary during periods of increased seasonal employment.

Profile

Working Conditions: Work Indoors
Physical Strength: Light Work
Education Needs: High School Diploma or GED, Technical/Community College
Licensure/Certification: Usually Not Required
Physical Abilities Not Required: No Heavy Labor
Opportunities For Experience: Internship, Military Service, Part-Time Work
Holland Interest Score*: CRS

* See Appendix A

Occupation Interest

Individuals attracted to the payroll administrator profession tend to be organized and detail-oriented people who find satisfaction in tracking financial information. Those individuals who excel as payroll administrators exhibit financial and mathematical acumen, intense focus, responsibility, accuracy, and effective time management. As they are responsible for compensation and employees' confidential financial information, prospective payroll administrators must be honest, trustworthy, meticulous, and highly organized. Payroll administrators should enjoy bookkeeping and have a background in accounting or human resources.

A Day in the Life—Duties and Responsibilities

The payroll administrator's specific daily occupational duties and responsibilities depend on the individual's job specifications and work environment. In general, a payroll administrator tracks and records employee attendance, hours, bonuses, commissions, sick leave, paid vacation days, and nontaxable wages. Payroll administrators may develop their own systems for employee timekeeping or follow their organization's existing system. At the end of every pay period, payroll administrators calculate required deductions, including insurance payments, income taxes, and social security payments. In addition to regular deductions, employees may owe one-time annual deductions, such as union dues or medical savings account contributions.

Payroll administrators are responsible for generating paychecks by manually preparing and signing checks or using an automated payroll program. They may manually record the calculated figures onto checks, stubs, and master payroll sheets, or in automated programs, they need only type the wage data into the computer system. Paychecks are either distributed to employees by hand or processed through direct bank deposit into their personal bank accounts. In instances of paycheck error, payroll administrators work with employees to correct the error and ensure proper payment.

Payroll administrators may participate in workshops or training programs offered by the personnel or human resources departments to educate employees about benefits, time sheets, and insurance options. Those employed by learning institutions may also be involved in discussions of work teams, workflows, dynamics, and best practices. In addition, all payroll administrators are responsible for complying with regulatory requirements for financial institutions as well as providing financial records and reports to accountants involved tax preparation and auditing

Duties and Responsibilities

- Calculating regular and overtime earnings
- Computing deductions such as income tax withholdings, social security, credit union payments, insurance, bond purchases and union dues
- Preparing checks and master payroll sheets or forms
- Preparing and distributing electronic payments and pay envelopes
- Maintaining records of sick leave, vacation and nontaxable wages
- Compiling and maintaining wage information forms for tax purposes
- Maintaining accurate year-to-date wage information on each employee

WORK ENVIRONMENT

Physical Environment

Payroll administrators generally work in bright, pleasant office environments in businesses and organizations that have paid employees. The work of a payroll administrator requires sitting at a desk and using computers for long periods each day.

Relevant Skills and Abilities

Interpersonal/Social Skills
- Cooperating with others
- Having good judgment
- Working as a member of a team

Organization & Management Skills
- Paying attention to and handling details
- Performing routine work

Research & Planning Skills
- Identifying problems

Technical Skills
- Performing scientific, mathematical and technical work
- Using technology to process information
- orking with data or numbers
- Working with machines, tools or other objects

Plant Environment

Payroll administrators working in plant or manufacturing environments supervise the organization's employee timekeeping and payroll. While a payroll administrator's office in a plant environment is most often kept separate from production lines, he or she may experience physical risks resulting from production fumes, noise, or plant accidents.

Human Environment

A payroll administrator's human environment may be social or isolated, depending on assignment and organization. Payroll administrators may interact regularly with employees, supervisors, or colleagues.

Technological Environment

During the course of their work, payroll administrators use Internet communication tools, financial software programs, adding machines and calculators, fax machines, photocopying machines, scanners, and postal machines. They must also consult tax and insurance tables and laws regarding employee compensation and work hours.

EDUCATION, TRAINING, AND ADVANCEMENT

High School/Secondary

High school students interested in pursuing a career as a payroll administrator should prepare themselves by building good study habits and by developing an ease with numbers and mathematical functions. High school classes in English, typing, bookkeeping, and mathematics will provide a strong foundation for work as a payroll administrator or college-level study in the field. Interested high school students should pursue internships or part-time employment opportunities that familiarize them with business and finance.

Suggested High School Subjects
- Bookkeeping
- Business
- Business & Computer Technology
- Business Data Processing
- Business Math
- College Preparatory
- English
- Keyboarding

Famous First

The first annual federal income tax was instituted in 1913 under the 16th Amendment to the US Constitution. The first filing deadline for income tax returns was March 1, 1914 and the form was four pages long. There were six different income brackets, with people in the highest bracket paying 6 percent. In just three years the top rate jumped to 67 percent and for many years afterward the top rate stayed above 75 percent. Since the 1980s, however, it has been below 40 percent.

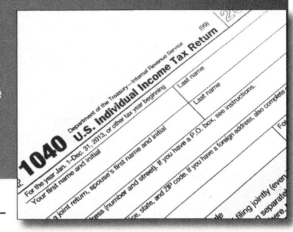

Postsecondary

Although an undergraduate degree is not strictly required for payroll administrators, students interested in becoming payroll administrators should work towards an associate's degree or a bachelor's degree in bookkeeping, accounting, secretarial science, or general business. Mathematics, communications, data processing, and business courses may also prove useful for their future work. Students can gain work experience and potential advantage in their future job searches through internships or part-time employment with local businesses or financial organizations.

Related College Majors
- Accounting Technician Training
- Business Administration & Management
- Office Supervision & Management

AAdult Job Seekers

Adults seeking employment as payroll administrators should have at least a high school diploma or an associate's degree. Most employers provide on-the-job training for new payroll administrators, but may prefer to hire candidates with higher education and/or familiarity with computer systems. Adult job seekers should educate themselves about the educational requirements of the organizations where they seek employment. Qualified adults seeking payroll administrator positions may benefit from joining professional payroll associations, such as the American Payroll Association, to help with networking and job searching. These associations generally offer professional development events and maintain lists and forums of available payroll jobs.

Professional Certification and Licensure

Certification and licensure is not required for general payroll administrators but may be required as a condition of employment or promotion. Options for voluntary payroll administrator certification include the Fundamental Payroll Certification (FPC) and the Certified Payroll Professional (CPP). The FPC and the CPP, offered by the American Payroll Association, are earned by passing a national examination. To qualify for the CCP certification, candidates must have at least three years of work experience in the field and complete approved training courses in payroll. There are no experience or training prerequisites for the FPC examination, although test preparation is recommended.

Additional Requirements

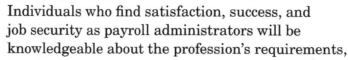

Individuals who find satisfaction, success, and job security as payroll administrators will be knowledgeable about the profession's requirements, responsibilities, and opportunities. Membership in professional payroll associations is encouraged among all payroll administrators as a means of building professional community. Payroll administrators who are members of a professional association must adhere to a strict code of ethics and conduct.

Fun Fact

America's 156 million wage earners and the payroll professionals who work with them contribute, collect, report and deposit approximately $1.97 trillion, or 68.9%, of the annual revenue of the U.S. Treasury.

Source: www.nationalpayrollweek.com and www.americanpayroll.org

EARNINGS AND ADVANCEMENT

Earnings of payroll administrators depend on the size and geographic location of the employer, and the employee's experience and skills. Median annual earnings of payroll administrators were $38,670 in 2013. The lowest ten percent earned less than $26,000, and the highest ten percent earned more than $57,000.

Payroll administrators may receive paid vacations, holidays, and sick days; life and health insurance; and retirement benefits. These are usually paid by the employer.

Metropolitan Areas with the Highest Employment Level in This Occupation

Metropolitan area	Employment	Employment per thousand jobs	Hourly mean wage
New York-White Plains-Wayne, NY-NJ	5,790	1.11	$21.64
Los Angeles-Long Beach-Glendale, CA	5,540	1.39	$21.38
Houston-Sugar Land-Baytown, TX	4,260	1.54	$19.15
Chicago-Joliet-Naperville, IL	4,160	1.12	$20.88
Dallas-Plano-Irving, TX	3,390	1.58	$20.90
Philadelphia, PA	2,730	1.48	$20.08
Minneapolis-St. Paul-Bloomington, MN-WI	2,730	1.52	$21.08
Atlanta-Sandy Springs-Marietta, GA	2,470	1.07	$20.14
Washington-Arlington-Alexandria, DC-VA-MD-WV	2,250	0.95	$23.93
Santa Ana-Anaheim-Irvine, CA	2,220	1.53	$22.92

Source: Bureau of Labor Statistics.

EMPLOYMENT AND OUTLOOK

There were approximately 180,000 payroll administrators employed nationally in 2012. They can be found in every industry, but a growing number work for accounting and payroll services firms that complete payroll functions for companies. Employment is expected to grow about as fast as the average for all occupations through the year 2022, which means employment is projected to increase 7 percent to 14 percent. Job growth will likely be limited due to the continuing automation of payroll functions which makes these workers more productive.

Employment Trend, Projected 2012–22

Payroll Administrators and Financial Clerks: 11%

Total, All Occupations: 11%

Office and Administrative Support Occupations: 7%

Note: "All Occupations" includes all occupations in the U.S. Economy. Source: U.S. Bureau of Labor Statistics, Employment Projections Program.

Related Occupations
- Bank Teller
- Billing Clerk
- Bookkeeper and Accounting Clerk
- Cashier
- Statistical Assistant

Related Military Occupations
- Finance & Accounting Specialist

Conversation With . . .
CARL YORK

Director of Certification and Systems Implementation
American Payroll Association
San Antonio, TX, 1 year
Payroll management profession, 12 years

1. **What was your individual career path in terms of education/training, entry-level job, or other significant opportunity?**

I started out working in an office environment. After four years I had an opportunity to work at a company that processed payroll for other companies. I started out as an entry-level payroll clerk and three years in realized I needed to get a degree if I wanted to move up and into management. So I started going to Amberton University near Dallas, TX while I was working. Part-way through my degree, I landed a position at La Quinta Inns and Suites — they knew I was working on my degree — and went on to spend five years as Director of Payroll for their 400 inns and suites.

Going to college wasn't in the cards at the time I graduated from high school, but I didn't give up. I worked hard and got my BBA in management accounting. I'm the first person in my family to go to college.

Hands-down, what really catapulted my career was getting involved with the American Payroll Association. I took a test from the APA to become a Certified Payroll Professional , then I started volunteering for their Dallas chapter and networking and meeting people in the industry. That's how I secured the position at La Quinta. I was on the APA chapter board in Dallas for eight years — president for two years — and I spoke at conferences and taught classes. Then the national organization offered me the position I have now, where I can hopefully help grow the profession.

With the help of volunteers and our certification board, I oversee our partnership with a company that delivers our tests across the globe. I oversee our certification programs and systems implementation with a lot of large projects

2. **What are the most important skills and/or qualities for someone in your profession?**

Payroll is an interesting blend of human resources, accounting, and legal issues. You have to like working with numbers.

To do payroll, it's imperative to have strong organizational skills, communication skills — verbal and written — and to be detail-oriented. Obtaining certifications is critical. Studies are showing that employers are placing just as much emphasis on certifications as certain degrees.

You need to be problem-solver and possess critical thinking skills. And you definitely want to be a people person because you're dealing with people's livelihoods. If there's a mistake or issue or problem, you have to know how to speak to people respectfully and help them accept the facts — say, their paycheck has been garnished for a legal reason — or otherwise come to resolution. There can be a lot of parties involved with payroll and you've got to figure out what's going on and get an answer

3. What do you wish you had known going into this profession?

Understanding the value of networking in a profession like this is critical. I wish I'd gotten involved with APA sooner.

4. Are there many job opportunities in your profession? In what specific areas?

Payroll is, by and large, made up of baby boomers so it's a good time for younger people to get into it. There will be room for growth, especially in management.

5. How do you see your profession changing in the next five years? What role will technology play in those changes, and what skills will be required?

Companies are starting to see payroll as an area that should come to the table and help with structure and policy-making and partner with IT, human resources, and certain areas of accounting. I also think — and this is huge — that getting experience or taking classes in global business and global culture is important. Companies are going global and in payroll, you're touching people's pay so you need to understand their culture.

6. What do you like most about your job? What do you like least about your job?

I enjoy knowing what I do is important not just to companies, but to employees' lives.

Sometimes it can be challenging to meet all the deadlines. And, since one of the busiest times in payroll is at the end of the year, occasionally it's challenging to figure out the holiday schedule and still get the job done.

In a lot of organizations, payroll professionals may feel underappreciated, because you don't hear from people when you're doing it right, you hear when there's a mistake. But if you actively pursue a seat at the table, you can show payroll's value to the organization

7. **Can you suggest a valuable "try this" for students considering a career in your profession?**

Because of the confidential nature of data in payroll, it's hard to get an inside view. I would suggest looking for a local APA chapter and visiting a meeting. We are also hoping to develop a student membership program that should be up and running soon.

SELECTED SCHOOLS

Most technical and community colleges offer programs in business administration, including payroll administration. Interested students are advised to consult with their school guidance counselor or to research area postsecondary schools and training programs.

MORE INFORMATION

American Payroll Association
660 North Main Avenue, Suite 100
San Antonio, TX 78205-1217
210.226.4600
www.americanpayroll.org

Association of Records Managers & Administrators
11880 College Boulevard, Suite 450
Overland Park, KS 66210
800.422.2762
www.arma.org

Simone Isadora Flynn/Editor

Purchasing Agent

Snapshot

Career Cluster(s): Business Administration; Government & Public Administration; Manufacturing

Interests: Sales, supply chain management, business management, negotiations, economics

Earnings (Yearly Average): $59,780

Employment & Outlook: Slower Than Average Growth Expected

OVERVIEW

Sphere of Work

Purchasing agents evaluate raw materials and other supplies for companies to use as an ingredient or component of their products. They assess the materials for quality, durability, and market value. The main responsibility of purchasing agents is to find the highest-quality supplies and equipment at the lowest cost while adhering to the desires of current customers and target markets. Purchasing agents work in nearly all realms of manufacturing.

Work Environment

Purchasing agents split their time between administrative and office settings and warehouse and manufacturing facilities. Agents employed in food production or medical manufacturing may spend time on farms and in other environments where products are grown and harvested. Purchasing agents also spend a lot of time at trade shows, product-demonstration seminars, and other industry meetings in order to evaluate new products and foster professional contacts with potential suppliers.

Profile

Working Conditions: Work Indoors
Physical Strength: Light Work
Education Needs:
  Technical/Community College,
  Bachelor's Degree
Licensure/Certification:
  Recommended
Physical Abilities Not Required: No
  Heavy Labor
Opportunities For Experience:
  Military Service, Part-Time Work
Holland Interest Score*: ESR

* See Appendix A

Occupation Interest

A job in purchasing attracts candidates who enjoy and are skilled at mathematics, economics, and sales. It is not uncommon for purchasing agents to be fluent in more than one language. The field also attracts professionals who enjoy the process of negotiation and maximizing profits. Purchasing agents are typically outgoing and confident individuals with deft interpersonal communication skills who are comfortable interacting with new people regularly.

A Day in the Life—Duties and Responsibilities

Purchasing agents fill their days with numerous duties and responsibilities, many of which need to be tended to simultaneously. Purchasing agents are in constant communication with people inside their own companies to understand and anticipate the company's needs from a purchasing standpoint. If current suppliers are not meeting quality standards, purchasing agents are responsible for recruiting their replacements.

One of the major tasks assumed by purchasing agents is the evaluation of potential suppliers and their products. Such evaluations can entail extensive travel and an in-depth familiarity with the manufacturing processes and quality standards of their employing organization.

Once suppliers are vetted and narrowed down to a small group of potential candidates, purchasing agents are responsible for negotiating bid proposals and contracts. Contract negotiations can involve large sums of money, depending on a purchasing agent's particular realm of industry. Agents must ensure that potential suppliers can meet requirements surrounding delivery dates and potential demand.

Purchasing agents should pay attention to markets and financial trends relevant to their particular industry in order to stay knowledgeable about potential cost-cutting avenues and to anticipate fluctuations in consumer demand. They are also responsible for the ongoing evaluation of vendors, and they maintain records of various vendors' track records in pricing and overall quality.

Duties and Responsibilities

- Developing standards for selecting specific material or services
- Reviewing written requests for products and services
- Obtaining information about products and prices
- Determining seller's ability to produce products and services
- Maintaining records on items purchased
- Discussing and taking corrective action on defective purchases

OCCUPATION SPECIALTIES

Contract Specialists

Contract Specialists negotiate with suppliers to draw up procurement contracts. They direct and coordinate the activities of workers engaged in formulating bid proposals, and administer, extend, terminate and renegotiate contracts.

Buyers

Buyers purchase goods for resale to consumers. Buyers who work for large organizations usually specialize in one or two lines of merchandise (for example, men's clothing or women's shoes or children's toys). Buyers who work for small stores may be responsible for buying everything the store sells.

Procurement Managers

Procurement Managers are purchasing agents who work in government agencies and buy items in bulk for a state, county, or locality. Procurement managers also work in the military and in high-tech industries, where they develop specifications and performance test requirements to facilitate the procurement of parts and equipment for specialized applications.

WORK ENVIRONMENT

Physical Environment

Purchasing agents alternate between office settings and on-site visits with suppliers. They also frequently attend large conferences and trade shows.

Plant Environment

Purchasing agents may travel to factories or plants to inspect a supplier's manufacturing processes or to examine their products.

Relevant Skills and Abilities

Communication Skills
- Persuading others
- Speaking effectively
- Writing concisely

Interpersonal/Social Skills
- Cooperating with others
- Working as a member of a team

Organization & Management Skills
- Coordinating tasks
- Following instructions
- Making decisions
- Managing people/groups

Research & Planning Skills
- Using logical reasoning

Technical Skills
- Performing technical work

Human Environment

Peer-to-peer and customer-client interaction is the hallmark of the purchasing industry. Purchasing agents are traditionally skilled conversationalists with strong negotiating skills.

Technological Environment

Purchasing agents utilize technologies ranging from telephone conferencing, e-mail, and video-conferencing software to financial analysis tools.

EDUCATION, TRAINING, AND ADVANCEMENT

High School/Secondary

High school students can best prepare for a career as a purchasing agent with course work in algebra, calculus, economics, finance, and introductory computer science. Gaining some hands-on business experience though internships, volunteer programs, or participation in school-run fundraisers or entrepreneurial programs can benefit those who are interested in a career in purchasing. Classes in rhetorical communication and participation in debate and forensic clubs can help students hone their negotiation tactics and strategies, which can be useful in the occupation

Suggested High School Subjects

- Accounting
- Business
- Business Data Processing
- College Preparatory
- Economics
- English
- Keyboarding
- Mathematics
- Merchandising
- Social Studies

Famous First

The first US procurement of arms following the Revolutionary War was the purchase of "rifle guns" in 1792 from makers of the Pennsylvania long rifle in Lancaster County, Pennsylvania. The arms were used to supply a battalion of 330 riflemen.

College/Postsecondary

Postsecondary education has not historically been a requirement for entry-level positions in purchasing due to the extensive on-the-job training new employees receive. However, recent trends indicate that candidates benefit from having completed postsecondary course work in engineering, business management, economics, or applied science. Undergraduate students interested in pursuing a career in purchasing should explore courses in retailing, advertising, supply-chain management, or international business.

Related College Majors

- Agricultural Supplies Retailing & Wholesaling
- General Retailing & Wholesaling Operations & Skills
- Hotel/Motel & Restaurant Management
- Institutional Food Workers & Administration, General

Adult Job Seekers

Seasoned purchasing agents are customarily those who have been fortunate enough to accrue several years of professional experience. As such, purchasing is not traditionally a field of professional transition or temporary employment for adult job seekers. That said, professionals with extensive corporate experience may be able to transition to the field with relative ease. Purchasing can require extensive travel and time away from home, which may make the job difficult for individuals interested in maintaining a clear work-life balance.

Professional Certification and Licensure

No specific certification or licensure is required to be a purchasing agent, although professional certification will give a purchasing agent a competitive advantage in the field. Organizations such as the American Purchasing Society, the Association for Operations Management, and the National Institute of Governmental Purchasing offer professional credentials to purchasing agents who have completed several years of professional experience and successfully passed the necessary exams. Certain permissions may be required for purchasers working in specific industries involving chemicals, energy, and other controlled substances or goods.

Additional Requirements

Patience, amicability, and honesty are all important traits for a successful purchasing agent. Purchasing is primarily about establishing and maintaining relationships, and individuals who are at ease negotiating with both individuals and small groups are often those who forge the most successful careers.

Fun Fact

In a typical firm with 100 – 500 employees, an average of seven people are involved in most buying decisions.

Source: Gartner Group via http://sales.linkedin.com/blog/sales-strategy-23-facts-about-buyers-and-purchasing/

EARNINGS AND ADVANCEMENT

Earnings depend on the size and geographic location of the employer and the employee's responsibilities and experience. Median annual earnings for purchasing agents were $59,780 in 2013. The lowest ten percent earned less than $37,000, and the highest ten percent earned more than $95,000.

Purchasing agents may receive paid vacations, holidays, and sick days; life and health insurance; and retirement benefits. These are usually paid by the employer. Retail buyers often earn cash bonuses based on their performance and may receive discounts on merchandise bought from the employer.

Metropolitan Areas with the Highest Employment Level in This Occupation

Metropolitan area	Employment	Employment per thousand jobs	Hourly mean wage
New York-White Plains-Wayne, NY-NJ	9,840	1.88	$32.75
Los Angeles-Long Beach-Glendale, CA	9,390	2.36	$32.32
Washington-Arlington-Alexandria, DC-VA-MD-WV	8,860	3.74	$40.33
Houston-Sugar Land-Baytown, TX	7,140	2.59	$32.17
Seattle-Bellevue-Everett, WA	6,460	4.46	$36.18
Philadelphia, PA	5,880	3.20	$33.95
Chicago-Joliet-Naperville, IL	5,340	1.44	$30.20
Dallas-Plano-Irving, TX	5,270	2.45	$30.81
Atlanta-Sandy Springs-Marietta, GA	5,080	2.20	$30.30
Santa Ana-Anaheim-Irvine, CA	4,140	2.85	$31.91

Source: Bureau of Labor Statistics.

EMPLOYMENT AND OUTLOOK

There were approximately 300,000 purchasing agents employed nationally in 2012. Employment of purchasing agents is expected to grow slower than the average for all occupations through the year 2022, which means employment is projected to increase 2 percent to 7 percent. A trend toward large companies increasing the size of their purchasing departments and requiring their agents to procure more services than in the past will be somewhat offset by technological advances that allow supplies to be purchased online. The best opportunities will be available for persons with a master's degree in business or public administration. Graduates of bachelor degree programs in business should have the best chance of obtaining a job in wholesale or retail trade or within government..

Employment Trend, Projected 2012–22

Total, All Occupations: 11%

Purchasing Agents and Buyers: 4%

Note: "All Occupations" includes all occupations in the U.S. Economy. Source: U.S. Bureau of Labor Statistics, Employment Projections Program.

Related Occupations

- Cost Estimator
- Fashion Coordinator
- Online Merchant
- Personal Financial Advisor
- Production Coordinator
- Wholesale & Retail Buyer
- Wholesale Sales Representative

Related Military Occupations

- Purchasing & Contracting Manager
- Supply & Warehousing Manager
- Supply & Warehousing Specialist

Conversation With . . .
JENNIFER STILLMAN

Butler Dearden, Boylston, MA, 1 1/2 years
Purchasing Agent/Manager field, 15 years

1. **What was your individual career path in terms of education/training, entry-level job, or other significant opportunity?**

I didn't know what I wanted to do when I started out, so I went into the Marine Corps for four years. I was a bulk field specialist; we re-fueled airplanes. I moved up quickly. By my second year, I managed the people who refueled the airport. When I came out of the military, I used my GI Bill to get my associate's degree and become a paralegal. My husband got out of the military about the time I finished school, and we moved home to Massachusetts. I soon went to work assisting with inventory control and purchasing as a temp worker for a packaging manufacturer and distribution company. I did that for six or eight months, at the end of which I was promoted to a temporary purchasing agent position for three months. At the end of that timeframe, they hired me permanently. I moved up to become a senior buyer, where you handle higher-commodity items and make bigger judgment calls in terms spending money and valuing inventory.

I stayed with that company for 11 years until my husband had to make a career move that took us to California for year. I did purchasing for a start-up company there. We moved back to Massachusetts and I got the position I hold now. My company sells paper, janitorial supplies, packaging, and safety supplies. As an example of what I do, typically I'll buy 60-plus truckloads of paper towels and tissues every year, which is $50-$65,000 per truckload.

My first job was one of those things I fell in to. I helped out in the buyer position and had a good personality for the work. I liked negotiating and dealing with vendors. This work is interesting, never boring, and very fast-paced. I picked it up very quickly.

2. **What are the most important skills and/or qualities for someone in your profession?**

You really have to know how to negotiate, and I don't mean giving a price and telling the other party where you need to be. You have to get them there without telling them what you need. It comes without training; you learn as you go. You have to have a natural knack to do it.

You also have to have patience because vendors and salesmen can be trying on the nerves. In addition, you need to be organized, as well as a good multitasker. You may be working on five to ten project at a time, and you have to be able to transition without hesitation.

3. What do you wish you had known going into this profession?

It's hard to get someone to fill your shoes when you're taking time off or vacationing because a buyer has a lot of connections. Being away typically requires cleanup when you get back.

4. Are there many job opportunities in your profession? In what specific areas?

In my profession, the upper-level positions such as purchasing manager and above are typically few and far between. By the time you hit that level, you stay there. The junior-level positions are those where people tend to move on because they want to move up. Absolutely, there are lower-level positions all over the place.

5. How do you see your profession changing in the next five years? What role will technology play in those changes, and what skills will be required?

Computer systems have evolved to help us manage inventory levels so they don't require as much guesswork on buyer's part. I think that might slightly affect personnel, but there's always going to be a need for human interaction to manage that behind-the-scenes flow.

6. What do you like most about your job? What do you like least about your job?

I like negotiating. I like interacting with my vendors, and those times where, at the end of the day, you can meet on a level ground and both be happy. I don't like negotiating as much from the sales side because there are sometimes sales staff, who can be very aggressive personalities, who, no matter what you do and how hard you try — it's not good enough. You better be thick-skinned.

7. Can you suggest a valuable "try this" for students considering a career in your profession?

When you go to buy a car, research the heck out of the deal and get good money on your trade-in. You should be able to represent yourself. If you can't do that, then you shouldn't be a buyer.

SELECTED SCHOOLS

Many colleges and universities, especially those with business schools, offer programs in subjects related to procurement and purchasing. The student can also gain initial training at a technical or community college. For some of the more prominent institutions in this field, see the list of selected schools in the "Advertising and Marketing Manager" and "Operations Manager" chapters.

MORE INFORMATION

American Purchasing Society
North Island Center, Suite 203
8 East Galena Boulevard
Aurora, IL 60506
630.859.0250
www.american-purchasing.com

APICS: The Association for Operations Management
8430 West Bryn Mawr Avenue
Suite 1000
Chicago, IL 60631
800.444.2742
www.apics.org

Institute for Supply Management Information Center
P.O. Box 22160
Tempe, AZ 85285-2160
800.888.6276
www.ism.ws

International Purchasing and Supply Chain Management Institute
16192 Coastal Highway
Lewes, DE 19985
206.203.4894
www.ipscmi.org

National Contract Management Association
21740 Beaumeade Circle
Suite 125
Ashburn, VA 20147
800.344.8096
www.ncmahq.org

National Institute of Governmental Purchasing
151 Spring Street
Herndon, VA 20170-5223
800.367.6447
www.nigp.org

John Pritchard/Editor

Receptionist and Office Assistant

Snapshot

Career Cluster(s): Business Administration

Interests: Administrative work, business, office technology, data processing, communications

Earnings (Yearly Average): $26,798

Employment & Outlook: Faster Than Average Growth Expected

OVERVIEW

Sphere of Work

Receptionists and office assistants welcome customers to a place of business, assist customers with any inquiries, and provide information and clerical support to their employers. Receptionists and office assistants may perform a wide variety of information related tasks, including greeting customers, answering the phone, taking and delivering messages, directing phone calls, providing customer support, scheduling appointments, collecting fees, escorting visitors, and responding to

information requests from employees and customers. Their general
clerical or administrative duties may include filing, making copies,
and preparing faxes and mailings.

Work Environment

Receptionists and office assistants work in offices within organizations
such as law firms, hospitals, insurance companies, and educational
institutions. Receptionists and office assistants, positioned at
information desks or kiosks, generally greet visitors entering the
building or department and notify their supervisors that a visitor
has arrived. Depending on employer and particular job description,
a receptionist and office assistant may work full-time or part-time.
Receptionists and office assistants generally work forty-hour weeks,
but overtime may be necessary during periods of increased business.
Part-time work is relatively common in this field.

Profile

Working Conditions: Work
Physical Strength: Light Work
Education Needs: High School Diploma
or GED, High School Diploma with
Technical Education
Licensure/Certification: Usually Not
Required
Physical Abilities Not Required: No
Heavy Labor
Opportunities For Experience:
Internship, Part-Time Work
Holland Interest Score*: CSE, ECS

* See Appendix A

Occupation Interest

Individuals attracted to the
receptionist and office assistant
occupation tend to be people-
oriented and organized. Those
individuals who excel as
receptionists and office assistants
are approachable, confident
speakers, responsive, and effective
with their time. Receptionists
and office assistants should enjoy
interacting with people and have
a background in typing, filing, and
basic computer use.

A Day in the Life—Duties and Responsibilities

Receptionists and office assistants often function as the first point
of contact for customers or clients, and as such, they influence the
customer's first impression of the organization for which they work.
Receptionists and office assistants greet customers, employees, and
visitors in person, over the phone, or by computer. In some instances,
receptionists and office assistants are required to collect fees and
physically guide or accompany visitors to their destination within

the organization. They provide information about the organization, answer the phone, take and deliver messages, resolve customer complaints, and schedule appointments, tours, and meetings, as well as prepare mailings, record financial information, and file office records.

The specific daily responsibilities of receptionists and office assistants are determined in part by the individual's work environment. In large businesses, such as airlines or hospitals, a receptionist and office assistant may exclusively perform very specialized tasks such as answering the customer support hotline or making schedule arrangements. In small businesses, such as a local hotel or moving company, a receptionist and office assistant will likely be responsible for all the information related tasks as well as some of the clerical tasks needed to run the business. These clerical tasks may include placing orders, managing inventory, and preparing faxes and mailings. Receptionists and office assistants employed by learning institutions may also participate in discussions of work teams, workflows, dynamics, and best practices.

The receptionist and office assistant's work experience also influences the type and amount of work assigned. For instance, experienced receptionists and office assistants often work in supervisory roles overseeing customer support departments and training new hires while inexperienced or junior receptionist and office assistants may be assigned entry-level tasks, such as taking and delivering phone messages. Receptionists and office assistants of all experience and skill levels use computers, calculators, photocopying machines, word processing software, fax machines, scanners, and postal machines to complete their work.

Duties and Responsibilities

- Receiving calls and directing callers to the appropriate contact
- Making and keeping track of appointments
- Receiving visitors' and answering their questions
- Typing letters and other material
- Filing
- Paging individuals
- Receiving, sorting and delivering mail
- Preparing travel vouchers
- Doing simple bookkeeping

WORK ENVIRONMENT

Physical Environment

Receptionists and office assistants work in office environments. The work of a receptionist and office assistant requires sitting at a desk and using computers and phones for long periods each day. In some cases, they may also be required to stand for long periods each day, greeting and escorting visitors and customers.

Relevant Skills and Abilities

Communication Skills
- Speaking effectively
- Writing concisely

Interpersonal/Social Skills
- Being patient
- Being sensitive to others
- Cooperating with others
- Working as a member of a team

Organization & Management Skills
- Following instructions
- Paying attention to and handling details
- Performing duties that change frequently
- Performing routine work

Unclassified Skills
- Keeping a neat appearance
- Remembering names and faces

Plant Environment

Receptionists and office assistants working in plant or manufacturing environments provide information and clerical support to the business. While a receptionist and office assistant's office in a plant environment is most often kept separate from production lines, receptionists and office assistants in a plant environment may experience physical risks resulting from production fumes, noise, or plant accidents.

Human Environment

A receptionist and office assistant's human environment tends to be very social and interactive. Receptionists and office assistants, depending on their work assignments and organization, may interact daily with visitors, colleagues (such as file clerks and office clerks), customers, and supervisors.

Technological Environment

In the course of their daily work, receptionists and office assistants use basic office equipment, such as computers, typewriters, Internet communication tools, word processing software, scheduling software, fax machines, photocopying machines, scanners, telephones, and postal machines.

EDUCATION, TRAINING, AND ADVANCEMENT

High School/Secondary

High school students interested in pursuing a career as a receptionist and office assistants should prepare themselves by building good study habits. High school-level study of typing and bookkeeping will provide a strong foundation for work as a receptionist and office assistant or college-level study in the field. Due to the diversity of receptionist and office assistant responsibilities, high school students interested in this career path may benefit from seeking administrative internships or part-time clerical work with local businesses.

Suggested High School Subjects
- Applied Communication
- Bookkeeping
- Business
- Business & Computer Technology
- Business Data Processing
- Business English
- Business Math
- Keyboarding
- Speech

Famous First

The first practical telephone answering machine was developed in 1948 by Joseph Zimmerman of Waukesha, Wisconsin. When the phone rang a device lifted the receiver, a record player played a greeting, and a recorder recorded the caller's message. The machine weighed nearly a hundred pounds. Per FCC rules, the machine was required to produce an intermittent "beep" signal to remind a speaker that his or her message was being recorded.

College/Postsecondary

Although an undergraduate degree is not strictly required for this occupation, postsecondary students interested in becoming receptionists and office assistants should work towards an associate's degree or bachelor's degree in secretarial science, bookkeeping, administrative work, communications, or general business. Coursework in mathematics and business may also prove useful in their future work. Formal postsecondary training may provide advantages in the field. Postsecondary students can gain work experience and potential advantage in their future job searches by securing administrative internships or part-time clerical employment with local businesses.

Related College Majors
- Administrative Assistant/Secretarial Science
- Receptionist Training

Adult Job Seekers

Adults seeking employment as receptionists and office assistants should have, at a minimum, a high school diploma or an associate's degree in a relevant field. Some senior receptionist and office assistant jobs require extensive experience, on-the-job training, and bachelor's degrees. Adult job seekers should educate themselves about the educational and professional requirements of the organizations where they seek employment. They may also benefit from joining professional administrative associations to help with networking and job searching. Professional administrative associations, such as the International Association of Administrative Professionals and the Office & Professional Employees International Union, generally offer job-finding workshops and maintain lists and forums of available jobs.

Professional Certification and Licensure

Certification and licensure is not required by law for receptionists and office assistants but may be required as a condition of employment, salary increase, or promotion. Options for voluntary receptionist and office assistant certification include the Certified Professional Secretary (CPS) and the Certified Administrative Professional (CAP) designations. The CPS and the CAP designations, offered by the American Association of Administrative Professionals, are earned by passing a national examination on topics such as office systems, technology, office administration, management, and best communication practices.

Additional Requirements

Successful receptionists and office assistants will be knowledgeable about the profession's requirements, responsibilities, and opportunities. As receptionists and office assistants often have access to confidential information, they must exhibit integrity and professional ethics. Membership in professional administrative associations is encouraged among all receptionists and office assistants as a means of building professional community.

EARNINGS AND ADVANCEMENT

Earnings depend on the type, size, and geographic location of the employer and the employee's experience, duties and skill. Median annual earnings of receptionists and office assistants were $26,410 in 2013. The lowest ten percent earned less than $19,000, and the highest ten percent earned more than $38,000.

Receptionists and office assistants may receive paid vacations, holidays, and sick days; life and health insurance; and retirement benefits. These are usually paid by the employer

Metropolitan Areas with the Highest Employment Level in This Occupation

Metropolitan area	Employment	Employment per thousand jobs	Hourly mean wage
New York-White Plains-Wayne, NY-NJ	54,240	10.35	$14.70
Los Angeles-Long Beach-Glendale, CA	25,950	6.53	$13.97
Chicago-Joliet-Naperville, IL	22,770	6.15	$14.01
Washington-Arlington-Alexandria, DC-VA-MD-WV	19,250	8.13	$14.93
Atlanta-Sandy Springs-Marietta, GA	18,360	7.95	$13.47
Philadelphia, PA	16,260	8.84	$13.60
Nassau-Suffolk, NY	16,090	13.02	$14.53
Minneapolis-St. Paul-Bloomington, MN-WI	14,720	8.22	$14.23
Houston-Sugar Land-Baytown, TX	13,680	4.96	$12.86
Edison-New Brunswick, NJ	13,650	13.90	$13.56

Source: Bureau of Labor Statistics.

EMPLOYMENT AND OUTLOOK

There were approximately one million receptionists and office assistants employed nationally in 2012. A rapidly growing number worked in the healthcare and social assistance industries in physicians' offices, hospitals, nursing homes and outpatient care centers. Personal and educational services, real estate industries, and finance and insurance companies also employed large numbers of receptionists and office assistants. Employment is expected to grow slightly faster than the average for all occupations through the year 2022, which means employment is projected to increase 10 percent to 18 percent. Jobs will result from a rapid growth in the services industries, such as physicians' offices, law firms and personal care services. Since many receptionists and office assistants also perform secretarial duties, persons with good computer and clerical skills should have the best job prospects.

Employment Trend, Projected 2012–22

Receptionists and Office Assistants: 14%

Total, All Occupations: 11%

Office and Administrative Support Occupations: 7%

Note: "All Occupations" includes all occupations in the U.S. Economy. Source: U.S. Bureau of Labor Statistics, Employment Projections Program.

Related Occupations

- Counter and Rental Clerk
- Customer Service Representative
- Executive Secretary
- File Clerk
- General Office Clerk
- Library Technician
- Telephone Switchboard Operator

Conversation With . . .
JOANNE CRIM

Denial Office Coordinator
Bowie, Maryland, 21 years

1. What was your individual career path in terms of education/training, entry-level job, or other significant opportunity?

When I was in high school, I knew I didn't want to start college right away so I signed up for Medical Assistant classes at a nearby vocational school. The plan was to attend half a day at the vocational school and half at high school. I was placed in the Dental Assisting class in error and decided to stay because my best friend was in the same class! When I graduated from high school I had two diplomas: one from my high school and my certification for Dental Assisting. I worked in three dental offices over a seven-year period and took some evening business courses at a community college. Six months into my first job, I discovered that I didn't like assisting for eight hours a day. It was too confining. I did, however, like helping the receptionist. I enjoyed the interaction with the patients and the other duties that went along with the front office. So, I became office receptionist in the next two dental offices where I worked. Then I moved to Maryland. Because of my certification as a dental assistant and my past office experience, I secured a position at Blue Cross and Blue Shield in Washington, DC processing dental claims. I started in the Claims Department and worked in different areas of the company pertaining to dental and spent my last eight years there investigating dental fraud. Once I started a family, I left BCBS and started working four days a week for wonderful dental office close to home. I found the job through a mutual colleague of the dentist who headed up the office.

2. What are the most important skills and/or qualities for someone in your profession?

Knowledge of dentistry is top priority when you are managing the front desk at a dental office. This is the heart of the practice. The receptionist choreographs each day for the doctors and the hygienist, maintains the flow of patients, makes sure the laboratory cases are back a few days prior a patient's appointment, keeps patients on a regular cleaning and exam schedule, and manages the medicine that patients should or shouldn't take before appointments — for instance, we may need to remind them to halt a particular medication if they are undergoing sedation for their dental work. You need to know and understand dental procedures and treatments to communicate logically or to answer questions for patients. You need to know how to schedule appointments so that the days flows well for the doctor and hygienist. Although our office has accountants who handle our payroll, the front desk handles all other administrative functions.

Finally, it's important for a person in my position to possess empathy. Many people have a fear of dental work and it's my job to be understanding with them. Don't sound like a robot on the phone when speaking to a patient who is fearful or having pain. You've got to remember you are dealing with a person and, to them, there's a lot of scary stuff that could be going on

3. What do you wish you had known going into this profession?

I can't think of anything I wish I had known before entering this field. I am fortunate to work in an office that puts family first and works as a team. We help each other out.

4. Are there many job opportunities in your profession? In what specific areas?

My experience is specific to the dental field. I would think that someone who wanted to do this in other areas of healthcare could gain the training needed to work in a doctor's office and find employment.

5. How do you see your profession changing in the next five years? What role will technology play in those changes, and what skills will be required?

The biggest changes will be are in computers, both in the opertories — the rooms where your dental work is done — and at the front desk. Many offices are going paperless and using a patient's thumb print to sign in for an appointment.

6. What do you like most about your job? What do you like least about your job?

I love everything about my job. The doctor I work with is a perfectionist. She will not settle for inadequate materials or supplies. It's a personal challenge to accomplish everything that needs to be done to keep our patients and our staff happy. It also helps to have a staff that, despite our age and personality differences, works well as a team because we respect each other. My one pet peeve is the few patients who don't respect our schedule and continually show up late for appointments. That has a domino effect on the rest of our day.

7. Can you suggest a valuable "try this" for students considering a career in your profession?

I think shadowing would be a great learning tool if someone is interested in the dental profession, or how an office works.

SELECTED SCHOOLS

Most technical and community colleges offer programs in business administration, including secretarial science. Interested students are advised to consult with their school guidance counselor or to research area postsecondary schools and training programs.

MORE INFORMATION

American Society of Administrative Professionals
121 Free Street
Portland, ME 04101
888.960.2727
www.asaporg.com

Association of Executive and Administrative Professionals
900 S. Washington Street, Suite G-13
Falls Church, VA 22046
703.237.8616
www.theaeap.com

International Association of Administrative Professionals
P.O. Box 20404
Kansas City, MO 64195-0404
www.iaap-hq.org

Office & Professional Employees International Union
265 W. 14th Street, 20th Floor
New York, NY 10011
800.346.7348
www.opeiu.org

Simone Isadora Flynn/Editor

Retail Store Sales Manager

Snapshot

Career Cluster: Business Administration Marketing, Sales & Service

Interests: Supervising sales personnel, hiring and training sales personnel, merchandise display, inventory, marketing, purchasing

Earnings (Yearly Average): $38,200

Employment & Outlook: Slower Than Average Growth Expected

OVERVIEW

Sphere of Work

Retail store sales managers are responsible for running profitable stores. They oversee the purchasing and arrangement of stock and may design the layout of the sales floor or window displays. Sales managers analyze customer trends, set sales targets, and create promotional campaigns in order to control expenses and meet company-wide goals. When on the sales floor, they may also answer questions and handle customer complaints. Retail store sales managers are

responsible for supervising their sales staff and hiring and training new sales associates as needed.

Work Environment

Retail store sales managers work in large or small retail establishments, managing either a department or an entire store. They may occasionally work from an office within the store, particularly when fulfilling their administrative obligations, but typically they spend much of their time moving around the sales floor, interacting with staff and customers or stocking and arranging inventory. They may be required to climb ladders and lift objects weighing up to fifty pounds. Sales managers work at least forty hours per week, and long, irregular hours are to be expected during holidays and other busy shopping periods. Retail store sales managers are expected to work some evening and weekend hours, which can change weekly. When emergencies occur or a store is understaffed, managers may be required to report to work on short notice.

Profile

Working Conditions: Work Indoors
Physical Strength: Light Work
Education Needs: On-The-Job Training High School Diploma or GED
Licensure/Certification: Usually Not Required
Physical Abilities Not Required: No Heavy Labor
Opportunities For Experience: Internship, Apprenticeship, Military Service, Part-Time Work
Holland Interest Score*: ESR

* See Appendix A

Occupation Interest

Individuals attracted to retail store sales management tend to be well-organized people who find satisfaction in accomplishing short-term tasks and seeing tangible results. Those with an affinity for psychology often flourish in sales management due to their ability to anticipate customer needs. Long-range planning skills are essential, as sales managers must frequently plan marketing events to drum up sales or anticipate staffing requirements for the future. Individuals interested in this career should be self motivated and able to manage a potentially large staff.

A Day in the Life—Duties and Responsibilities

The profitability and overall success of retail stores often depend upon the efforts of sales managers. As such, retail store sales managers must spend a good deal of their time planning for the future. They set sales goals, which may be based on company-wide goals or other requirements, and create strategies for reaching these goals. Such strategies may include sales and other promotions, as well as displays or store layouts that draw attention to specific products. Sales managers order and may stock inventory to ensure that the appropriate items are available for purchase and located in the correct places. In addition, they may determine how many sales associates must be on duty and organize a schedule that accommodates the flow of customers, maximizes efficiency, and reduces costs. Retail store sales managers then study customer traffic patterns and sales records to determine whether their strategies are working. Based on such data, they make changes to the visuals or highlight particular items that may not have been selling well previously in order to meet their goals.

Retail store sales managers are also typically responsible for supervising sales associates, who assist customers in selecting items and complete sales transactions, and stock clerks, who ticket and display items. Sales managers identify which staff members need more training or deserve special recognition and respond accordingly. Since the maximization of sales is usually a primary goal, managers monitor associates and evaluate their use of good sales techniques, making suggestions for improvement when necessary. Sales managers may also hold meetings or meet informally with sales associates to explain the features and benefits of specific merchandise, information which can then be relayed to the customer.

While many sales management duties involve the planning of sales strategies or training of staff, sales managers working in retail stores may also interact with customers. They should handle questions or concerns in a calm and approachable manner, and step in to manage interactions between staff and customers as needed.

Duties and Responsibilities

- Recommending purchase of new stock
- Analyzing customer wants and needs
- Listening to customer complaints and resolving problems
- Preparing sales and inventory reports
- Planning department layouts, shelf arrangements and displays
- Setting sales territories, quotas and goals
- Reviewing market analyses to determine customer needs, volume potential, price levels and discount rates
- Planning advertising campaigns and sales promotions
- Hiring, training and supervising personnel

OCCUPATION SPECIALTIES

Department Managers

Department Managers supervise and coordinate the activities of workers in one department of a retail store.

WORK ENVIRONMENT

Physical Environment

Retail store sales managers work in large or small retail environments and may manage a department within a larger store. They may work long and irregular hours and be required to spend much of their time on their feet.

Human Environment

Retail store sales managers work in a busy environment and interact with a wide variety of people. As satisfying individual customers is a key aspect of the retail business, it is important for sales managers to remain calm and patient at all times.

Relevant Skills and Abilities

Communication Skills
- Speaking effectively
- Writing concisely

Interpersonal/Social Skills
- Asserting oneself
- Cooperating with others
- Working as a member of a team
- Coordinating tasks
- Making decisions
- Managing people/groups

Organization & Management Skills
- Managing time
- Meeting goals and deadlines
- Organizing information or materials
- Paying attention to and handling details

Research & Planning Skills
- Using logical reasoning

Technical Skills
- Performing scientific, mathematical and technical work
- Working with data or numbers

Technological Environment

Retail store sales managers generally use computers to catalog inventory, collect and interpret sales data, and create employee schedules. They may also operate cash registers or point-of-sale terminals.

EDUCATION, TRAINING, AND ADVANCEMENT

High School/Secondary

High school students interested in pursuing a career in retail store sales management should take courses in mathematics and communications. Psychology classes may also be useful. Students can obtain relevant experience by working part time in a retail environment.

Suggested High School Subjects
- Accounting
- Applied Communication
- Bookkeeping
- Business
- Business & Computer Technology
- Business English
- Business Math
- College Preparatory
- Merchandising
- Psychology
- Speech

Famous First

The first department store was opened in Vincennes, Indiana, by Adam Gimbel in 1842. His store offered a wide variety of goods organized into separate departments under a single roof. He also provided a money-back guarantee to ensure that the customer was satisfied. Later, Gimbel's seven sons exported the idea to other cities in the United States.

College/Postsecondary

While many employers do not require sales managers to hold postsecondary degrees and accept extensive sales experience in lieu of formal education, some aspiring retail store sales managers may choose to pursue an associate's or bachelor's degree in business management or a related field. Business management coursework includes topics such as economics, statistics and data processing, personnel management, decision-making theory, and principles of finance. A foundation in psychology and marketing may also be useful. It is beneficial for postsecondary students to work in the retail field in order to gain practical experience.

Related College Majors
- Apparel & Accessories Marketing Management
- Fashion Merchandising
- Food Products Retailing & Wholesaling Operations
- General Retailing & Wholesaling Operations & Skills
- Marketing & Merchandising

Adult Job Seekers

Adults seeking retail store sales management positions must typically work as assistant managers first, unless they previously held a comparable position at another company. Adults may also enter the management track by working as a management trainee or participating in a formal training program. Professional associations, such as the Sales and Marketing Executives International, may offer career resources and networking opportunities.

Professional Certification and Licensure

Certification and licensure are not legally required for retail store sales managers. However, some states may require registration or other qualifications from sales managers working in specific retail environments, such as liquor stores. As such, sales managers should educate themselves about the legal and professional requirements of the state in which they work.

Additional Requirements

Individuals dedicated to working and advancing in the retail store sales management field must have a high degree of flexibility. Sales managers should be decisive and sales oriented, with good communication skills and the ability to motivate others

Fun Fact

The word "retail" derives from the French word "retaillier," which means to cut a piece off or to break bulk.

Source: p. 6, Retailing Management, by Michael Levy, Barton A. Weitz, and Sheryn Beattie.

EARNINGS AND ADVANCEMENT

Earnings of retail store sales managers depend on the type, size and geographic location of the employer, the clientele they serve and the amount of merchandise they sell. Many retail store sales managers receive a commission or a combination of salary and commission. Under a commission system, retail store sales managers receive a percentage of department or store sales. This system offers retail store sales managers the opportunity to increase their earnings.

Retail store sales managers had mean annual earnings of $38,200 in 2013. The lowest ten percent earned less than $18,000, and the highest ten percent earned more than $74,000.

Retail store sales managers may receive paid vacations, holidays, and sick days; life and health insurance; and retirement benefits. These are usually paid by the employer. Some employers may also provide merchandise discounts.

Metropolitan Areas with the Highest
Employment Level in This Occupation

Metropolitan area	Employment	Employment per thousand jobs	Hourly mean wage
New York-White Plains-Wayne, NY-NJ	560,010	106.83	$27.88
Los Angeles-Long Beach-Glendale, CA	414,720	104.34	$19.45
Chicago-Joliet-Naperville, IL	405,560	109.59	$20.98
Houston-Sugar Land-Baytown, TX	292,790	106.17	$21.13
Atlanta-Sandy Springs-Marietta, GA	258,150	111.85	$19.44
Dallas-Plano-Irving, TX	242,510	112.82	$21.06
Phoenix-Mesa-Glendale, AZ	210,640	118.25	$18.37
Washington-Arlington-Alexandria, DC-VA-MD-WV	201,750	85.23	$19.59
Philadelphia, PA	196,930	107.02	$22.23
Minneapolis-St. Paul-Bloomington, MN-WI	186,810	104.28	$20.70

Source: Bureau of Labor Statistics.

EMPLOYMENT AND OUTLOOK

There were approximately 1.5 million retail store sales managers employed nationally in 2012. Some of the largest employers are grocery stores, department stores, motor vehicle dealerships and clothing and accessory stores. Employment of retail store sales managers is expected to grow slower than the average for all occupations through the year 2022, which means employment is projected to increase 7 percent to 12 percent. The Internet and electronic commerce continue to create new opportunities to reach and communicate with potential customers. Some firms are hiring Internet sales managers, who are in charge of maintaining an Internet site and answering inquiries relating to the product, prices and the terms of delivery.

Employment Trend, Projected 2012–22

Total, All Occupations: 11%

Retail Sales Occupations: 10%

Parts Salespersons: 7%

Note: "All Occupations" includes all occupations in the U.S. Economy. Source: U.S. Bureau of Labor Statistics, Employment Projections Program.

Related Occupations

- Fashion Coordinator
- Food Service Manager
- General Manager and Top Executive
- Hotel/Motel Manager
- Manufacturers Representative
- Online Merchant
- Pharmaceutical Sales Representative
- Postmaster and Mail Superintendent
- Supervisor
- Wholesale and Retail Buyer

Related Military Occupations

- Sales & Stock Specialist

Conversation With . . . *CHRISTOPER WIRTH*

Bookstore Manager, 2 years
Anne Arundel Community College, Arnold, MD
Retail, nearly 30 years

1. **What was your individual career path in terms of education/training, entry-level job, or other significant opportunity?**

I received an AA in business from this community college and a BS in business and public administration from the University of Maryland. I started in retail in the bookstore as a summer clerk and over the years worked my way up to textbook buyer, accounts payable, operations, assistant manager, then manager. However, I always had aspirations to work in politics so at age 30 I left to take an internship on Capitol Hill in Washington, DC. My representative ended up not being reelected, but the experience gave me confidence as a writer and taught me good communications skills, consensus-building, and teamwork. It also created a ten-year break in my time at the college bookstore, including three years at a now-defunct electronics retail chain where I learned salesmanship, customer service, budgeting, staffing, and inventory control. I was manager at the time they let us know the company would be phasing out over two or three years. So, after weighing my options, I decided the college was where I had found a nurturing environment and decided to try to build my career. I was fortunate to come back.

I manage three locations, approximately 80-100 employees, and handle budgeting and finance, conduct audits and inventories, oversee projects assigned to various departments, do employee evaluations, and manage a host of other duties. I act as the liaison between the bookstore and various campus stakeholders such as students, faculty and staff, as well as external stakeholders such as publishers

2. **What are the most important skills and/or qualities for someone in your profession?**

You have to have a customer-centric approach. Retail relies on repeat business and customer loyalty to flourish. I'm always in a position where, first and foremost, the customer is served.

You have to be an effective communicator. You cannot rise to any level of responsibility without verbal and written communication skills because you cross paths with so many people of different levels of education. You also need good listening skills. I like to hear all data first, and once I'm clear on an issue I react. That helps disarm people, especially individuals who are agitated or have some issue with the store.

In addition, you need to be able to multi-task, prioritize commitments, meet deadlines, and provide timely feedback

3. What do you wish you had known going into this profession?

My first job was a summer position here as a clerk right out of college, and I lacked the vision that maybe that was an opportunity. Even small jobs that seem inconsequential at the moment may be an opportunity. I was fortunate because my bosses recognized something they liked in me and asked me to stay on.

4. Are there many job opportunities in your profession? In what specific areas?

We have people shipping and receiving, doing procurement, accounts payable and receivable, operations, customer service, IT systems support, e-commerce, mobile commerce, and seasonal support. There are a lot of positions.

5. How do you see your profession changing in the next five years? What role will technology play in those changes, and what skills will be required?

There are multiple places a student can buy or rent a book. So, you have to join e-commerce and m-commerce or you will be left in the dust. Your best bet is to bring new technologies into your stores.

Textbooks are slowly shifting to digital formats. Many conventional textbooks contain access codes with expanded online contest. Technology is central to our operations, whether it's VOIP telephone or online sales, smart phone apps, the remote servers to our inventory, or the college's growing virtual campus. Our challenge is to stay abreast of changes and take advantage of industry-sponsored training, workshops and webinars to keep our skills up-to-date. We have to remain relevant to our students.

6. What do you like most about your job? What do you like least about your job?

I like to mentor my staff; it lets me share in their successes and encourage their potential. I always push my people to tell me what they're good at. For example, some of my workers do graphics — great things I didn't realize when we hired them — and now they are doing display windows. We might be a temporary way station for them career-wise, but we want to be relevant.

There's very little I don't like, although as a manager you have to be available more or less all the time. You also have to be competitive, and online competition sometimes creates an uneven playing field.

7. **Can you suggest a valuable "try this" for students considering a career in your profession?**

For retail, get a holiday season temporary job. Any internship gives you a chance to give a field a dry run. It's a short-term investment, but it gives you an insider's look. You can't put a dollar value on that.

SELECTED SCHOOLS

Most colleges and universities offer programs in business administration, often with a concentration in sales and marketing. The student can also gain initial training at a technical or community college. Interested students are advised to consult with their school guidance counselor or to research area postsecondary schools and training programs.

MORE INFORMATION

National Retail Federation
325 7th Street NW, Suite 1100
Washington, DC 20004
800.673.4692
www.nrf.com

Retail, Wholesale and Department Store Union
30 East 29th Street
New York, NY 10016
212.684.5300
www.rwdsu.org

Susan Williams/Editor

Services Sales Representative

Snapshot

Career Cluster: Business Administration; Sales & Service

Interests: Sales, marketing, business, customer relations, communication

Earnings (Yearly Average): $51,030

Employment & Outlook: Average Growth Expected

OVERVIEW

Sphere of Work

Services sales representatives sell their company's services to other companies or individuals. Services sales representatives work across a broad range of industries and offer both technical and nontechnical services. Technical services may include financial services, construction and building services, design, engineering, and software customization. Nontechnical services may include Internet and cable television services, vehicle leasing, outdoor advertising, cleaning, and home or office maintenance. Services sales representatives can be found

in any industry where a company provides a service to businesses, government, or individual consumers.

Work Environment

The work environment for services sales representatives is influenced by their industry, and the type of services they represent. Those who work in technical services tend to be outside service sales representatives. Outside services sales representatives visit prospective clients at their homes, offices, or work sites such as farms, factories, construction sites, or manufacturing facilities. Inside services sales representatives usually work in an office or call center environment and sell their company's services by telephone and the Internet. Services sales representatives, especially outside representatives, may have little face-to-face interaction with their colleagues and supervisors, but they must have excellent interpersonal skills and communicate confidently with people from a wide variety of backgrounds.

Services sales representatives may frequently be required to work more than forty hours a week when travel, evening, or weekend activities demand it, but they also often enjoy the flexibility to set their own schedules. For outside representatives, extensive travel is usually mandatory. Inside representatives may be required to work evenings and weekends, depending on the best time to contact their prospects. The benefits of this occupation may include a fully maintained vehicle. A services sales representative's income may be derived from a combination of salary and commission or from commission only.

Profile

Working Conditions: Work Indoors
Physical Strength: Light Work
Education Needs:
  Technical/Community College,
  Bachelor's Degree
Licensure/Certification: Required
Physical Abilities Not Required: No
  Heavy Labor
Opportunities For Experience: Part-
  Time Work
Holland Interest Score*: ESA

* See Appendix A

Occupation Interest

This occupation attracts self-motivated people who love sales, enjoy autonomy, and desire flexible work arrangements. An outgoing, assertive personality is an advantage. Maintaining a positive attitude and remaining persistent are especially important since sales representatives must frequently deal with resistant and uncooperative prospects.

Services sales representatives should possess good organization skills because they must manage their own time and priorities to meet sales goals and deadlines. They must also be able to respond positively to customer and supervisors' feedback in order to succeed. Those who desire work in a technical field must acquire appropriate knowledge, skills, and qualifications.

A Day in the Life—Duties and Responsibilities

Services sales representatives work in one of two ways: business-to-business, or "B2B," sales describe sales transactions in which the seller and buyer are both businesses while sales that occur between a business and an individual consumer are known as business-to-customer, or "B2C," sales.

A typical services sales representative's day involves a combination of planning, prospecting (looking for potential new customers), presenting, and following up with contacts. The sales process begins with an activity called "lead generation." Some services sales representatives are provided sales leads by their company, while others need to develop their own leads from referrals, networking, and contact lists. Depending on the nature of the services they represent, services sales representatives may contact leads by telephone, while others may drop in on leads at their homes or workplaces. Outside representatives may spend much of the day traveling to meet with prospects.

Services sales representatives are likely to attend sales appointments with prospects and clients. Some appointments may be to initiate new sales, while others may be to manage ongoing relationships or to develop further sales opportunities. The services sales representatives conduct sales presentations in which they explain the features, benefits, and costs of the services they represent. Technical sales (sometimes known as solution sales) may demand an extensive audit, interview, and needs assessment process before presenting a customized solution to the prospect.

A significant portion of a services sales representative's day is dedicated to completing paperwork. This includes recording notes from their sales calls, ordering new supplies, managing a budget, preparing expense claims, and writing sales reports, proposals, presentations, and orders.

Duties and Responsibilities

- **Developing client lists**
- **Looking for new clients in assigned territory**
- **Contacting prospects to determine needs**
- **Outlining types and prices of services**
- **Recommending services**
- **Writing, phoning or visiting prospective clients or contributors**
- **Following up with clients**

WORK ENVIRONMENT

Relevant Skills and Abilities

Communication Skills
- Persuading others
- Speaking effectively
- Writing concisely

Interpersonal/Social Skills
- Asserting oneself
- Being persistent
- Cooperating with others
- Motivating others
- Providing support to others
- Working as a member of a team

Organization & Management Skills
- Coordinating tasks
- Managing people/groups
- Managing time
- Meeting goals and deadlines

Unclassified Skills
- Keeping a neat appearance
- Using set methods and standards in your work

Physical Environment

The work environment for services sales representatives depends largely on the industry in which they work and the services they represent. Inside representatives usually work in an office or call center environment, while some may also work from home. Outside representatives travel frequently to visit prospects and clients at their homes or workplaces.

Human Environment

Services sales representatives enjoy a high level of interaction with prospects and customers. They must be able speak confidently with new people and with people from a wide variety of backgrounds. Face-to-face interactions with colleagues and supervisors may be minimal, although daily contact by telephone is to be expected.

Technological Environment

Daily operations require the use of standard office technologies, including a laptop computer, mobile telephone, e-mail, and the Internet. Proficiency in the use of word processing, spreadsheet, and presentation programs is expected. Services sales representatives may also need to use specialized systems, such as sales databases, presentation aids, and enterprise-wide resource platforms.

EDUCATION, TRAINING, AND ADVANCEMENT

High School/Secondary

High school students can best prepare for a career as a services sales representative by studying English and applied communication, business, applied mathematics, and economics. Typing and computer science classes may help prepare the student for the technology requirements of the role, while studies in psychology may provide an understanding about human behavior, motivation, and different communication styles. Foreign language proficiency may also be useful. Part-time sales, retail, or customer service employment during high school may provide an opportunity to gain valuable experience and insight into the sales profession.

Suggested High School Subjects
- Business
- College Preparatory
- Composition
- Economics
- English
- Speech

Famous First

The first chamber of commerce was New York's chamber, founded in 1768 by twenty New York City merchants interested in "promoting and encouraging commerce, supporting industry, adjusting disputes relative to trade and navigation, and procuring such laws and regulations as may be found necessary for the benefit of trade in general."

College/Postsecondary

Prior sales experience is often considered more important than formal qualifications in the services sales profession. Nonetheless, the competitive nature of employment in this field means that many employers are seeking candidates who possess an associate's or bachelor's degree in business or another relevant field. Some technical sales positions require a bachelor's degree as minimum requirement, and many employers may prefer a relevant postgraduate degree or professional certification. Examples of technical sales specialties include financial services, technology and software development, engineering, architecture, design and manufacturing services, and medical devices. A relevant degree along with sales experience provides applicants with an advantage over other candidates.

Related College Majors
- Business & Personal Services Marketing Operations
- General Retailing & Wholesaling Operations & Skills
- Hospitality & Recreation Marketing Operations
- Hotel/Motel & Restaurant Management

Adult Job Seekers

Adults seeking a career transition to a services sales representative role are advised to refresh their skills and update their resume. Meeting sales goals is extremely important in this job, so good sales results and any sales awards should be emphasized. Registering with an employment agency that specializes in sales employment or obtaining further education about a specific product or industry may be helpful.

Professional Certification and Licensure

In real estate sales, financial services, insurance, transportation services, and certain other industries or professions, sales representatives are required to hold state certification and licensure. Individuals interested in pursuing employment in these fields should research and fulfill the industry-specific requirements of their home state.

Additional Requirements

A clean driving record is often required by employers. A criminal background check may also be mandatory. Services sales representatives who have a college degree, advanced product knowledge, and an outgoing, persuasive personality will be the most successful

Fun Fact

Consumers are more likely to give a company repeat business after a good service experience (81%) than they are to never do business with a company again after a poor experience (52%).

Source: https://blog.kissmetrics.com/happy-campers/

EARNINGS AND ADVANCEMENT

Earnings of services sales representatives depend primarily on sales performance. Earnings of services sales representatives who sold technical services generally were higher than earnings of those who sold non-technical services. Successful services sales representatives who establish a strong customer base can earn more than managers in their firm. Services sales representatives are paid in a variety of ways. Some receive a straight salary; others are paid solely on a commission basis. Most firms use a combination of salary and commissions.

Median annual earnings of services sales representatives were $51,030 in 2013. The lowest ten percent earned less than $25,000, and the highest ten percent earned more than $110,000.

Services sales representatives may receive paid vacations, holidays, and sick days; life and health insurance; and retirement benefits. These are usually paid by the employer

Metropolitan Areas with the Highest
Employment Level in This Occupation

Metropolitan area	Employment	Employment per thousand jobs	Hourly mean wage
New York-White Plains-Wayne, NY-NJ	36,390	6.94	$38.84
Los Angeles-Long Beach-Glendale, CA	29,690	7.47	$29.70
Houston-Sugar Land-Baytown, TX	22,100	8.02	$30.32
Chicago-Joliet-Naperville, IL	22,010	5.95	$31.29
Dallas-Plano-Irving, TX	20,610	9.59	$30.86
Atlanta-Sandy Springs-Marietta, GA	16,390	7.10	$29.45
Washington-Arlington-Alexandria, DC-VA-MD-WV	16,010	6.76	$36.55
Phoenix-Mesa-Glendale, AZ	15,560	8.73	$26.63
Minneapolis-St. Paul-Bloomington, MN-WI	14,260	7.96	$29.16
Santa Ana-Anaheim-Irvine, CA	13,190	9.08	$32.39

Source: Bureau of Labor Statistics.

EMPLOYMENT AND OUTLOOK

Services sales representatives held about 800,000 jobs nationally in 2012. Employment is expected to grow about as fast as the average for all occupations through the year 2022, which means employment is projected to increase 6 percent to 11 percent. Turnover in this field is relatively high, particularly among those services sales representatives who sell non-technical services.

Employment Trend, Projected 2012–22

Total, All Occupations: 11%

Services Sales Representatives: 8%

Sales and Related Occupations (All): 7%

Note: "All Occupations" includes all occupations in the U.S. Economy. Source: U.S. Bureau of Labor Statistics, Employment Projections Program.

Related Occupations

- Advertising Agent
- Automobile Salesperson
- Insurance Sales Agent
- Manufacturers Representative
- Online Merchant
- Pharmaceutical Sales Representative
- Real Estate Sales Agent
- Retail Salesperson
- Sales Engineer
- Technical Sales Representative
- Wholesale Sales Representative

> ## *Conversation With . . .*
> ## *MICHAEL RHIM*
>
> Principal and retirement services expert, 6 years
> PRM Consulting, Washington, DC
> Financial Services field, 20 years

1. What was your individual career path in terms of education/training, entry-level job, or other significant opportunity?

I was a business management major at Howard University in Washington, DC. After my first year, a new insurance program was created and top-level students were encouraged to apply. I entered the program because it offered a scholarship that allowed me to stay at the university and gain summer employment through internships. I was pleasantly surprised by the career opportunities in the insurance industry. My first job was at the Wyatt Co., an actuarial consulting firm, as a technician writing computer programs for actuaries. I later was recruited to TIAA CREF, one of the country's largest financial services companies. I took a job as an institutional consultant – in essence, an account manager. My job was to keep the retirement clients happy, to introduce new services, and to handle any client service needs. I later moved into management and became an assistant vice president in Detroit. There, I managed a team of financial planners and a team of account managers. We worked with institutional clients such as colleges and universities to help them refine and manage their retirement plans. I later moved back to DC, moved up, and my career took off. I stayed at TIAA CREF for 20 years, but got to the point where I had had enough of corporate life. I came to work at PRM, a small minority-owned human resources consulting firm. I liked the firm's entrepreneurial spirit. We provide human resource services across the gamut, from benefits to executive searches to diversity training. I came in as a principal and was put in charge of a growing retirement practice since that is my area of expertise. I evaluate clients' retirement plan designs, look at their investment options, and work with them to hire appropriate financial firms. It's kind of like being a watchdog for the client.

Since I am a principal, my main role is to create revenue for the firm and bring in new clients.

2. What are the most important skills and/or qualities for someone in your profession?

Without people skills, you can't even get to sales. I am talking about the skillset of really being able to understand a client's needs by listening and anticipating, and then being able to address their needs. You also need analytical skills to dissect and evaluate benefits or retirement plans. When people come to us, they want things fixed.

Sometimes, clients may not know they have needs, and I must be astute enough to ask the right questions to find out what they need. I also need technical skills, such as knowledge of legal issues surrounding benefits and labor laws, and awareness of legislation and how that impacts benefits. I need to understand how investments work. Finally, I need compliance skills. For instance, most 401K plans require ongoing discrimination testing. You must be able to articulate to clients why these tests are important; it's because they could be fined significantly if their plans are out of compliance with Internal Revenue Services laws that affect retirement plans.

3. What do you wish you had known going into this profession?

The value of relationship building. We're in the people business and every person I meet is an opportunity.

4. Are there many job opportunities in your profession? In what specific areas?

Yes, although sometimes it's cyclical. In recent years, due to the Affordable Care Act, firms have needed analytical work on health care. Right now, retirement is a growth area as financial services firms are hiring more people to provide services to the retiring Baby Boomer generation. In addition, there are three generations currently in the workplace so institutions are hiring people to provide more online services — such as those for mobile devices — to address each generation's needs. Institutions are also looking to firms like ours to help them manage their retirement plan investment options.

5. How do you see your profession changing in the next five years? What role will technology play in those changes, and what skills will be required?

Institutions are wrestling with how to deliver the different generations' retirement needs. Firms like ours have to be able to assess the best way for institutions to take advantage of technology to manage their retirement programs, or to attract the kind of people they want. And we need to use technology such as social media or blogs to grow our own business and demonstrate our expertise.

You need a license to practice skills such as investment advising. Plus, certifications in various areas of human resources consulting are a must.

6. What do you like most about your job? What do you like least about your job?

When I was a manager in the corporate world, I managed people and I was too far removed from what I enjoy most, which is dealing with clients. That's what I enjoy here - providing solutions. However, it's a constant challenge to find new business

7. Can you suggest a valuable "try this" for students considering a career in your profession?

Find an internship in a consulting firm and see what goes on. There may be one segment of the business you like, and one you don't. For instance, if you like math, you might enjoy working in the compensation area.

SELECTED SCHOOLS

Most colleges and universities offer programs in business administration, often with a concentration in sales. The student can also gain initial training at a technical or community college. Interested students are advised to consult with their school guidance counselor or to research area postsecondary schools and training programs..

MORE INFORMATION

National Association of Sales Professionals
555 Friendly Street
Bloomington Hills, MI 48341
www.nasp.com

Sales and Marketing Executives International, Inc.
P.O. Box 1390
Sumas, WA 98295
312.893.0751
www.smei.org

Technology Services Industry Association
17065 Camino San Bernardo, Suite 200
San Diego, CA 92127
858.674.5491
www.tsia.com

United States Reps Association
www.usra.info

Kylie Hughes/Editor

Technical Sales Representative

Snapshot

Career Cluster: Business Administration; Manufacturing; Sales & Service

Interests: Sales, marketing, communications

Earnings (Yearly Average): $74,520

Employment & Outlook: Average Growth Expected

OVERVIEW

Sphere of Work

Technical sales representatives sell their company's products or services primarily to other companies and institutions. Most technical sales, sometimes referred to as solution sales, are business-to-business (B2B) sales, in which both the seller and buyer are businesses or institutions. Technical sales representative opportunities exist in a broad range of industries but are likely to be concentrated in fields such as agriculture, manufacturing, engineering, construction, military, science, computing, technology, mining, and education.

Work Environment

The work environment for technical sales representatives depends on the industry in which they work and the type of products or services they represent. Representatives of computer solutions may visit potential customers, or prospects, in their offices, while those who sell agricultural products may visit prospects on farms. Travel across a defined sales territory is generally mandatory. As such, the benefits of this occupation may include a fully maintained vehicle. Technical sales representatives may have little face-to-face interaction with their colleagues and supervisors, but they must be able to initiate contact with new people and confidently communicate with people from a wide variety of backgrounds. They may frequently be required to work more than forty hours a week when traveling, or when evening or weekend activities demand it, but they usually have the flexibility to set their own schedules.

Profile

Working Conditions: Work Indoors
Physical Strength: Light Work
Education Needs: On-The-Job Training, Bachelor's Degree
Licensure/Certification: Usually Required
Physical Abilities Not Required: No Heavy Labor
Opportunities For Experience: Part-Time Work
Holland Interest Score*: ESR

* See Appendix A

Occupation Interest

A career as a technical sales representative suits self-motivated people who enjoy autonomy and flexible work arrangements. A gregarious personality is a further advantage, as this role regularly involves meeting new people. However, it should be balanced with empathy, cooperativeness, and an awareness of different communication styles in order to develop good relationships with a broad range of people. A technical sales representative should have the confidence to interact with new people and the assertiveness to close sales. The ability to cope with rejection is also important, as sales representatives must frequently deal with resistant and uncooperative prospects.

Technical sales representatives should possess good organization and prioritization skills, as well as expert knowledge in their particular field, which may be gained through practical experience or formal training. They must be able to manage their own time and priorities in order to meet deadlines. Despite working independently, they must also possess a positive approach to teamwork, including the ability to receive and act on feedback and coaching from supervisors and trainers.

A Day in the Life—Duties and Responsibilities

A technical sales representative's day will involve a combination of planning, searching for potential new customers, presenting sales proposals, and following up with clients. The sales process begins with an activity called lead generation. Some technical sales representatives will have sales leads provided to them by their company, while others will need to develop their own leads from referrals, networking, and contact lists. Searching for potential customers, or prospecting, can be accomplished in a variety of ways, including contacting prospects via telephone, mail, or e-mail, calling on them in person, or meeting them at conferences, networking events, and other functions. Technical sales representatives may spend a significant proportion of the day driving or traveling.

Technical sales representatives are likely to attend sales appointments with prospects and clients. Some of these appointments may be to initiate new sales, while others may be to manage ongoing relationships or develop further sales opportunities.

The key to technical sales is to develop cost-effective solutions to customers' problems and challenges. This involves researching the problem to gain a thorough understanding of it. Therefore, the sales process may include auditing, interviewing, or conducting a detailed needs assessment before developing a customized solution. Technical sales representatives plan and conduct sales presentations, during which they explain the features, benefits, and cost-effectiveness of the products and services they recommend.

A portion of the technical sales representative's day is dedicated to paperwork. This includes recording notes from sales calls, ordering new supplies, managing budgets, preparing expense claims, and writing sales reports, proposals, presentations, and orders.

Duties and Responsibilities

- Calling on regular customers to obtain orders
- Preparing lists of prospective customers and scheduling appointments
- Presenting samples, pictures or catalogs illustrating products to customers
- Checking inventories of retail stores and ordering needed items
- Assisting retailers in updating inventory and ordering systems
- Advising retailers on pricing, advertising and arranging window and counter displays
- Checking on delivery dates
- Preparing reports
- Entertaining customers

WORK ENVIRONMENT

Physical Environment

The work environment for technical sales representatives depends largely on the industry in which they work and the products and services they represent. Some may spend their time in laboratories, manufacturing plants, or corporate offices, while others visit farms, factories, or military facilities. Extensive travel by car or air may be expected.

Human Environment

Technical sales representatives have a high level of interaction with prospects and customers. They must be able speak confidently with new people from a wide variety of backgrounds. Face-to-face interactions with colleagues and supervisors may be minimal, although daily contact by telephone is to be expected. Teamwork and collaboration skills are important.

Relevant Skills and Abilities

Communication Skills
- Persuading others
- Speaking effectively
- Writing concisely

Interpersonal/Social Skills
- Being able to work independently
- Cooperating with others
- Working as a member of a team

Organization & Management Skills
- Making decisions

Research & Planning Skills
- Developing evaluation strategies

Technical Skills
- Performing scientific, mathematical and technical work

Technological Environment

Daily operations will demand the use of standard office technology, including laptop computers, mobile telephones, e-mail, and the Internet. Proficiency in the use of word processing, spreadsheet, and presentation programs is expected. Technical sales representatives may also need to utilize specialized systems, such as sales databases, presentation aids, and enterprise-wide resource platforms.

EDUCATION, TRAINING, AND ADVANCEMENT

High School/Secondary

High school students can best prepare for a career as a technical sales representative by studying English and applied communication. Subjects such as business, applied mathematics, and economics may also be beneficial. Computing and keyboarding will prepare the student for the technology requirements of the role, while studies in psychology may provide an understanding of human behavior, motivation, and different communication styles. Foreign languages may also be useful. Part-time sales, retail, or customer service work will provide an opportunity to gain valuable experience and insight into the sales profession.

Suggested High School Subjects
- Applied Communication
- Bookkeeping

- Business Math
- English
- Merchandising
- Speech

Famous First

The first shipment of merchandise by airplane occurred in 1910, when five bolts of silk manufactured by the New York firm of Rogers & Thompson were delivered to the Morehouse-Martens Company of Columbus, Ohio. The first leg of the journey, to Dayton, Ohio, was accomplished by conventional land transport. But in Dayton the silk was placed onto a Wright bi-plane and flown to Columbus, 60 miles away. The flight, part of a publicity stunt, took just under one hour.

College/Postsecondary

Prior sales experience is often considered more important than formal qualifications in the sales profession. Nonetheless, the competitive nature of employment in this field means that many employers prefer candidates who possess an associate's or bachelor's degree in a relevant subject. Some employers may also expect a postgraduate degree or professional certification, as well as practical experience in an appropriate industry.

Related College Majors

- Agricultural Supplies Retailing & Wholesaling
- General Retailing & Wholesaling Operations & Skills
- General Selling Skills & Sales Operations
- Industrial/Manufacturing Technology
- Physical Science Technologies

Adult Job Seekers

Many employers prefer candidates for technical sales roles who have extensive experience using their products or services, while others seek candidates with sales experience. Applicants from sales backgrounds should note their experience representing specific companies, products, or services; specify the territories in which they have worked; and highlight outstanding sales results and any awards received. Candidates who come from a non-sales background should emphasize their expertise and experience in their field and may consider undertaking sales training with a private organization or professional association, which can also provide valuable networking opportunities.

Professional Certification and Licensure

In certain industries, sales representatives are required to hold state-based certificates and licenses. Technical sales representatives should consult reputable professional associations in the appropriate technical field to determine whether certification is needed.

Additional Requirements

Technical sales representatives often must have a clean driving record and may need to pass a criminal background check

Fun Fact

Nearly 12.3% of all the jobs in the U.S. are full time sales positions, and over one trillion dollars is spent annually on sales force salaries.

Source: http://www.salesforcetraining.com/sales-training-blog/sales-training-2/friday-fun-facts-interesting-stats-about-sales/

EARNINGS AND ADVANCEMENT

Earnings depend on the type of employer, the type of product sold, the assigned sales territory and the employee's experience and ability. Technical sales representatives are paid a combination of salary and commission. Median annual earnings of technical sales representatives were $74,520 in 2013. The lowest ten percent earned less than $38,000, and the highest ten percent earned more than $145,000.

Technical sales representatives may receive paid vacations, holidays, and sick days; life and health insurance; and retirement benefits. These are usually paid by the employer. Most employers provide technical sales representatives with an expense account and a car or mileage allowance

Metropolitan Areas with the Highest Employment Level in This Occupation

Metropolitan area	Employment	Employment per thousand jobs	Hourly mean wage
Chicago-Joliet-Naperville, IL	16,600	4.48	$37.20
Houston-Sugar Land-Baytown, TX	11,590	4.20	$46.06
Los Angeles-Long Beach-Glendale, CA	10,590	2.66	$38.84
New York-White Plains-Wayne, NY-NJ	9,400	1.79	$46.37
Atlanta-Sandy Springs-Marietta, GA	8,800	3.81	$38.95
Boston-Cambridge-Quincy, MA	8,470	4.84	$44.47
San Jose-Sunnyvale-Santa Clara, CA	7,960	8.55	$58.34
Santa Ana-Anaheim-Irvine, CA	7,680	5.28	$40.55
Dallas-Plano-Irving, TX	7,350	3.42	$36.24
Phoenix-Mesa-Glendale, AZ	6,910	3.88	$42.58

Source: Bureau of Labor Statistics.

EMPLOYMENT AND OUTLOOK

In 2012, technical sales representatives held about 350,000 jobs nationally. Employment of technical sales representatives is expected to grow about as fast as the average for all occupations through the year 2022, which means employment is projected to increase 6 percent to 12 percent. This is due to the increasing variety and number of goods to be sold. Many job openings will result from the need to replace workers who transfer to other occupations or leave the labor force.

Employment Trend, Projected 2012–22

Total, All Occupations: 11%

Technical Sales Representatives: 9%

Sales and Related Occupations (All): 7%

Note: "All Occupations" includes all occupations in the U.S. Economy. Source: U.S. Bureau of Labor Statistics, Employment Projections Program.

Related Occupations
- Automobile Salesperson
- Insurance Sales Agent
- Manufacturers Representative
- Pharmaceutical Sales Representative
- Real Estate Sales Agent
- Retail Salesperson
- Sales Engineer
- Services Sales Representative
- Wholesale Sales Representative

Conversation With . . .
KAREN BEALE

Business Unit Executive, 21 years
NorthAmerica Server Sales
IBM

1. **What was your individual career path in terms of education/training, entry-level job, or other significant opportunity?**

When I was young, I liked puzzles that required logic, such as crosswords, jigsaws and cryptograms. In high school I took AP classes in logic-based subjects. I wasn't sure what direction to take, but knew that math majors scored the highest on the GMAT, LSAT, and MCAT exams. That told me I could be a math major and delay a decision about my career for four years. In my sophomore year at Spelman College in Atlanta, one of my teachers was an IBM employee on loan to teach. He asked if I'd do an internship with IBM. The project I worked on helped me see I could use the logic I'd developed—like finding a pattern through cryptograms—and get paid. I learned to write computer programs and went on to minor in computer science. I was only one of two girls in my computer science class to do so. IBM invited me back, and at the end of that internship said they would hire me after graduation. I hesitated because IBM was the only place I'd worked. John Hancock Insurance offered me an internship in actuarial science, so I did that for six months. I started to write programs to automate some of their tasks. That made me want to go back to programming, so I returned to IBM as a programmer. I went into sales a few years later.

I had flexible hours, could work from home, and could raise my kids—unusual at the time—so I stayed in the sales force until my children were grown. My projects included helping a major retailer get garments to stores in the appropriate season. For example, if Store A in Kansas wasn't selling blue mohair sweaters, while Store B in New York City couldn't keep them on the shelves, how do you know and how do you get the sweaters to stores where they're needed? We helped them streamline their processes and run their stores more efficiently.

In my first management job, I consolidated the jobs of selling hardware and software so we could move to solution sales. I started in the Mid-Atlantic area managing a technical sales team that supported IBM's largest clients, then led a team for the eastern U.S., helping to architect server and solution areas, as well as Linux. Now I manage technical sales teams and managers for the entire U.S.

When I started, the closest person in age was 15 years older—and I was one of only two women in a group of 400 to 500 men. I've typically always been the only person of color. African-American women in this field remain unique.

2. **What are the most important skills and/or qualities for someone in your profession?**

Knowing what questions to ask and how to listen. You need to get to the root cause of any problem your client wants you to solve.

If your client can't install the coolest widget because their current infrastructure won't support it, their software doesn't integrate, or they have no one to manage it, it doesn't matter if you've made the most architecturally sexy thing ever. You must listen.

3. **What do you wish you had known going into this profession?**

I wish I'd better known how to step outside my daily responsibilities to see what other people do, and to network. I am surrounded by highly intelligent people and haven't always understood the value that I could bring to other positions. My extensive IBM-certified training honestly probably amounts to a doctorate or two.

4. **Are there many job opportunities in your profession? In what specific areas?**

Yes. Sales skills are transferable, and being able to translate the complex into something more simple than non-technical people can understand is rare.

5. **How do you see your profession changing in the next five years? What role will technology play in those changes, and what skills will be required?**

The huge question is this: how do you take advantage of social media without becoming just another voice in the crowd? Also, sensors reside in 90 percent of products being sold today. How do you make something meaningful of it? How do you leverage the global connectivity people have and maintain a competitive advantage?.

6. **What do you like most about your job? What do you like least about your job?**

I enjoy interacting with so many people across so many areas. I have many high-level clients, so I see all types of industries, people, and problems. Their needs are a new puzzle to solve.

I least like the amount of time that I'm sitting – for example, on conference calls. I don't think that's good for my–or anyone's–health.

7. **Can you suggest a valuable "try this" for students considering a career in your profession?**

Seek out internships. Look for online contests and challenges posted by companies that interest you. They may ask you to figure out a cool app that could transform the way somebody does business. Then submit. People are winning money, or even getting internships or jobs this way. It's important exposure.

SELECTED SCHOOLS

Most colleges and universities offer programs in business administration, often with a concentration in sales and marketing. The student can also gain initial training at a technical or community college. Interested students are advised to consult with their school guidance counselor or to research area postsecondary schools and training programs.

MORE INFORMATION

American Supply Association
222 Merchandise Mart Plaza, Suite 1400
Chicago, IL 60654
312.464.0090
www.asa.net

Manufacturers' Agents National Association
16-A Journey, Suite 200
Aliso Viejo, CA 92656
877.626.2776
www.manaonline.org

Manufacturers' Representatives Educational Research Foundation
8329 Cole Street
Arvada, CO 80005
303.463.1801
info@mrerf.org
www.mrerf.org

Sales & Marketing Executives International
P.O. Box 1390
Sumas, WA 98295-1390
312.893.0751
www.smei.org

Kylie Hughes/Editor

What Are Your Career Interests?

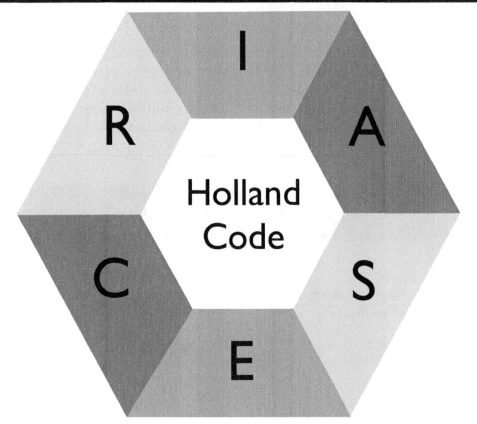

This is based on Dr. John Holland's theory that people and work environments can be loosely classified into six different groups. Each of the letters above corresponds to one of the six groups described in the following pages.

Different people's personalities may find different environments more to their liking. While you may have some interests in and similarities to several of the six groups, you may be attracted primarily to two or three of the areas. These two or three letters are your "Holland Code." For example, with a code of "RES" you would most resemble the Realistic type, somewhat less resemble the Enterprising type, and resemble the Social type even less. The types that are not in your code are the types you resemble least of all.

Most people, and most jobs, are best represented by some combination of two or three of the Holland interest areas. In addition, most people are most satisfied if there is some degree of fit between their personality and their work environment.

The rest of the pages in this booklet further explain each type and provide some examples of career possibilities, areas of study at MU, and co-curricular activities for each code. To take a more in-depth look at your Holland Code, take a self-assessment such as the SDS, Discover, or a card sort at the MU Career Center with a Career Specialist.

Realistic *(Doers)*

People who have athletic ability, prefer to work with objects, machines, tools, plants or animals, or to be outdoors.

Are you?		**Can you?**	**Like to?**
practical	independent	fix electrical things	tinker with machines/vehicles
straightforward/frank	ambitious	solve electrical problems	work outdoors
mechanically inclined	systematic	pitch a tent	be physically active
stable		play a sport	use your hands
concrete		read a blueprint	build things
reserved		plant a garden	tend/train animals
self-controlled		operate tools and machine	work on electronic equipment

Career Possibilities
(Holland Code):

Air Traffic Controller (SER)	Dental Technician (REI)	Laboratory Technician (RIE)	Property Manager (ESR)
Archaeologist (IRE)	Farm Manager (ESR)	Landscape Architect (AIR)	Recreation Manager (SER)
Athletic Trainer (SRE)	Fish and Game Warden (RES)	Mechanical Engineer (RIS)	Service Manager (ERS)
Cartographer (IRE)	Floral Designer (RAE)	Optician (REI)	Software Technician (RCI)
Commercial Airline Pilot (RIE)	Forester (RIS)	Petroleum Geologist (RIE)	Ultrasound Technologist (RSI)
Commercial Drafter (IRE)	Geodetic Surveyor (IRE)	Police Officer (SER)	Vocational Rehabilitation
Corrections Officer (SER)	Industrial Arts Teacher (IER)	Practical Nurse (SER)	Consultant (ESR)

Investigative *(Thinkers)*

People who like to observe, learn, investigate, analyze, evaluate, or solve problems.

Are you?		**Can you?**	**Like to?**
inquisitive	intellectually self-confident	think abstractly	explore a variety of ideas
analytical	Independent	solve math problems	work independently
scientific	logical	understand scientific theories	perform lab experiments
observant/precise	complex	do complex calculations	deal with abstractions
scholarly	Curious	use a microscope or computer	do research
cautious		interpret formulas	be challenged

Career Possibilities
(Holland Code):

Actuary (ISE)	Chemical Engineer (IRE)	Geologist (IRE)	Physician, General Practice (ISE)
Agronomist (IRS)	Chemist (IRE)	Horticulturist (IRS)	Psychologist (IES)
Anesthesiologist (IRS)	Computer Systems Analyst (IER)	Mathematician (IER)	Research Analyst (IRC)
Anthropologist (IRE)	Dentist (ISR)	Medical Technologist (ISA)	Statistician (IRE)
Archaeologist (IRE)	Ecologist (IRE)	Meteorologist (IRS)	Surgeon (IRA)
Biochemist (IRS)	Economist (IAS)	Nurse Practitioner (ISA)	Technical Writer (IRS)
Biologist (ISR)	Electrical Engineer (IRE)	Pharmacist (IES)	Veterinarian (IRS)

Artistic (*Creators*)

People who have artistic, innovating, or intuitional abilities and like to work in unstructured situations using their imagination and creativity.

Are you?
creative
imaginative
innovative
unconventional
emotional
independent
Expressive

original
introspective
impulsive
sensitive
courageous
complicated
idealistic
nonconforming

Can you?
sketch, draw, paint
play a musical instrument
write stories, poetry, music
sing, act, dance
design fashions or interiors

Like to?
attend concerts, theatre, art
  exhibits
read fiction, plays, and poetry
work on crafts
take photography
express yourself creatively
deal with ambiguous ideas

Career Possibilities
(Holland Code):

Actor (AES)
Advertising Art Director (AES)
Advertising Manager (ASE)
Architect (AIR)
Art Teacher (ASE)
Artist (ASI)

Copy Writer (ASI)
Dance Instructor (AER)
Drama Coach (ASE)
English Teacher (ASE)
Entertainer/Performer (AES)
Fashion Illustrator (ASR)

Interior Designer (AES)
Intelligence Research Specialist
  (AEI)
Journalist/Reporter (ASE)
Landscape Architect (AIR)
Librarian (SAI)

Medical Illustrator (AIE)
Museum Curator (AES)
Music Teacher (ASI)
Photographer (AES)
Writer (ASI)
Graphic Designer (AES)

Social (*Helpers*)

People who like to work with people to enlighten, inform, help, train, or cure them, or are skilled with words.

Are you?
friendly
helpful
idealistic
insightful
outgoing
understanding

cooperative
generous
responsible
forgiving
patient
kind

Can you?
teach/train others
express yourself clearly
lead a group discussion
mediate disputes
plan and supervise an activity
cooperate well with others

Like to?
work in groups
help people with problems
do volunteer work
work with young people
serve others

Career Possibilities
(Holland Code):

City Manager (SEC)
Clinical Dietitian (SIE)
College/University Faculty (SEI)
Community Org. Director
  (SEA)
Consumer Affairs Director
  (SER)Counselor/Therapist
  (SAE)

Historian (SEI)
Hospital Administrator (SER)
Psychologist (SEI)
Insurance Claims Examiner
  (SIE)
Librarian (SAI)
Medical Assistant (SCR)
Minister/Priest/Rabbi (SAI)
Paralegal (SCE)

Park Naturalist (SEI)
Physical Therapist (SIE)
Police Officer (SER)
Probation and Parole Officer
  (SEC)
Real Estate Appraiser (SCE)
Recreation Director (SER)
Registered Nurse (SIA)

Teacher (SAE)
Social Worker (SEA)
Speech Pathologist (SAI)
Vocational-Rehab. Counselor
  (SEC)
Volunteer Services Director
  (SEC)

Enterprising *(Persuaders)*

People who like to work with people, influencing, persuading, leading or managing for organizational goals or economic gain.

Are you?
self-confident
assertive
persuasive
energetic
adventurous
popular

ambitious
agreeable
talkative
extroverted
spontaneous
optimistic

Can you?
initiate projects
convince people to do things
  your way
sell things
give talks or speeches
organize activities
lead a group
persuade others

Like to?
make decisions
be elected to office
start your own business
campaign politically
meet important people
have power or status

**Career Possibilities
(Holland Code):**

Advertising Executive (ESA)
Advertising Sales Rep (ESR)
Banker/Financial Planner (ESR)
Branch Manager (ESA)
Business Manager (ESC)
Buyer (ESA)
Chamber of Commerce Exec
  (ESA)

Credit Analyst (EAS)
Customer Service Manager
  (ESA)
Education & Training Manager
  (EIS)
Emergency Medical Technician
  (ESI)
Entrepreneur (ESA)

Foreign Service Officer (ESA)
Funeral Director (ESR)
Insurance Manager (ESC)
Interpreter (ESA)
Lawyer/Attorney (ESA)
Lobbyist (ESA)
Office Manager (ESR)
Personnel Recruiter (ESR)

Politician (ESA)
Public Relations Rep (EAS)
Retail Store Manager (ESR)
Sales Manager (ESA)
Sales Representative (ERS)
Social Service Director (ESA)
Stockbroker (ESI)
Tax Accountant (ECS)

Conventional *(Organizers)*

People who like to work with data, have clerical or numerical ability, carry out tasks in detail, or follow through on others' instructions.

Are you?
well-organized
accurate
numerically inclined
methodical
conscientious
efficient
conforming

practical
thrifty
systematic
structured
polite
ambitious
obedient
persistent

Can you?
work well within a system
do a lot of paper work in a short
  time
keep accurate records
use a computer terminal
write effective business letters

Like to?
follow clearly defined
  procedures
use data processing equipment
work with numbers
type or take shorthand
be responsible for details
collect or organize things

**Career Possibilities
(Holland Code):**

Abstractor (CSI)
Accountant (CSE)
Administrative Assistant (ESC)
Budget Analyst (CER)
Business Manager (ESC)
Business Programmer (CRI)
Business Teacher (CSE)
Catalog Librarian (CSE)

Claims Adjuster (SEC)
Computer Operator (CSR)
Congressional-District Aide (CES)
Cost Accountant (CES)
Court Reporter (CSE)
Credit Manager (ESC)
Customs Inspector (CEI)
Editorial Assistant (CSI)

Elementary School Teacher
  (SEC)
Financial Analyst (CSI)
Insurance Manager (ESC)
Insurance Underwriter (CSE)
Internal Auditor (ICR)
Kindergarten Teacher (ESC)

Medical Records Technician
  (CSE)
Museum Registrar (CSE)
Paralegal (SCE)
Safety Inspector (RCS)
Tax Accountant (ECS)
Tax Consultant (CES)
Travel Agent (ECS)

BIBLIOGRAPHY

Finance, Management, and Operations

Anderson, Mary Ann, Edward J. Anderson, and Geoffrey Parker. *Operations Management for Dummies*. Hoboken, NJ: For Dummies, 2013.

Armstrong, Michael. *How to Be an Even Better Manager: A Complete A-Z of Proven Techniques and Essential Skills*. Philadelphia: Kogan Page, 2014.

Chick, Doug. *What All Network Administrators Know*. thenetworkadminstrator.com, 2013.

Fitch, Thomas P. *Career Opportunities in Banking, Finance, and Insurance*. New York: Checkmark Books, 2007.

Grossman, Theodore, and John Leslie Livingston. *The Portable MBA in Finance and Accounting*, 4th ed. Hoboken, NJ: Wiley, 2009.

Grotke, Robert Louis. *All You Need to Know about Accounting and Accountants: A Student's Guide to Careers in Accounting*. CreateSpace, 2013.

Label, Wayne A. *Accounting for Non-Accountants: The Fast and Easy Way to Learn the Basics*, 3rd ed. Naperville, IL: Sourcebooks, 2013.

Meyer, Susan. *Careers as a Bookkeeper and Auditor*. New York: Rosen, 2014.

Ross, Stan. *The Inside Track to Careers in Accounting*. New York: AICPA, 2010.

Sales, Marketing, Human Resources, and Office Management

Armstrong, Michael, and Stephen Taylor. *Armstrong's Handbook of Human Resources Management Practices*, 13th ed. Philadelphia: Kogan Page, 2014.

Davis, Alison, et al. *The Definitive Guide to HR Management Tools*. Upper Saddle River, NJ: FT Press, 2013.

France, Sue. *The Definitive Personal Assistant and Secretarial Handbook*, 3rd ed. Philadelphia: Kogan Page, 2012.

Levit, Alexandra. *They Don't Teach Corporate in College: A Twenty-Something's Guide to the Business World*, 3rd ed. Pompton Plains, NJ: Career Press, 2014.

Pincus, Marilyn. *Your Bright Future in Business Administration*. New York: Simon & Schuster, 2002.

Pride, William M., Robert J. Hughes, and Jack R. Kapoor. *Business*, 12th ed. Boston: Cangage Learning, 2013.

Sandberg, Sheryl. *Lean In: For Graduates*. New York: Knopf, 2014.

Solomon, Michael R., Greg W. Marshall, Elnora W. Stuart. *Marketing: Real People, Real Choices*, 7th ed. Upper Saddle River, NJ: Prentice Hall, 2011.

Stinson, Paul. *Retail, Marketing, and Sales*. New York: Ferguson, 2007.

Stroman, James, Kevin Wilson, and Jennifer Wauson. *Administrative Assistant's and Secretary's Handbook*, 5th ed. New York: AMACOM, 2014.

INDEX

A

AACE International 118
AA degree 240
academic training 235
accountant 2, 5, 9, 13, 70, 71, 79
account executives 44
accounting assistants 70, 71, 72, 73, 75, 77, 78
accounting associations 7, 125, 137, 174, 175
Accounting Clerk 12, 25, 268
accounting courses 80
Accounting Hall of Fame, The 9
Accounting Manager 12, 26, 89
accounting professionals 179
accounting software 2, 8, 19, 73, 85, 169
Accounting Technician Training 22, 75, 265
account manager 321
accounts payable 17, 18, 19, 20, 21, 22, 23, 25, 26, 72, 307, 308
Accounts Payable Clerk 26
Accounts Payable Network 28
Accounts Payable Specialist 17
Accreditation Council for Accountancy and Taxation 16, 69
Accredited Purchasing Practitioner 100
Accredited Systems Engineer certification 236
actuarial science 334
Actuary 66, 89, 177, 208
Adding Machine, The 22
administrative assistant 26, 29, 30, 31, 32, 33, 34, 38, 166
administrative associations 291
Administrative Chief of Staff 162
administrative personnel 156
Administrative Services Manager 162
administrative staff 157, 229
Administrative Support Occupations 25, 37, 78, 151, 164, 268, 293
Administrative Support Specialist 37
administrative support staff 38, 39
Administrative Support Supervisor 37, 164

Advanced Management Program 67
Advancing Government Accountability 87
Advertising Agent 320
Advertising and Marketing Manager 45
Advertising and Promotions Managers 51
Advertising Director 51
Advertising Managers 44
Advertising Research Foundation 55
Advertising Sales Agent 51
Advertising Women of New York 55
AEAP 161
Affordable Care Act 322
Agricultural Supplies Retailing & Wholesaling 278, 330
Algebra 6, 61, 173, 218, 234
Altamonte Springs 16, 69, 182
AMA 251
AMBA 23, 28
Amberton University 269
American Accounting Association 16, 81
American Advertising Federation 55
American Airlines 235
American Association for Budget and Program Analysis 87, 92
American Association of Administrative Professionals 291
American Association of Advertising Agencies 55
American Express Company 188
American Institute of Certified Public Accountants 16, 62, 69, 175
American Institute of CPA Student Scholarships, The 16
American Institute of Professional Bookkeepers 81
American Management Association 198, 213, 251
American Marketing Association 55, 220, 227
American Medical Billing Association 23, 28
American Payroll Association 266, 269, 272

American Society for Training and Development 198

American Society of Administrative Professionals 40, 296

American Society of Professional Estimators 118

American Staffing Association 198

American Supply Association 337

American University 90

American with Disabilities Act 190

analytics 215, 225

Anderson, Arthur 61

Anne Arundel Community College 38, 165, 307

anthropology 52

AOL 235

APA 269, 270, 271

AP classes 334

APICS 105, 284

APP 100

Apparel & Accessories Marketing Management 303

Applied Communication 21, 61, 74, 98, 124, 135, 159, 173, 234, 249, 289, 302, 329

Applied Math 218, 234

Applied & Resource Economics 220

applied science 278

Apprenticeship 30, 42, 184, 298

architects 110, 117

architectural studies 116

Architecture 106

art and design courses 52

art directors 46

Arts 47, 98

asset management 256

assistant buyer 103

assistant manager 307

Associate's Degree 255

Association for Financial Professionals 142, 175

Association for Investment Management and Research 174

Association for Operations Management 279, 284

Association of Executive and Administrative Professionals 40, 161, 167, 296

Association of Government Accountants 92

Association of Management Consulting Firms 213

Association of National Advertisers 55

Association of Records Managers & Administrators 272

audit executive 67

auditing 1, 2, 3, 5, 11, 19, 56, 57, 60, 61, 62, 63, 65, 170, 262, 327

Auditor 12, 56, 57, 59, 61, 63, 65, 66, 67, 69, 89, 139, 177

AutoCAD 117

Automobile Salesperson 320, 333

Automotive Service Advisor 115

B

Babbitt, B. T. 47

Baby Boomer 322

balance sheets 72, 171

Baltimore Research 224, 240

bank branch managers 171

bankers 63, 175

Banking 1, 56, 70, 82, 119, 124, 131, 168

Banking & Financial Support Services 124

banking manager 170

Bank of America 225

Bank of New York 194

Bank Teller 25, 78, 268

basic accounting 7, 13, 204

BBA 255, 269

beneficiaries 188

benefits clerk 79

Benefits Managers 186

benefits specialists 183, 260

benefits training 184, 187

Bentley University 67

Big Data 179

Big Four 61

Bill & Account Collector 139

Billing Clerk 78, 268

billing manager 19

biotechnology 208

Bloomsburg 255

Blue Cross and Blue Shield 294

Blueprint Reading 111

bookkeeper 71, 79

bookkeeping 2, 3, 5, 8, 20, 21, 22, 62, 70, 71, 72, 74, 75, 76, 80, 123, 135, 173, 240, 249, 261, 264, 265, 287, 289, 290
Booth School of Business 197
Boston University 38
brand strategists 46
Brigham Young University 15
Broaker, Frank 7
Budget Analyst 12, 66, 82, 83, 85, 87, 89, 90, 91, 115
budgeting 58, 72, 90, 91, 307
Building Trades & Carpentry 111
bulk field specialist 282
Burroughs, William Seward 22
Business Administration & Management 34, 62, 87, 112, 160, 205, 250, 265
Business and Professional Women's Foundation 259
business communications 46
Business & Computer Technology 6, 21, 32, 74, 124, 147, 159, 234, 264, 289, 302
business courses 6, 61, 265, 294
Business Data Processing 6, 21, 33, 47, 74, 86, 98, 124, 136, 234, 236, 264, 278, 289
Business English 21, 74, 159, 289, 302
business executives 205, 209
business finance 92
Business Law 6, 33, 61, 74, 86, 98, 124, 173, 218
business management 70, 98, 112, 153, 219, 220, 249, 250, 257, 273, 278, 303, 321
Business Marketing 220
Business Math 21, 47, 74, 86, 136, 264, 289, 302, 330
Business Operations Specialists 115, 223
business schools 15, 54, 69, 92, 105, 118, 130, 142, 181, 197, 212, 227, 258, 284
business support staff 71
business telecommunications 235
business training 205
Buyers 93, 94, 95, 97, 99, 100, 101, 102, 104, 206, 279, 280

C

calculus 203, 218, 234, 277
California Institute of Technology 243
campaign development 42

CAP 34, 291
Capitol Hill 307
career counseling 184, 187
career management professionals 205
Carnegie Mellon University 181, 243, 258
cashier 240
Cash managers 170
Casino credit departments 141
casino industry 140
Casino Operations 141
CBA 125, 137
CBF 125, 137
CCE 125, 137
CCH 179
CCP certification 266
CER 83
certification program 34, 63, 161
Certified Administrative Professional 34, 161, 291
Certified Credit Executive 125, 137
Certified Financial Risk Manager 175
Certified Government Financial Manager 87, 175
Certified Healthcare Financial Manager 175
Certified Information Systems Auditor 63
Certified Internal Auditor 63
Certified Management Accountant 175
Certified Payroll Professional 266, 269
Certified Professional Purchasing Manager 100
Certified Professional Secretary 161, 291
Certified Public Accountant 7, 14, 175
Certified Purchasing Manager 100
Certified Purchasing Professional 100
Certified Treasury Professional 175
CES 120, 132, 144
CFA Institute 175, 182
CFO 80, 178
Champaign 15, 243
CHANGE 67
Chapel Hill 54, 181
Charlotte 118, 138
Charlottesville 182
Chartered Financial Analyst 175
Chief Executive Administrator 162
chief financial officer 247
City Manager 177, 208, 254
Claims Department 294

Clearwater 126, 150

clerical support 285, 288

clerk 8, 18, 19, 22, 62, 76, 79, 121, 261, 269, 307, 308

client service 321

client services supervisor 42

Clothing & Textiles 98

club secretary 47

College of Business 15, 182, 197

College of Business Administration 182

Columbia Business School 212, 258

Columbia International University 165

Columbia University 212, 258

commerce 55, 104, 238, 306, 308, 316

commercials 210

commission 114, 120, 304, 312, 318, 332

communication business 209

Communications 41, 47, 48, 143, 206

Community College 30, 38, 71, 94, 120, 156, 165, 240, 261, 274, 307, 312

compensation analyst 79

computer administration 229

Computer courses 159

Computer Engineer 238

Computer & Information Systems Manager 238, 254

Computer Installation & Repair 235

Computer Maintenance Technology 235

Computer Network Architect 238

Computer Occupations 238

Computer Programmer 239

Computer Programming 234, 235

computer programs 321, 334

Computer Science 6, 47, 61, 86, 218, 234, 235, 249

computer security professionals 229

computer security specialists 230

Computer Support Specialist 151, 239

Computer Systems Analyst 208, 239

Computer Systems Officer 239

Computer Systems Specialist 239

Computer Technology 6, 21, 32, 74, 124, 147, 159, 234, 264, 289, 302

computing programs 73

Concept of the Corporation, The 204

Construction 26, 106, 109, 112, 115, 118

Construction/Building Technology 112

Construction Estimators 109, 118

construction management 112, 115

construction science 112, 115

Consultancy 209

consultant 203, 204, 209, 210, 224, 321

consulting services 11, 65

consumer 128, 171, 214, 215, 216, 217, 224, 226, 275, 313

consumer behavior 224

consumer credit managers 171

Contract Managers 96

contractor 2, 57, 108, 132, 169, 261

Contract Specialists 276

Coopers & Lybrand 61

Copywriter 51

Cornell University 243

corporate executives 194

corporate marketing 41

corporate researcher 225

Cost Estimator 89, 106, 107, 109, 111, 113, 115, 116, 117, 281

Council of American Survey Research Organizations 227

Counter and Rental Clerk 293

County/City Auditors 59

Court Administrator 177, 193

Court Reporter 37

CPA 7, 8, 14, 16, 62, 63, 79, 175, 178, 179, 180, 211

CPM 100

CPP 100, 266

CPPM 100

CPS 291

CRC 125, 137

CRE 71

creative specialists 45

credit administrators 131

credit analysts 131

credit and loan managers 120

Credit and loan officers 119, 120, 121, 122, 123, 125, 127

credit applicants 119, 120, 122, 134

Credit Authorizer 139

credit bureaus 120, 133

Credit Business Associate 125, 137

Credit Business Fellow 125, 137

Credit Checkers 122

credit management 132, 136

Credit Manager 12, 66, 127, 131, 133, 135, 137, 139, 140, 141, 177
credit representative 140
Credit Risk Certified 125, 137
credit unions 120, 122, 132, 134, 136, 139, 169
criminal justice 26
Critical thinking 45, 103
CRM 52, 53
CRS 2, 18, 261
cryptograms 334
Crystal Lake 244
CSE 18, 71, 120, 286
cultural studies 46, 147
customer care representative 140
customer relations 311
customer relationship management 52
customer service 17, 26, 119, 120, 143, 144, 145, 146, 147, 148, 149, 150, 151, 154, 257, 307, 308, 315, 329
Customer Service Representative 37, 143, 145, 147, 149, 151, 153, 293
customer service support 148
customer support 146, 285, 287
cyberattacks 232

D

Darden School of Business 182, 213
Dartmouth College 212
Database Administrator 239
Data Processing Technology 236
Davis, Allan 33
Deloittes, The 210
Deloitte & Touche 61
dental assistant 294
dentistry 294
departmental director 42
Department Managers 300
designers 42, 46, 104, 110
design services 109
Development Economics 90
diagnostic assessment 152
Digital Equipment Corporation 13
digital technology 236
Diners Club card 124
diplomatic coordinators 49
Director of Administration 49
director of advertising 42

Director of First Impressions 162
Director of Payroll 269
director of research 224
directors 44, 46, 84, 232, 245, 246, 247, 248, 250, 251, 252, 254
doctor 295
doctorate 224, 335
Drucker, Peter 204
DVR 210

E

e-commerce 104, 238, 308
Econometrics 220
Economics 6, 47, 62, 82, 90, 98, 136, 173, 174, 218, 220, 278, 315
Economist 208, 223
ECS 286
editors 46
Education Administrator 254
Education and Training Managers 186
Education Department 130, 142
e-financing 129
Electronic Commerce Specialist 51, 223
electronic education 240
Electronics 240
Eli Broad College of Business 197
e-marketing campaigns 52
Emergency Management Officer 193
e-Mortgages 129
employee benefits 186
employee commissions 260
employee mismanagement 58
employee recruitment 187
employee training programs 185
employment agencies 185
employment law 195
Employment Specialist 193
Energy Auditor 12, 66, 89
engineering 99, 106, 107, 111, 112, 115, 194, 208, 278, 311, 316, 325
engineers 96, 108, 117, 232, 240
Enterprise Management & Operation 205, 250
entrepreneurial programs 277
Ernst & Young 61
ESA 94, 156, 312
ESC 30

ESR 107, 169, 184, 246, 274, 298, 326

estimator 107, 108, 109, 111, 112, 113, 117

ethics 7, 8, 23, 61, 63, 124, 125, 128, 136, 174, 190, 219, 266, 291

Executive Assistant 34, 38, 165

executive management 155, 178

Executive Officer 254

Executive Secretary 37, 155, 157, 159, 161, 163, 165, 167, 293

executive staff 156, 157, 158, 161, 162, 232

external auditing 56

External auditors 56, 58

external vendors 30, 31

Extra-curricular activities 203

EY 61

F

Fairleigh Dickinson University 140

Fair Trade Act 99

Fannie Mae 128

fashion classes 103

Fashion Coordinator 281, 306

Fashion Institute of Technology 140

Fashion Merchandising 303

FBI 128

FCC 290

federal employment 190

federal government 86, 91

federal laws 58

FHA loan 128

File Clerk 293

Finance 1, 12, 28, 37, 56, 70, 78, 82, 87, 89, 90, 92, 119, 131, 136, 141, 168, 174, 250, 268

Finance & Accounting Manager 12, 89

Finance & Accounting Specialist 37, 78, 268

finance associations 125, 137

Finance, General 87

finance managers 132

finance staff 170

financial administration 71

financial aid director 165

Financial Analyst 12, 66, 89, 175, 177

financial and investment managers 133

Financial Clerks 268

financial controllers 75

financial counseling 3

Financial Institution Managers 134, 171

financial institutions 18, 119, 120, 151, 169, 254, 262

Financial Management 7, 182

Financial Management Association Int'l. 182

Financial Manager 12, 66, 87, 92, 130, 139, 142, 168, 169, 171, 173, 175, 177, 179, 181, 254

Financial Managers Society 125, 130, 137, 142, 182

financial officers 132

Financial Operations 89, 124, 208

financial planners 321

financial publications 216

financial report 168

financial service providers 71

financial services 1, 2, 80, 131, 168, 224, 254, 311, 316, 317, 321, 322

Fisher College of Business 15

FIT 103, 140

fleet (vehicle) management 26

Food Products Retailing & Wholesaling Operations 303

Food Service Manager 306

Foreign languages 74, 147, 159, 249, 329

forensic clubs 277

FPC 266

Frederick Community College 240

freelancers 46

Fulfillment Department 198

full-time work 71, 144

Fundamental Payroll Certification 266

G

GED 30, 261, 286, 298

General Insurance 13

General Manager 177, 193, 208, 306

General Mills stockholders 174

General Motors 204

General Office/Clerical & Typing Services 34

General Office Clerk 25, 37, 78, 293

General Retailing 148, 278, 303, 316, 330

General Selling Skills 148, 330

Geometry 61, 234

Georgia Institute of Technology 243

GI Bill 282

Gimbel, Adam 302

global economy 140

Global Management Analysts Association 213

Global Professional in Human Resources 189

GMAT 334

government agencies 31, 56, 82, 96, 111, 131, 241, 261, 276

Government Finance Officers Association 92

GPHR 189

Grainger Hall 55, 198

Graphic Arts 47

graphic designer 52

guidance counselor 28, 40, 81, 154, 167, 272, 296, 310, 324, 337

H

Haas School of Business 54, 181, 197, 212

Haloid 160

Hanover Insurance 13

Harding, Warren G. 86

Harvard Business School 67, 212, 258

health benefits 183, 185

healthcare 208, 238, 293, 295

health care industry 25

health insurance 9, 24, 36, 50, 64, 77, 88, 101, 114, 126, 138, 150, 162, 176, 186, 191, 206, 221, 237, 252, 267, 280, 292, 304, 318, 332

health services 25, 254

Heffelfinger, Charles 174

High School Diploma 18, 30, 71, 120, 144, 156, 261, 286, 298

high school education 240

high-tech applications 96

history 46, 120, 121, 152, 185, 190, 229

home appliance manufacturer 109

Hospitality 316

Hotel/Motel Manager 306

Hotel/Motel & Restaurant Management 278, 316

Howard University 321

HR 79, 194, 195, 257

HR manager 195

human resource management 189, 204, 250

human resources associations 190

Human Resources Certification Institute 189, 198

human resources development 189, 197

human resources director 247

human resources employees 185

human resource services 321

Human Resources Management 189

Human resources managers 183, 184, 185, 187, 191, 192

human resources professionals 183

Human Resources Specialist 208, 254

human resources specialists or managers 189

Human Services 183

hygienist 294, 295

I

IAAP 161, 162

IBM 235, 334, 335

ICR 201

Ideal X 250

IEP 153

Inbound marketing 53

income tax 178, 262, 265

Independent management consultants 210

Indiana University 15, 54, 181, 258

Industrial Engineer 115, 208

industrial engineering 112

Industrial/Manufacturing Technology 330

Industrial Relations Directors 186

industry associations 2, 133, 170

industry-sponsored training 308

Information Center 105, 284

Information Clerk 151, 164

information management 29, 30

information management technology 29

Information Sciences & Systems 236

information security 235

Information Security Analyst 239

Information Security Specialists 232

Information Systems Audit and Control Association 69

Information Technology 228, 254

Information Technology Project Manager 254

INS Certificate 13

Inside representatives 312, 314

Institute for Public Procurement, The 105

Institute for Supply Management 100, 105, 284

Institute of Finance and Management 28

Institute of Internal Auditors 16, 69, 182

Institute of Management Accountants 16, 69, 175

Institute of Management Consultants 209, 213

institutional consultant 321

Institutional Food Workers & Administration, General 278

Instructor 193

insurance carriers 139

insurance manager 170

Insurance Sales Agent 320, 333

Insurance Underwriter 66

internal accounting 1

Internal audit 68

Internal Auditors 4, 16, 59, 69, 182

Internal Revenue Service 58

Internal Revenue Services laws 322

International Association of Administrative Professionals 34, 40, 161, 162, 167, 291, 296

International Association of Workforce Professionals 198

International Business 205

International Customer Management Association 154

International Customer Service Association 154

International Development 90

International Federal Reporting Standards 78

International Foundation of Employee Benefit Plans 198

International Public Management Association for Human Resources 198

International Purchasing and Supply Chain Management Institute 284

International Studies 90

International Virtual Assistants Association 34, 40

Internet sales managers 306

Internship 2, 18, 42, 57, 71, 94, 107, 169, 184, 201, 215, 229, 261, 286, 298

intranets 231

inventory 58, 72, 94, 97, 282, 283, 287, 297, 298, 299, 300, 301, 307, 308, 328

investment guidance 1, 168

investors 169, 247

IRC 229

IRS 58

ISC 215

IT 57, 67, 231, 236, 270, 308

IT managers 231

IT Professional certification 236

J

job-finding workshops 62, 291

job shadowing 32

job training programs 189

John Hancock Insurance 334

Journalism 47, 48

junior auditors 62

junior executives 247

J. Walter Thompson Agency 219

K

Kelley School of Business 15, 54, 181, 258

Kellogg School of Management 197, 212, 258

Kenan-Flagler Business School 54, 181

Kennedy, Gerald 174

Kennedy Group, The 209

Keyboarding 21, 74, 124, 146, 147, 159, 234, 264, 278, 289

Key Performance Indicators 255

KPMG 61

Krannert School of Management 197, 258

Kumon North America Inc. 178

L

labor laws 185, 322

Labor/Personnel Relations & Studies 189, 205

Ladies' Home Journal 219

La Quinta Inns and Suites 269

law 7, 31, 33, 34, 38, 61, 62, 74, 99, 137, 148, 165, 195, 204, 210, 286, 291, 293

Lawyer 193

leadership development 194

lead generation 313, 327

League of Professional System Administrators 244

ledgers 72, 75

Legal Secretary 37, 164

Legal Specialist 37

liberal arts college 15

Library Technician 293

life insurance 185

life sciences 21

Linux 236, 334

loan and credit applicants 119, 120, 134

loan associations 120, 122, 132, 169

loan authorizers 124, 125

Loan Clerk 139

Loan Interviewers 122

Loan Officers 134

Loan Processors 122

local area networks 228, 231

logistics 116, 245, 256

LSAT 334

M

Macy's 104

Mail Superintendent 306

major retailer 334

Management Accountants 4, 16, 69, 175

Management Analyst 37, 89, 193, 208

Management Consultant 200, 201, 203, 205, 207, 209, 211, 213, 254

management development specialist 194

Management Information Systems 236

Management Occupations 177, 193

management professionals 205

Management Science 48, 205

management staff 201

management trainee 303

Managerial Economics 174

managing director 224

manufacturers 93, 94, 95, 110

Manufacturers' Agents National Association 337

Manufacturers Representative 306, 320, 333

Manufacturers' Representatives Educational Research Foundation 337

Manufacturing buyers 99

Manufacturing Cost Estimators 109

mapping 219

Marine Corps 282

Marketing automation 53

marketing degrees 99

Marketing Management 99, 220, 303

Marketing managers 44

Marketing & Merchandising 48, 303

Marketing Research Association 220, 224, 227

marketing specialists 223

Market Research Analyst 51

Market researchers 214, 215, 217, 220, 221, 223

Marriott School of Management 15

Marshall School of Business 16, 54, 197

Massachusetts Institute of Technology 181, 212, 243, 258

master's of business administration 62, 125, 174, 181, 212, 258

Mathematics 6, 33, 61, 62, 98, 106, 124, 136, 147, 168, 188, 218, 234, 265, 278

MBA 7, 62, 125, 136, 174, 179, 180, 181, 197, 209, 211, 212, 250, 258

MCAT 334

McCombs School of Business 16, 54, 182

McIntire School of Commerce 55

McKinsey & Companys 210

McLean, Malcolm 250

McNamara, Frank 124

m-commerce 308

mechanics 140

Media 41, 143

media directors 44

Medical Assistant 37, 164, 294

Medical Billing Assistant Certificate of Proficiency 23

medical billing clerks 23

Medical & Health Services Manager 254

Medical Records Administrator 78

Medical Transcriptionist 164

Mendoza College of Business 15

mentors 8, 62

merchandise coordinator 103

merchandise manager 95

Merchandising 48, 98, 173, 278, 302, 303, 330

Michigan State University 197

Microsoft Access 14

Microsoft Office 13

Microsoft Windows 111

Microsoft Word 13

Mid-Atlantic area 334

Military Service 2, 30, 71, 83, 184, 201, 229, 246, 261, 274, 298

mobile commerce 308

modeling 110, 219

Morehouse-Martens Company 330

Morris Shepard Federal Credit Union 136

Mortgage loan officers 125

mortgage officer 129

Mount Ida College 103
MRA 224
multimedia communications 47
multimedia technicians 46

N

National Association of Certified Public
    Bookkeepers 81
National Association of Colleges and
    Employers 9, 50, 64, 190, 251
National Association of Credit Management
    125, 130, 137, 142
National Association of Personnel Service 198
National Association of Sales Professionals
    324
National Association of State Auditors,
    Comptrollers and Treasurers 69
National Association of State Boards of
    Accountancy 16
National Association of State Budget Officers
    87, 92
National Association of System Administrators
    244
National Cash Register Company 190
National Contract Management Association
    284
National Employment Counseling Association
    189, 199
National Institute of Governmental
    Purchasing 279, 284
National Management Association 251, 259
National Retail Federation 105, 310
National Secretaries Association 35
NCR 190
negotiators 49, 97
network and computer systems administration
    234
Network and computer systems
    administrators 228, 229, 230, 232, 233,
    236
network and systems administration 235, 243
Networking 48, 67, 76, 161, 251
Network Professional Association 244
newsletters 47, 165
New York University 15, 54, 181
NGIP 105
NMA 251

Non-Profit Management & Operation 250
Nontechnical services 311
Northwestern University 197, 212, 258
Notre Dame 15
nursing degree 152

O

Occupational Analysts 186
office administration 33, 34, 167, 291
Office and Administrative Support 25, 37, 78,
    151, 164, 268, 293
Office and Professional Employees
    International Union 23, 40
office assistant 286, 287, 288, 289, 290, 291
office clerks 288
Office Machine Operator 25, 78
Office management 29
office manager 19, 150, 161
Office of Management and Budget 86, 90
Office of Personnel Management 213
office personnel 30, 31
office professional 29
Office & Professional Employees International
    Union 28, 291, 296
office receptionist 294
Office Supervision & Management 34, 160,
    265
OfficeTeam 162
Ohio State University 9, 15
OMB 86
Online Merchant 102, 151, 177, 223, 281, 306,
    320
online services 127, 322
on-the-job training 22, 34, 112, 148, 265, 278,
    290
Operations directors 245, 246, 248, 252, 254
Operations Management 205, 279, 284
Operations Manager 105, 118, 255, 256, 257,
    284
Operations Officer 254
Operations Research Analyst 208
Organizational studies 200
Organization Management 26
outbound marketing 53
Outside representatives 313, 314
Owen Graduate School of Management 198

P

packaging manufacturer 282

Packard BioScience Company 240

paralegal 282

part-time administrative 159, 249

part-time assistant 166

payroll 1, 2, 3, 17, 19, 58, 70, 72, 76, 178, 186, 194, 195, 260, 261, 262, 263, 264, 265, 266, 267, 268, 269, 270, 271, 272, 295

payroll administration 272

Payroll Administrators 268

payroll associations 266

Payroll Clerk 25, 78

payroll professionals 266, 270

Payroll Specialists 186

Penn State 224

pensions 186, 192

Personal Financial Advisor 12, 66, 89, 115, 177, 281

Personal Services Marketing Operations 316

personnel administration 189

personnel management 190, 303

Personnel Manager 193

Personnel Specialist 37

Pharmaceutical Sales Representative 306, 320, 333

PHR 189

Physical Science Technologies 330

placement programs 187

policy development 247

Political Science 173

Postal Specialist 37

postgraduate degree 316, 330

postgraduate professional certification 75

Postmaster 306

postsecondary degree 33, 111

Postsecondary education 22, 219, 278

PRC 224

Pricewaterhouse Coopers 61

PRM 321

problem solvers 18, 49, 107, 113

Proctor & Gamble 225

procurement 276, 278, 284, 308

Procurement Managers 96, 276

product-demonstration seminars 274

product development 44, 216, 247

production assistants 42, 46

Production Coordinator 115, 281

product managers 46

Professional accounting associations 7

Professional administrative associations 291

Professional auditing associations 62

professional auditors 63

Professional Construction Estimators Association 118

professional development 75, 190, 204, 224, 229, 266

Professional finance associations 125, 137

Professional in Human Resources 189

professional payroll associations 266

Professional Researcher Certification 224

Program Assistant 38

Program Coordinator 38

program director 209

programmer 334

project contractor 2, 132, 169

project management 42, 43, 48, 110, 116, 203

project manager 224

Promotions 45, 51

Promotions managers 45

Property Accountants 4

Psychologist 193

Psychology 47, 48, 98, 136, 147, 188, 218, 302

Public Accountants 4, 16, 62, 69, 175

public accounting 1, 2, 8, 58, 67, 178, 179

Public Administration 1, 56, 82, 168, 200, 273

Public Administrator 12, 66, 177, 254

public employment programs 185

Public Relations 48, 51, 254

public relations executives 46

public relations personnel 42

Public Relations Specialist 51, 254

Public Service 245

publishers 307

purchasers 93, 100, 223, 279

Purchasing Agent 102, 115, 273, 275, 277, 279, 281, 282, 283

purchasing clerk 76

Purchasing & Contracting Manager 281

Purchasing Manager 26, 100

Purchasing, Procurement & Contracts Management 99, 112

Purdue University 197, 258

Q

Quantitative Economics 220
Quickbooks accounting program 80

R

Raytheon Company 67
real estate broker 128
Real Estate Sales Agent 320, 333
reasoning 45, 73, 85, 97, 110, 277, 301
Receptionist 148, 151, 164, 285, 287, 289, 290,
    291, 293, 295
Receptionist Training 148, 290
reconciliation specialist 13
Recreation Marketing Operations 316
Recruiting Manager 193
Religious Program Specialist 37
research assistants 221
Researchers 217, 223, 225
research study 226
Retail 95, 96, 99, 102, 104, 105, 151, 254, 280,
    281, 297, 298, 299, 300, 301, 303, 304, 305,
    306, 307, 309, 310, 320, 333
Retail buyers 95, 280
retailers 93, 151, 328
Retailing & Wholesaling Operations 148, 250,
    278, 303, 316, 330
retail management 93
Retail Sales Occupations 306
Retail Salesperson 102, 151, 320, 333
retail store sales management 298, 302, 303,
    304
Retail Store Sales Manager 102, 254, 297,
    299, 301, 303, 305, 307, 309
Retail, Wholesale and Department Store
    Union 310
Retail & Wholesale Operations 99
retirement benefits 9, 24, 36, 50, 64, 77, 88,
    101, 114, 126, 138, 150, 162, 176, 183, 185,
    191, 206, 221, 237, 252, 267, 280, 292, 304,
    318, 332
retirement planning 80
retirement programs 322
Revolutionary War 278
risk analysts 131
risk assessment 131, 132

Risk Management Association 125, 130, 137,
    142
Risk Managers 134, 171
Rock & Roll Hall of Fame 9
Rogers & Thompson 330
Ross School of Business 15, 54, 181, 197, 212,
    259
Ross Stores 103
Rutgers University 178

S

SABRE 235
sales and marketing directors 247
Sales and Marketing Executives International,
    Inc. 324
sales associates 298, 299
Sales Engineer 115, 320, 333
sales management 298, 299, 302, 303, 304
Sales Manager 51, 102, 254, 297, 299, 301,
    303, 305, 307, 309
Sales & Marketing Executives International
    337
Sales Operations 148, 330
sales representatives 42, 311, 312, 313, 314,
    315, 317, 318, 320, 325, 326, 327, 328, 329,
    331, 332, 333
sales staff 44, 95, 283, 298
Sales & Stock Specialist 306
savings and loan association managers 171
savings and loan associations 120, 122, 132,
    169
Scheider, Ralph 124
scholarship 321
SEC 58, 62
secretarial duties 157, 293
Secretarial Science 34, 148, 160, 290
Secretary 34, 37, 151, 155, 157, 159, 161, 163,
    164, 165, 167, 291, 293
Secretary Training 34
Securities and Exchange Commission 58
securities dealers 139
Semi-Automated Business Research
    Environment 235
senior administrative staff 229
senior buyer 282
Senior Professional in Human Resources 189
senior receptionist 290

sensors 335

service engineers 240

service providers 46, 71

service sales representatives 312

shareholders 247

Shipping & Receiving Clerk 25

Shorthand 159

SHRM 196

Sloan School of Management 181, 212, 258

social media 46, 52, 53, 179, 206, 225, 256,
 322, 335

social media analytics 225

social science 219

social security 260, 262

Social Studies 6, 173, 188, 218, 278

Society for Human Resource Management
 189, 196, 199

Society of Financial Service Professionals 174,
 182

Sociologist 223

Sociology 218

software customization 311

Software Developer 239

software development 109, 228, 229, 316

special education 194

Spelman College 334

Sperry Corporation 22

SPHR 189

staffing 184, 187, 202, 298, 307

Stanford Graduate School of Business 197,
 212, 258

Stanford University 197, 212, 243, 258

state boards of accountancy 62

Statistical Assistant 25, 78, 268

Statistician 208

Stern School of Business 15, 54, 181

St. Louis 22, 88, 126

stock brokers 63, 175

stock clerks 299

store manager 104

subcontractors 108, 110, 117

Success Estimating and Cost Management
 System 111

SuccessEstimator 111

summer clerk 307

summer employment 321

superintendent 245

Supervisor 37, 164, 306

suppliers 71, 96, 100, 274, 275, 276

supply chain management 273

Supply & Warehousing Manager 281

Supply & Warehousing Specialist 281

supporting managers 160

support services 146, 183, 192

support staff 38, 39, 71, 247

system administration 234, 235

system administrators 229, 230, 237, 238

Systems Accountants 4

T

tax accountant 71

Tax Auditors 59

tax collectors 63, 175

taxpayer 59

Technical/Community College 30, 71, 94, 120,
 156, 261, 274, 312

Technical Education 286

technical sales 316, 325, 326, 327, 328, 329,
 330, 332, 333, 334

Technical Sales Representative 320, 325, 327,
 329, 331, 333, 335, 337

technical services 192, 312, 318, 320

technical training 240

technician 321

Technology Services Industry Association 324

telecommunication 5, 60

Telephone Switchboard Operator 293

temp worker 282

Tepper School of Business 181, 258

TIAA CREF 321

timekeepers 260

timekeeping 261, 263

Top Executive 177, 193, 208, 306

trade association 224

trade schools 112

Training & Education Director 193

training programs 28, 33, 40, 81, 99, 100, 154,
 167, 185, 189, 192, 262, 272, 296, 310, 324,
 337

training seminars 185, 230

transportation services 317

Travelocity 235

Treasurers 69, 170, 171

Trenton 244

Trigonometry 61, 234

trust company managers 171
Tuck School of Business 212

U

Unisys 22
United States Reps Association 324
University of California 54, 181, 197, 212, 243
University of Chicago 197
University of Edinburgh 224
University of Illinois 15, 243
University of Manchester 90
University of Maryland 307
University of Michigan 15, 54, 181, 197, 212,
    243, 259
University of New Orleans 79
University of North Carolina 54, 181
University of Notre Dame 15
University of Pennsylvania 15, 54, 181, 213,
    259
University of Southern California 16, 54, 197
University of South Florida 182
University of Texas 16, 54, 182, 243
University of Virginia 55, 182, 213
University of Wisconsin 55, 198
university programs 123
UNIX 235
Urban & Regional Planner 223
U.S. accountants 179
U.S. Bureau of Labor Statistics 12, 25, 37, 51,
    66, 78, 89, 102, 115, 139, 151, 164, 177,
    179, 193, 208, 223, 238, 254, 268, 281, 293,
    306, 320, 333
US Constitution 265
U.S. Cost 111
U.S. News and World Report 179

V

Vanderbilt University 198
vendors 27, 30, 31, 32, 71, 73, 83, 94, 95, 97,
    100, 121, 145, 230, 275, 282, 283
vocational assessment 184
vocational education program 33
vocational school 33, 205, 294
vocational training 22
VOIP 308
volunteer programs 234, 277

Volunteer Work 42, 156, 184, 229
VP 255

W

wage earners 266
Washington Business High School 33
WBZ radio 209
Web Administrator 239
Web Developer 239
webinars 152, 153, 308
Wharton School, The 15, 54, 181, 213, 259
Wholesale and Retail Buyer 306
wholesalers 71, 93, 94
Wholesale Sales Representative 102, 281, 320,
    333
Wholesaling Operations & Skills 148, 278,
    303, 316, 330
Wisconsin School of Business 55, 198
Wolters Kluwer 179
Woodbury Soap 219
workshops 62, 185, 262, 291, 308
World at Work 199
Wright bi-plane 330
writing courses 218
written exam 220
Wyatt Co. 321

X

xerography 160
Xerox Corporation 160

Y

Young, Arthur 61

Z

Zimmerman, Joseph 290